The Rise and Reason of Comics and Graphic Literature

The Rise and Reason of Comics and Graphic Literature

Critical Essays on the Form

Edited by Joyce Goggin
and Dan Hassler-Forest

McFarland & Company, Inc., Publishers
Jefferson, North Carolina, and London

LIBRARY OF CONGRESS CATALOGUING-IN-PUBLICATION DATA

The rise and reason of comics and graphic literature : critical essays
    on the form / edited by Joyce Goggin and Dan Hassler-Forest.
        p.   cm.
    Includes bibliographical references and index.

    ISBN 978-0-7864-4294-2
    softcover : 50# alkaline paper ∞

    1. Comic books, strips, etc.— History and criticism.
    2. Graphic novels — History and criticism.   I.   Goggin, Joyce,
    1959–   II. Hassler-Forest, Dan.
    PN6714.R57   2010
    741.5'9 — dc22   2010030564

British Library cataloguing data are available

Cover art created or licensed by: (top row, left to right) William
Hogarth, Brushing Up Studios, Nancy Presley; (bottom row)
Getty Images, David Grigg, Korionov.

Manufactured in the United States of America

*McFarland & Company, Inc., Publishers
    Box 611, Jefferson, North Carolina 28640
        www.mcfarlandpub.com*

Table of Contents

Introduction

Out of the Gutter: Reading Comics and Graphic Novels

Joyce Goggin and
Dan Hassler-Forest

Welcome to the gutter: not only the proverbial cultural ghetto to which the comics medium has been traditionally relegated throughout most of its existence, but also the term that defines the formal and theoretical characteristics that determine the way meaning is created in sequential art. As the commonly used term for the space between the panels on the comics page, the gutter also signifies the theoretical space in which the reader performs the suturing operation that ultimately enables the interpretive act, based on the assumption that the relationship between two consecutive images is not an arbitrary one. This is similar in some ways to the use of editing and montage in cinema, and in other ways to how readers of prose texts continuously fill in various kinds of gaps and elisions to create dynamic forms of meaning from the static symbols that make up any text.

But the gutter, as the deliberately open space where some form of suturing or hermeneutic activity is required in order for the reader to attain a first level of closure, is also distinct from similar formal characteristics of other media. The gutter could be said to constitute the single element that defines comics as a separate medium rather than a subgenre of literature or the graphic arts. Individual comics texts may feature conventional gutters in the form of open white spaces between panels or, as in much of comics pioneer Will Eisner's work, they may employ page layouts in which the images bleed into each other in different ways. But whatever the design particulars may be, there still remains a theoretical space identifiable as a "gutter," where readers

1

must intuit and define the relationships between different (elements of) images. It is this kind of reader activity that remains central to understanding the comics medium, and it is still the defining element for both author and reader interaction with the medium. Within the diverse body of texts that make up what we recognize culturally as comics the only medium-specific element that cannot be removed or altered without affecting comics' identity as such remains the gutter.[1] This is not the case, for example, of speech balloons or cartoonish design elements.

It hardly seems a coincidence that the term we have come to use for this single defining quality of the medium has such negative real-world connotations. For no matter how much energy is poured into efforts aimed at improving comics' reputations both inside and outside of academic circles, they have so far remained firmly situated in the gutter of Western culture. Obviously, euphemistic and distinctly apologetic terms like "graphic novel" are employed in a bid for cultural legitimacy by academics and readers not wishing to be misidentified as someone who would enjoy the lurid adventures of superheroes and swamp monsters. Will Eisner and comics theorist/author Scott McCloud have been at the forefront of this battle to rescue the medium from the prejudices and negative associations that continue to surround it, offering more serious-sounding alternatives like "sequential art" and "sequential narrative" that have — predictably — failed to catch on in general usage.

Whether this fight to legitimize comics as a medium "like any other" is gaining ground in our culture or not (and it does slowly but surely appear to be doing so), the battleground formed by this debate is fascinating in its own right, and that is where this book enters the fray. *The Rise and Reason of Comics and Graphic Literature* collects contributions from a diverse group of international scholars on various aspects of comics, lending a critical academic perspective to debates surrounding the medium's history and its formal characteristics. The essays in this volume also investigate problematic aspects of comics terminology and semiotics, as well as the major genres that have come to play defining roles in our associations and preconceptions surrounding, and sometimes clouding, the ways in which we perceive and decode it.

Part One, entitled "Origin Stories: History and Development of the Genre," showcases a selection of articles that provide historical frameworks for understanding the recent development of the comic book from various academic perspectives. The authors in this section have focused on the contemporary academic and critical re-appraisal of comic books as a form of literature, while introducing readers to forefathers of the genre like Hogarth and George L. Carlson, as well as to the development of the genre in publishing history.

Part Two, "What We Talk About When We Talk about Comics: Theory and Terminology," addresses some of the more problematic aspects of academic approaches to the medium, such as the lack of consensus on what terms to use, or even what theoretical framework to apply to narratives that combine words and images. The complicated nexus of meaning and cultural prejudice surrounding the medium has prompted a large number of terms, each of which has proved problematic in its own way, from comic strips to the more recent "graphic novel" or "sequential art." This section then, offers a variety of interdisciplinary critical perspectives on the debates surrounding theory and terminology.

In Part Three, "Out of the Gutter: Comics and Adaptations," authors discuss a number of intermedial adaptations that have been sourced from comic books. As these authors suggest, one of the reasons that the comic book medium has become the locus of increased critical, public, and academic debate in recent years is the growing number of films, video games, TV series, and even acclaimed novels by authors like Neil Gaiman based entirely or in part on comic books. This section of the book features in-depth case studies of comic book adaptations, and addresses the wide cultural impact of such adaptations.

From the late 1930s onward, superhero narratives have dominated the American comic book industry. Even after the celebrated deconstructionist work of Alan Moore and Frank Miller in the late 1980s, men in tights have remained the defining force within the American comic book marketplace, as well as the basis of the most common prejudice surrounding the medium. Part Four of this volume, "Men in Tights? The Superhero Paraodigm," looks at how superheroes have traditionally been linked to dominant agendas in American politics throughout history, and how this tradition has become increasingly problematic in a post–9/11 world. This section also analyzes the heritage of the superhero tradition in contemporary graphic novels and comic books from a political perspective.

Finally, Part Five, "Drawing History: Nonfiction in Comics," investigates how non-fiction comics have become a growing subgenre in the comic book medium that has met with sustained commercial success since the introduction of works such as Art Spiegelman's *Maus*. Such work has become part of the literary "graphic novel" movement, as well as an essential element of new methods in pedagogy. The articles in this section likewise address some of the medium-specific ways in which the comic book form opens up both problems and opportunities for the presentation of non-fictional narratives ranging from (auto)biography to historiography.

The editors of *The Rise and Reason of Comics and Graphic Literature* invite readers to engage with this remarkably dynamic, yet consistently underrated medium. The essays collected here provide historical and theoretical inroads into the comics medium, and analyze it in concert with other media, themes and narrative genres. We have brought together essays that, in various ways, address both meanings of "gutter," and have sought to explore a range of issues in comics studies, making this a particularly adaptable reference work. As comics studies grow — and they do so at an almost exponential rate — many instructors in disciplines such as film, art history, literature and new media feel a growing push from colleagues and students alike to acquaint themselves with the comics medium. We hope that anyone with an interest in comics — professional or otherwise — will find in this volume a useful and informative collection of essays that address the main issues in current comics studies and debates.

Notes

1. Given the frequently discussed problematic nature of the term "graphic novel," we have attempted to avoid it as a general descriptive term throughout this volume, using "comics" unless a specific context or debate brings up issues of terminology.

PART ONE

Origin Stories: History and Development of the Genre

1

Of Gutters
and Guttersnipes
Hogarth's Legacy

JOYCE GOGGIN

I have been lately allarm'd with some Encroachments of my Belly upon
the Line of Grace & Beauty, in short I am growing very fat.
— David Garrick, 1746.

Although we often think of comics as being endowed with an essential
contemporaneity, informed fans know that the medium has a long history,
spanning many centuries, and including forms that predate anything that
Comic Book Guy might sell. In this essay I will focus on a precursor of the
contemporary comics medium that arrived on the scene long after cave paintings and medieval tapestries, but which constitutes, nonetheless, a venerable
progenitor of the medium. My focus is the work of 18th-century English artist
William Hogarth (1697–1764), whom Scott McCloud, in *Understanding
Comics*, mentions as a significant innovator in the history of comics.[1] I will
also discuss, through the work of Hogarth, a number of aspects of modernity
that were gathering steam in his time, and which are now endemic to the
comics medium — all of which have had a profound effect on the development
of comics as a medium; on the look of comics; and on how they communicate
with readers and viewers.

In his prolific career, Hogarth painted and printed many "progresses,"
or visual narratives composed of elaborate comic panels that sequentially
related tales of social climbing and financial crisis. As McCloud remarks,
"despite the low '*panel count*,'" Hogarth's 18th-century graphic progresses
were "rich in detail and motivated by strong social concerns," such as the

plight of prostitutes and the snares of modern urban living. This said, however, McCloud's principle interest in Hogarth's panels is the way they "were designed to be viewed *side-by-side — in sequence!*" (1994, 16–17). So although *Marriage à la Mode, The Rake's Progress*, and *The Harlot's Progress* contain only six to eight panels, they tell comedic rags-to-riches-to-rags stories of aristocrats and women of questionable virtue in baroque intricacy, and are among the first graphic tales to attempt such narrative depth both within and across panels.

Hogarth's own precursor, following McCloud's genealogy of comics, is Egyptian painting, which also functioned as a form of sequential pictorial narrative.[2] To illustrate his point, McCloud reproduces, in considerable detail, an Egyptian mural that relates the story of farmers who neglect to pay taxes on their harvest, and are subsequently beaten by tax collectors (McCloud 1994, 14–15). While this is certainly a dynamic sequential narrative, Egyptian painting is separated from Hogarth's progresses by a considerable expanse of time and, as I will argue, the advent of modernity; hence McCloud makes no specific attempt to connect the two apart from formal considerations. Yet there is an important, if somewhat obscure, link to be made between Egyptian sequential art and Hogarth's 18th-century prints, through the latter artist's bizarre, hybrid jumble of Freemasonic iconography, which I would like to explore briefly.

As is commonly known, the Masons claim to borrow a good deal of their doctrine and their iconography from the ancient Egyptians. Hence, along with the trowels, compasses and aprons that function as signifiers of the original Freemasonic Craft, they adopt the "great doctrine of the inner light" from ancient Egyptian mythology, as well as a panoply of icons, including the all-seeing eye pyramid, which has graced American paper money since the 18th century (Jeffers, 6).[3] Hogarth was himself "an observing member [of the Freemasons] at least into the mid–1730s," and was made a Grand Steward of the Craft in 1735 (Paulson, qtd. in Hogarth, xxxv).[4] Throughout his career, Hogarth painted and caricatured influential Masons like his father-in-law James Thornhill and politician John Wilkes, while incorporating many Masonic icons and emblems into his work. So when Hogarth published *The Analysis of Beauty*, a treatise on his own somewhat controversial aesthetics, he designed the frontispiece around a serpent of Isis contained within a transparent pyramid.

The artist chose this image because, in his own aesthetic program, the source of all beauty coalesces in Lines of Beauty, represented in their purest and most ancient forms by serpentine lines and pyramid shapes.[5] *The Analysis of Beauty* (Fig. 1) is then announced by a semiotically dense compilation of Egyptian and Freemasonic iconography, which, according to Hogarth, had

THE
ANALYSIS
OF
BEAUTY.

Written with a view of fixing the fluctuating I D E A S of
T A S T E.

BY *W I L L I A M   H O G A R T H.*

So vary'd he, and of his tortuous train
Curl'd many a wanton wreath, in fight of Eve,
To lure her eye.--------   Milton.

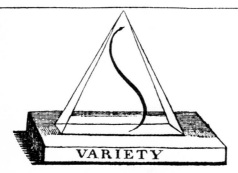

L O N D O N:

Printed by *J. R E E V E S* for the *A U T H O R,*
And Sold by him at his Houfe in L E I C E S T E R - F I E L D S.

MDCCLIII.

Fig. 1, Hogarth's frontispiece for *The Analysis of Beauty*

precisely the desired effect. As he explained in the preface to the 1753 edition of *The Analysis of Beauty*:

> The bait soon took; and no Egyptian heirogliphic [*sic*] ever amused more than it did [...] painters and sculptors came to me to know the meaning of it, being as much puzzled [...] as other people, till it came to have some explanation [...] [6].

By the time the 1753 edition was published, the "bait," a wriggling serpent dubbed "the Line of Beauty," had entered common parlance. Indeed, as the epigraph to this essay makes clear, by mid-century London celebrities like actor David Garrick were euphemistically using Hogarth's Line of Beauty to describe their own corpulence.[6] But what was it that so attracted Hogarth and his readers to the gentle curve of the serpent and the abrupt shape of the pyramid? As he wrote, "the triangular form [...] and the serpentine line itself, are the two most expressive figures that can be thought of to signify not only beauty and grace, but the whole *order of form*" (Hogarth, 11).[7] More specifically, the "sharpe pointe wherewith [the pyramid] seemeth to divide the aire" and "serpent-like" lines have "motion in them" (Hogarth, 3). It was this *illusion of motion* that Hogarth called "the greatest grace and life that a picture can have [...] which the painters call the *spirite* of a picture" because it "expresses *Motion*," through curved lines and triangular shapes (ibid).

... *to* lead *the eye a* kind of chace...[8]

While it is tempting to understand the movement of triangles and Lines of Beauty as a metaphor, because they have "*seeming* motion in them, which very much *resembles* the activity of the flame and of the serpent," one might do well to take Hogarth more literally for a variety of reasons (3, my italics). The most immediate of these is the motion involved in the creation of a line drawing, "insomuch [as] the hand takes a lively movement in making it with pen or pencil" (Hogarth, 42). In other words, the movement that went into making a drawing inheres in the lines of which it is composed, and is then communicated directly to the viewer. As Hogarth muses, this knowledge is so innate that the movement that gives rise to Lines of Beauty in any act of creation is not lost, even on the "day-labourer who constantly uses the leaver, [that gives the] machine [...] a mechanical power" (Hogarth, 6).

While the motion that goes into creating images is a source of pleasure, the movement of the eye is of capital importance, as the eye "is peculiarly entertained and relieved in the pursuit of [...] serpentine lines, as their twistings their concavities and convexities are alternately offer'd to its view" (Hogarth, 52).[9] So for Hogarth, in his comic progresses, and indeed in all that is aesthetically pleasing, the viewer derives enjoyment from the movement of the eye as it "must course [...] to and fro with great celerity [...] yet amazing ease and swiftness," because ocular pleasure "is still more lively when [the eye] is *in motion*" (Hogarth, 33). Or, as Hogarth scholar Frédéric Ogée has explained so succinctly, "the beholder's pleasure comes from his/her gradual and free pursuit of the windings of the pictures' lines [...] by cause-and-effect, left-to-right movement" (Ogée, 72). In short, for Hogarth, visual aesthetic pleasure is derived from the kinetic activity of the eye.

This pleasant ocular activity is, moreover, rooted in a more deeply meditative "movement" that aesthetic objects, like Hogarth's drawings and panels, set in motion. Ronald Paulson has referred to this kind of movement as synecdochal, because it assumes that a part can stand in "for the whole that embodie[s] the formal essence of a person" (Paulson, qtd. in Hogarth, xxxvi). This is perhaps best illustrated by the section on proportion in the *Analysis*, wherein Hogarth shows how two crossed lines can suggest a human figure in various attitudes.[10] This operation produces cognitive engagement in the viewer as s/he reads *between* the lines, fleshing out that which has been suggested, rather than completely "filled in." Hogarth was acutely aware that he could "inclose any substance" while leading the eye "a merry chase" over undulating lines, by inviting the viewer to project substance into the space created by his "undulating" lines (Hogarth, 61). In the process, he could enlist the viewer's imagination to "perform *motion, purchase, stedfastness*," and to produce the "*joint-sensations* of bulk and *motion*" (ibid.).

... *the face is the index of the mind...*[11]

To illustrate the various elements examined in *The Analysis of Beauty*, Hogarth included two pullout panels, each containing a central compound image, framed by upwards forty smaller panels. Many of these panels show gradients in the curvature of the Line of Beauty for varying effects, such as fat and thin. Similarly, the panels that contain Hogarth's illustrations of how to draw faces (Fig. 2, plate 1, panels 97–105, bottom, right) cover a gradient from "the features of a face of the highest taste (panel 97) [...] taken from an antique head [copied by] Raphael Urbin, and other great painters and sculptors," to a face (panel 105) "composed merely of such plane lines as children make" (Hogarth, 94–95). In other words, the panels illustrate how to draw a face in decreasing order of detail and realism, ending with a collection of circles and straight lines that merely suggest physiognomy. Likewise, Fig. 3, plate 2, panels 110—118 (bottom, left) begin with a baby's head composed of four circles, to which details and shading are progressively added to produce a "realistic" portrait of an old woman (panel 118).[12]

Writing more than 200 hundred years after Hogarth designed these panels to explain how comic artworks, Scott McCloud ventured his own theory

Fig. 2. William Hogarth, *The Analysis of Beauty*, Plate 1, 1753.

of comics with a chapter on viewer identification that echoes Hogarth with uncanny resonance.[13] McCloud's theory is laid out by means of illustrations of a man's face, progressing from photographic realism to examples that decrease in degree of realistic detail, culminating in a face composed of dots and lines.[14] McCloud wants us to notice that the last figure communicates "face," and prompts an emotive response, by engaging us with the simplest of lines. As he explains:

> When you enter the world of the cartoon you see yourself [...] the cartoon is a vacuum into which our identity and awareness are pulled. An empty shell that we inhabit which enables us to travel in another realm. We don't just observe the cartoon, we *become* it [McCloud 1994, 36].

Spectators project or "extend" identity into scant line drawings because such cartoons invite us to think ourselves into the frame emotively, to "fill in" the characters with our own sense of identification: we give comics "life by reading [them] and by 'filling up' this very iconic form" (McCloud 1994, 39). One could also see comics images as a "vacuum" that pulls, or sucks, the

Fig. 3. Hogarth, *The Analysis of Beauty*, Plate 2, 1753.

viewer in, creating a powerful emotive suturing of the observer onto the observed, resulting in the kind of "sensual, haptic pleasure" often attributed to Hogarth (Fort and Rosenthal, 6). In other words, comics art works engage readers' imaginations and thought processes to connect with simple images like those above, and to read "the face as the index of the mind" (Hogarth, 95). Or, as McCloud has explained, the simple, iconic images of the comics engage and suture readers into the medium because "[i]cons demand our participation to make them work" (McCloud 1994, 59).

Closure and "the assistance of the imagination"[15]

Along with the elements of comics art just discussed — the movement of the artist's hand, followed by the movement of the eye of the spectator; the interpellation of the spectator who must flesh out and read between simple lines — narrative has yet to enter the fray. Although in Hogarth, image and text are separated with few exceptions (signposts, calling cards, epigrams or epitaphs in images, for example), Paulson has claimed that Hogarth's progresses "dramatized in a uniquely powerful way — *because* in graphic images, but in images *deeply dependent on verbalization*" and narrative (my emphasis, Paulson 1996, 36).

Whatever the case may be, *The Analysis* suggests that Hogarth was conscious of the interplay of his panels with language and narrative at both micro and macro levels:

> It is a pleasing labour of the mind to solve the most difficult problems: allegories and riddles, trifling as they are, afford the mind amusement: and with what delight does it follow the well-connected thread of a play, or novel, which ever increases as the plot thickens, and ends most pleas'd, when that is most distinctly unravell'd? [33].

At the micro-level then, any number of elements in each panel of Hogarth's work initiates a sort of hermeneutic play wherein the spectator is prompted to do something analogous to solving an allegory or riddle, while projecting personality into simple line drawings. At this level, observers must pick their way "through a complex iconographic orchestration [of] interlacing references and meaningful juxtapositions [that] make sense within a system of differences [...] through complex visual markings that work with and against one another, producing significance" (Fort and Rosenthal, 3). At the macro level however, viewers cognitively extract another narrative that runs from one panel to the next; moving the narrative across time as well as space, and building "the narrative thrust of the image [that] draws it toward history" and, therefore, toward story (De Bolla, 66).[16]

Like McCloud, Ogée has also suggested that Hogarth's boldest innovations were his use of the serial format and of graphic proliferation, "descriptions of the causes and effects of the passing of time [... and the] representation of several forms of disorder [as ...] they invite the beholder into a visually tactile and 'moving' apprehension" (Ogée, 71). What I take to be the most significant factor here is the involvement of viewers in structuring a chronological narrative by means of panels — viewers who, as Hogarth confessed, would not be able to make sense of his progresses "without the assistance of the imagination" (Hogarth, 42). Hence, as scholars who write about Hogarth so often remark, beauty is experienced "by the beholder whose eye travels and creates lines from one character to the other, one plate to the next, and who thus experiences Hogarth's artistic 'process' as in flux rather than residing in the final product" (Fort and Rosenthal, 6).

This dynamic mental connecting of events in one panel sequentially to the events in the following panels, across the "gutter" that separates them, is what McCloud calls "closure." With this term, McCloud refers to a process of logical extrapolation whereby if we were to see a man with an axe threatening a Hogarthian guttersnipe in one panel, and the guttersnipe dead of head wounds in the next, we would (il)logically assume that the man with the axe from the first panel had killed her. By connecting two panels in this way, either temporally or thematically, we are performing the kind of cognitive operation on which meaning in comics art depends.[17] As McCloud wrote, "[t]his phenomenon of observing the parts but perceiving the whole has a name. It's called *closure*" (McCloud 1994, 63). Or, in Ronald Paulson's terms once again, it's called "synecdochal" logic (Paulson 1996, 63).

Before leaving this topic, I would like to argue that this method of guiding readers/viewers is no trivial development in the history of narrative media production. This technique, and particularly the way in which Hogarth practiced it, had a deep impact on other modes of storytelling, and Ronald Paulson goes so far as to claim that the panel composition of Hogarth's sequential, image-based narratives was actually borrowed by Richardson for the structuring of *Pamela* (1740) into "divisions, demarcations, 'scenes,' and closures (in Fielding, chapters)" (Paulson 1996, 38). Whereas Defoe's writing earlier in the century "simply ran on and on without stopping to form (or at least develop, shape, and *close*) scenes," rambling on "without division or *closure*," writers in Hogarth's circle "hooked" readers, inviting them to connect and close episodes across the narrative (Paulson 1996, 38). Hence, if Paulson's theory holds water, Hogarth's pictorial, sequential narratives, and the ways in which they suture viewers in and invite them to actively perform closure, gave rise to the sequential structure of the 18th-century, serialized novel of the type published by Richardson and Sterne, and for which Hogarth also contributed illustrations.[18]

Motion and Modernity

> Action is a sort of language which perhaps one time or other may come to be taught by a kind of grammar-rules.
>
> — Hogarth

It should by now be clear that Hogarth was obsessed with communicating a sense of movement in his work, and virtually all of Hogarth's artistic output is invested with a dual movement across space and through time. On the one hand "[t]he heterogeneous display [in each panel] presents itself performatively, since the objects on display appear animated and enter into a dialogue" (Fort and Rosenthal, 13). And while at the micro level of each panel, the spectator is guided in following lines of beauty and interpreting the various intrigues incorporated in each panel, at the macro level readers are encouraged to move exegetically across panels. Given that Hogarth himself explained that the noble "dimensions which appear to have given [his art] so much dignity, are the same that are best fitted to produce the utmost speed," it is little wonder that his progresses communicate rapidity as well as movement, and hence modernity (Hogarth, 73).

Moreover, just as the kinesis of the artist's brushstrokes was to inhere in the final product, drawing the spectator's eye into an amusing joy-ride in and across panels, Hogarth's techniques of observation and execution grew directly out of his life as a devotee of London and big-city life in industrial modernity.[19] The pleasure that the viewer's eye takes in Hogarth's serpentine lines was supposedly a direct translation of the enjoyment that the artist took in "winding walks," retaining images "as he strolled the streets, reducing scenes to mental diagrams" out of which "he presumably abstracted the Line of Beauty" (Paulson, qtd. in Hogarth, xxxvi). His self-taught method was "to draw by memory [...] lineally such objects as fitted any purpose best," and to keep "images in [his] mind's Eye without drawing upon the spot" so that his tableaux were produced quite literally from a state of flux (ibid.).

While his focus on speed and mobility distinguishes Hogarth as particularly modern, it has also been remarked that his modernity is manifest in the objects he chose to represent, such as industrial drill bits (plate 1, panel 15) and candlesticks (plate 1, panels 12, 33, 34).[20] It is possible that at least some of these objects encountered on his walks belonged to the art of the "common sign-painter," who "instantly becomes [...] a Rubens, a Titian, or a Corregio" if "he lays his colours smooth" (Hogarth, 93). Long Lane, a street that Hogarth often visited and admired, housed many establishments with impressive signs (The Anchor, Golden Ball, Black Boy, Indian Queen, Golden Key) that he supposedly "enjoyed as others did trees and gardens" (Paulson 1971, 232). Indeed, when Hogarth, a man keenly aware of his times, was roaming the streets of London on image-gathering missions, the notion of "seeing sights" in commercial centers was on the rise (Burney, 29). As novelist, and Hogarth contemporary, Frances Burney so vividly described in her fiction, the practice of meandering through "auctions, curious shops and so forth"— in short, the pleasures of going "a-shopping"— was just being discovered (Burney, 41).[21] One is reminded here of Benjamin's later essays on the flâneur— the quintessential figure of city life— for whom "the shiny enameled signs of businesses are at least as good a wall ornament as an oil painting is to a bourgeois in his salon" (Benjamin 1997, 37). Like Hogarth, Benjamin's flâneur takes in the dominant aesthetic of commodity culture, expressed in an endless commercial collage of signs, posters, handbills and merchandise, to be imbibed as one strolls.

Similarly, Benjamin scholar Anne Friedberg has pointed out that, "by the middle of the 18th century, shopkeepers began to realize that the window might be a prime proscenium for commodity display" (Friedberg, 65). This moment marked an early juncture in the history of the mobilized shopper's gaze that knows how to "read the social hieroglyphs of the commodit[ies] on display" (ibid., 57). For Friedberg, the visual pleasure of commodity culture is predicated on the theatricality of the shop window as "the site of seduction for consumer desire," and as a place to watch the endless parade of goods which would later develop into the continuous visual pleasure of film (ibid., 65). The excitement of moving images would, a century and a half after Hogarth, become a prime means of presenting the mobilized pedestrian gaze in modern culture.

In this light, it is not difficult to see how Hogarth's comics art, in which he strove to render motion and invite the beholder into a visually tactile and "moving apprehension," is part of a continuum that includes the moving-image entertainment (TV, film, computer games) that is such an essential part of commodity culture. As suggested above, the movement and thrust of this kind of democratized commercial aesthetics was supposedly obvious to Hogarth's industrial laborer who "constantly uses the leaver" and powers the modern machine that mass-produced consumable goods like comic prints (Hogarth, 6). It was also apparent to producers of many products in the 18th century, including those of women's fans, which were marketed at that time as an essential semiotic accoutrement of social interaction. Such fans were often decorated with illustrations including Hogarth's processes, which unfolded like a short film across the face of the modern coquette.[22]

... the art of seeing...

> The more prevailing the notion may be, that painters and connoisseurs are the only competent judges of things of this sort; the more it becomes necessary to clear up and confirm [...] that no one may be deterr'd [...] from entering into this enquiry.
>
> — Hogarth

In their introduction to *The Other Hogarth*, Fort and Rosenthal cite, among the most salient features of the artist's *oeuvre* "[c]onsumption and commercialization in an expanding global market" (5). Hogarth was, as I have hinted, a savvy businessman who was not opposed to applying his trade to the purpose of advertising. He produced business cards for his sisters' millinery that "showed the actual interior of a shop with bolts of material, clerks and customers," captioned "Wholesale or Retale, at Reasonable Rates" (Paulson 1971, 233). He was no less shrewd where his own livelihood was concerned, and placed an early announcement for the publication of *The Analysis of Beauty* in Henry Fielding's *Covent-Garden Journal* March 24, 1752, in the hope of securing advanced sales. The announcement featured the "bait" in the form of the Freemasonic pyramid and curving serpent, and advertised publication in four installments including "Two Explanatory Prints, serious and comical engraved on large Copper-Plates, fit to frame for Furniture" (Paulson, xvii). Early subscribers could pre-purchase the first installment for the special rate of 5 shillings until November, and then opt to pay another 5 shillings upon delivery of the next installments and prints. Late subscribers paid 15 shillings for the complete *Analysis* as well as the accompanying "ready to frame" prints, which themselves enjoyed further editions in their own right, and which out-sold the book.

While Hogarth was well aware of the market in which his prints circu-lated and the profits they could generate, it is important to consider how the greater context enters into the picture. As De Bolla has pointed out, the mid-point of the 18th century saw a "growth in the audience for culture [that was] stimulated by greater capacities for reproducing and disseminating" aesthetic objects of varying "quality" (DeBolla, 6). Similarly, Friedberg has argued that a major cultural shift resulted from this moment, which saw the "organization of the look in the service of consumption, and the gradual incorporation of the commodified experience into everyday life" through popular culture (DeBolla, 3). And, as authors including De Bolla, Ogée, McCloud, and Hog-arth himself have reasoned, the commercial, mass-produced art that came to the fore in the 18th century elicited an active, sensuous, emotive — in short, sentimental — spectatorial identification:

> The *sentimental* look operates via a fully somatic insertion into the visual field. It makes the body present to sight, folding it into a set of gestures or attitudes that enable the viewer to feel his or her presence in the visual sphere, feel the self in sight, and in so doing it stimulates the cognitive process of affective response [...] the sentimental look presents the viewer to the object and to vision, allows the viewer both to recognize itself in the place of the seen and to identify with the process of seeing [De Bolla, 11, my italics].

The sentimental look and its capacity to draw spectators in and *hold* them, while making them feel part of the spectacle or image is, as I have been arguing, precisely what makes Hogarth's progresses, and the comics medium in general, so very engaging. This was part and parcel of "a culture that was increasingly comfortable with the notion of being-in-the-picture, in the plane of representation," not just as a function of the projection of the self into images, but also where the circulation of spectators in new public spaces such as museums and shopping streets was concerned (De Bolla, 60). Hence, while the canvas or image itself is an eye-catcher within the spacings of the exhibition room, it also structures the exchange of glances that may take place in public places at a time when more and more of the "'middling sort' began to figure more forcibly in the public sphere" (ibid., 23). And this, of course, threatened social order by opening a *porte d'entrée* for both artists and admirers of the "inferior sphere" of "mechanical arts" into the culture of the cognoscenti.

Herein lay the crux of a number of issues for people in the 18th century, which persist largely unresolved today. Faced with an ever-increasing body of commercial, sentimental art and a "very vivacious production [from] popular imagery and sign painting," the upper classes lamented "those Objects, that everywhere [were] thrusting themselves out to the Eye, and envdeavouring to become visible" (Georgel, 97, 99). This gave rise to a voluble public debate on the notion of the "connoisseur," those socially superior persons who distinguished themselves from every Sally Housecoat and Johnny Lunchbucket now participating in culture, by virtue of their superior appreciation of high art, and their disdain for mechanical or mass-produced art.[23] At the same time, however, artists, like everyone else, were becoming increasingly dependant on the market for their income. So whereas artists previously relied on the patronage of "persons of quality," they were now often obliged to finance themselves publicly, while treading a fine line between appealing to the trained eye of the connoisseur and diminishing their potential market in sales to the uninformed masses.

Hogarth's involvement in this debate was poorly received, and cartoons of the artist with his Line of Beauty began circulating directly following the publication *The Analysis*.[24] This reception is unfortunate, given that his "intervention represents the most ambitious counterargument to the academic view concerning the need for 'book learning' in the appreciation of the visual arts" in 18th-century debates on aesthetics (De Bolla, 25). What makes Hogarth's argument so radical is his isolation of the Line of Beauty, which disrupts the "more prevailing notion" that "painters and connoisseurs are the only competent judges of things of this sort," and considerably democratizes the "art of seeing" because such lines are familiar to all (ibid., 18).[25]

This point is perhaps best illustrated by the collection of art objects at the centre of plate 1 of *The Analysis*, which represented Henry Cheere's statuary yard at Hyde Park Corner. Cheere's enterprise was one in a row of such yards that specialized in mass-produced, cheap lead copies of classical sculptures, whose execution was "so monstrously wretched, that one [could] hardly guess at their Originals" (James Ralph, quoted in Paulson 1993, 101). By including a drawing of his friend's statue yard, and suggesting that people learn about aesthetics from it, Hogarth was providing advertising for Cheere, while directly flying in the face of academicians who favored instructing artists by having them copy more accurate casts of canonical sculptures from antiquity.[26] While Hogarth effectively falls in with the "Ignorance and Folly of the Buyers [...] resolv'd to [...] purchase their Follies as cheap as possible" and "Workmen in a wrong Taste of Designing" who are "hasty and rude in Finishing," he is also suggesting that beauty and aesthetic value have more to do with basic Lines of Beauty than with a culturally constructed, class-driven canon (ibid.). In other words, Hogarth's line holds out the means with which to by-pass the high/low art distinction that was being so rigorously policed by the mid–18th century, and which continues to keep comics art in the proverbial gutter today.

The Financial Revolution and Comic Art

There is one common, if perhaps not immediately obvious, thread that runs through my argument, just as the Line of Beauty runs through Hogarth's *Analysis*. I would argue that this thread is the direct or indirect source of all the forms of mid 18th-century movement and dynamism to which I have referred thus far. While the industrial revolution quite obviously facilitated mobility and sped production, it was the financial revolution, which occurred roughly from 1688 to 1776, that radically altered the class system by creating surplus wealth which permitted social mobility.[27] At the same time, the notion of credit at the center of this revolution created new ways of obtaining and producing wealth, while necessitating the forward projection of profits and interest, thereby shifting attention to the future.

It was, moreover, a highly volatile market that came to occupy such a central role in all aspects of daily life beginning in the 18th century. Fueled by intense dissatisfaction with the royal mishandling of debt, and spurred on by the excitement of a credit-based economy managed by new public institutions like banks, the market picked up a dizzying head of speed. And while the giddy force of the market made it possible for everyone to buy shares, profit, and enjoy new commodities, the economy it drove was also new, naïve, and open to wild experimentation. For example, the South Sea Bubble, known as the first episode in a now familiar cycle of booms and crashes, was the demise of hundreds of small enterprises licensed almost purely for the purposes of creating public stock for trade and speculation. When a rush on shares caused a colossal crisis in 1720, Hogarth immediately commemorated the event in a popular comic print that sold for 1 shilling.[28] As scholars have suggested, "the creation of various types of memorabilia" around the South Sea Bubble "depended upon pleasing the public rather than upon" accurately representing the events of 1720.[29] Hence, The South Sea Bubble became a popular motif for artists because this rapid upset was dramatic and exciting, yet it also provided an arena for satire and moralizing about greed and mob madness.

If Hogarth's South Sea Bubble print is merely a popularization of commonly held (mis)apprehensions of this first market crash, Hogarth's *Marriage à la Mode* (Fig. 4) reveals a keen understanding of the economy and its new drivers. This progress, commonly thought of as "attacking the 'property marriage'" and the financialization of that aspect of daily life in the 18th century, also fully articulates the dynamic of the market which animates Hogarth's own commercial art (Paulson 1996, 43). Here, I want to focus briefly on the first panel, depicting the negotiation of a marriage between Earl Squander's son and the daughter of a wealthy city merchant, in a six-panel progress that ends in death and disaster. The negotiation takes place in Earl Squander's mansion, which provides a perfect setting for the vibrant interchange of Hogarthian Lines of Beauty in details such as the back wall, displaying eight detailed paintings arranged to suggest a parallel sequential narrative. Likewise, in characteristic fashion, Hogarth suggests the passage of time through his horizontal arrangement of character clusters arrested in "suspended action," with "every person at one instant of time" of the narrative tableau (Hogarth, 103).

But the action at the center of the panel is where movement converges, and where marriage is focused through markers of the new, volatile financial market. Hogarth illustrates exchange in this market through an element of still life, depicting a pile of coins and a number of documents on a table between Earl Squander and the merchant. This segment recalls Foucault's analysis of Velázquez's *Las Meninas* (1656), in which he describes the painting as "present[ing] us with the entire cycle of representation" in the 17th century, including mirrors, an artist's canvas, palette, and brush ("the material tools of representation"), all contained in another representation, which dissolves and returns as the viewer moves in and out of the illusion (Foucault 1994, 11). In a similar gesture, Hogarth renders the entire cycle of the representation of money during a paradigmatic shift in economic thought and practice, as money was becoming ever more abstract and virtual. Hence, set off against coin and

Fig. 4. Hogarth, *Marriage à la Mode*, panel 1, "The Marriage Settlement," 1720.

a title, the old "material tools of representation," are instruments of credit like the mortgages, paper money, and shares proffered by the merchant. These financial instruments are also set off against the *real* estate visible through a window directly behind the Earl. Here, that least liquid form of wealth includes a building project that the Earl is unable to finance. In other words, the *landed* gentry represented by Earl Squander is giving way to a growing merchant class that moves wealth quickly by projecting credit and interest into the future and conducting trade through the abstract medium of paper.

In choosing such a transaction as the central theme for a progress that Hogarth both painted and printed to be sold as an inexpensive sequential narrative or comic to an expanding middle class, he was challenging and critiquing notions of class and of what constitutes art for the privileged few. The artist was also acknowledging, however implicitly, that his progresses and panels were a new kind of aesthetic production that delivered a fast-paced, haptic form of narrative for the entertainment of a specialized, emergent reader, namely the modern economic subject.

Conclusion

In this essay, I have advanced the notion that Hogarth's art, and consciously commercial art more generally, grew up in the 18th century alongside a booming and fast-moving market economy, heavily invested in the new finance.[30] *The Analysis of Beauty*, published as it was in quick succession to any number of treatises on the Beautiful and aesthetic pleasure, made visible the complicity of art with the (art)market, and destabilized theories of the beautiful that sought to establish and justify a canon. *The Analysis* explicitly welcomed the "mechanik" arts so that "no one should be deterr'd from discussing" questions of beauty because, for Hogarth, taste was not limited to the upper classes and their "connoisseurs" (18). If the aesthetic pleasure that emanates from the Line of Beauty consists in ocular kinesis (the movement of the eye), haptic sensual involvement (the thrills and chills), and the illusion of movement, then beauty is to be found in the mass-produced candlesticks and corkscrews with which Hogarth demonstrated his theory, as much as in Caravaggios.

Moreover, because Hogarth's Line of Beauty permeates high and low art alike, it resolves the issue of commerciality, with which Scott McCloud struggles at length in the seventh chapter of *Understanding Comics*. The argument he presents consists in fine-tuning the relationship of comics to the market by offering a comics gradient from less commercial, more artist-driven, to more commercial comics created with little or no aesthetic morality or sense of purpose other than making money. This gesture effectively establishes yet another canon (a highly questionable concept in and of itself) in the world of "mechanic" art where it does not belong. I would like to close by advancing the polemical notion that it is precisely comics art's constant involvement with the market that gives it the dynamic look, speed and feel that readers so enjoy. And Hogarth's Line of Beauty, as simple a concept as it may be, helps us to recognize the aesthetic merit of those arts that continue to remain, in McCloud's idiom, "invisible."

Notes

1. For more on "forerunners" of comics, see Shesgreen, 577.
2. Although one might intuit that hieroglyphs fall under McCloud's definition of the comics medium as "juxtaposed, pictorial and other images in deliberate sequence, intended to convey information, and/or to produce an aesthetic response in the viewer," the author insists that hieroglyphics are related to "the written word and not comics" (9, 13).
3. The Masonic pyramid first appeared on the American fifty-dollar bill, issued September 26, 1778. The all-seeing eye pyramid, also of Masonic origin, has been printed on the back of American one-dollar bills since 1935. On this point see Standish, 121. Cf. Jeffers, 165.
4. See W. Bro. Yasha Beresiner, "William Hogarth: The Man, the Artist and his Masonic Circle," *Masonic Papers*, http://www.freemasons-freemasonry.com/beresiner11.html. For more on Hogarth's specific contributions to Masonry, see Ridley 257, 277.

5. Note that the Line of Beauty and the pyramid are supported by variety, which is an obvious and important aspect of Hogarth's output. See Chapter II, "Of Variety," in *The Analysis*.

6. Although he had not yet published his work on the Line of Beauty when Garrick famously quoted him, Hogarth frequently discussed his philosophy within his circle of famous friends so that the Line of Beauty had considerable currency even before *The Analysis* was published. Cf. Paulson's introduction to Hogarth, xx.

7. All italics are in Hogarth's original text unless otherwise indicated.

8. Hogarth, 34.

9. The pyramid is supposedly equally dynamic because: "There is no object composed of straight lines, that has so much variety, with so few parts, as the pyramid; and it is its constantly varying from its base gradually upwards in every situation of the eye, (without giving the idea of sameness, as the eye moves round it) that has made it esteem'd in all ages" (Hogarth, 30). On Balzac's later use of the pyramid in *La Peau de Chagrin* (1831) to create this same illusion of movement and to express the instability of the fictional world of his novel, see Bell 190 and Weber 44–50.

10. "It is easy to conceive that the attitude of a person upon the cross, may be fully signified by the two straight lines of the cross" (102). See also Fig. 3, plate 2, middle right, panels 69 and 70.

11. Hogarth, 95.

12. The baby's face composed of four circles is panel 116, followed by panels 110–114, and then 117 and 118. This is a prime example of Hogarth's erratic numbering system, which was ridiculed by his detractors. See Paulson 1991, 134–141.

13. See chapter 2, "The Vocabulary of Comics." It is worth noting that, although McCloud's work bears a remarkable resemblance to Hogarth's *Analysis of Beauty*, it is unlikely that the author of *Understanding Comics* was directly influenced by the 18th-century artist — the simplest reason being that the *Analysis of Beauty* was a rather obscure work with limited circulation until 1997 when Hogarth's *Analysis* was edited and re-published, some three years after the publication of McCloud's work.

14. See McCloud 29.

15. Hogarth, 42.

16. Both Hogarth and McCloud devote a considerable portion of their argument to discussing single panels in which time can be read as moving across the panel. For Hogarth, this is the case in his composite ballroom scene at the center of panel 2, which he proposes reading as moving across time chronologically from left to right (Hogarth, 33). Compare this with McCloud's chapter 4, "Time Frames on individual panels that contain time sequences and the temporal structure of comics in general" (McCloud, 96–97).

17. These are just some of the kinds of sense that readers make across gutters and, of course, there are many different kinds of gutters. For more on this topic, see McCloud chapter 3, "Blood in the Gutter," 60–93.

18. Cf. Riehl 38–41 and Lamb, 183. Paulson also argues that Richardson borrows "from Hogarth's progresses the particular Hogarthian graphic version of play, with big scenes, symbolic gestures and objects" (Paulson 1996, 39). Elsewhere, Paulson has written that, along with Hogarth's images in *Tristram Shandy*, "the Shandean inheritance from Hogarth's *Analysis* [includes the] Shandean reading structure (serpentine, not straight lines; avoid all rules; digressive is progressive)," based "on the practice of reading a Hogarth print" (Paulson, "Introduction" to *The Analysis of Beauty*, l). While this claim is perhaps subject to criticism, the appeal and bravado of advancing the notion that visual sequential narrative shaped the traditional 18th-century English novel is tremendously evocative. Cf. Bartual, *passim*.

19. "Hogarth's ambition was to present himself, an English artist and a Londoner, as the visual interpreter of contemporary urban life [...]. Today the phrase 'Age of Hogarth' is often used to describe the early–Georgian period, just as 'Hogarthian London' has come to characterize its capital city. In his own time, William Hogarth (1697–1764) was appreciated as the most dynamic and influential artist working in Britain" (Riding, 1).

20. Cf. Klucinskas: "Sa [Hogarth] modernité se manifeste d'abord par son choix de sujets" (5).

21. According to Elizabeth Kowaleski-Wallace, this passage in Burney is "the first recorded instance of the verb *to shop*" (91).

22. On this point, see Angela Rosenthal's fascinating essay entitled "Unfolding Gender: Women and the 'Secret' Sign Language of Fans in Hogarth's Work," passim. See also Crary, Chapter 1, passim.

23. The main players in these debates were Joseph Addison who published *Pleasures of the Imagination*, in 1712 as numbers 411 through 421 of *The Spectator*, Lord Shaftsbury, Joshua Reynolds and Jonathan Richardson, to whom Hogarth disparagingly refers below.

24. See Paul Sandby's *The Author Run Mad* (1754), published in the 1997 edition of *The Analysis of Beauty*.

25. "[...] it is not unreasonable to suppose, that this discernment [of the eye] is still capable of further improvements by instructions from a methodical enquiry; which the ingenious Mr. Richardson, in his treatise on painting, terms *the art of seeing*" (Hogarth, 94).

26. In a similar vein, Shesgreen writes that Hogarth eschewed "the usual sources of material like the Bible, history, mythology, and pervious art, drawing instead on his own experience and imaginations" (573).

27. See North and Weingast. Their article is often credited as one of the first to identify the "financial revolution."

28. For a detailed account of the South Sea Bubble see Dale, 96–140.

29. See for example, Helen Julia Paul, forthcoming.

30. As I have argued elsewhere (Goggin, forthcoming) along with many others, art and money are not separable, and this includes art in general. Probably the most forceful argument in this regard can be found in Marc Shell's *Art and Money*, passim.

2

Ridiculous Rebellion
George L. Carlson and the Recovery of Jingle Jangle Comics
Daniel F. Yezbick

> Carlson was a *rara avis*. One of a kind. His like has never been seen before, and since him it has all been the sincerest form of flattery.
> — Harlan Ellison

The cover of the June 1945 issue of *Jingle Jangle Comics* depicts a bizarre scene: Little Bo Peep, Prince Charming, Peter Rabbit, and Humpty Dumpty all gawking as a slick, red-headed dandy and his impish sidekick drive an automobile through the gate of an archetypal fairytale castle. Next, the voyagers attempt to refuel their supped-up jalopy, flashing a "Gas Ration Card" at Humpty, who tends the pump in sensible shoes and a dashing brown bowler. Amidst this queer assembly stands a signpost: "Fairy-Tale Land: Dream at Your own Risk!" Regular readers of *Jingle Jangle* would presumably recognize the drivers as Bingo and Glum, Woody Gelman's precocious adventurers, on their way off into the unknown once again. Their madcap escapades in Storybook Land exemplified the series' self-conscious fusion of classic and contemporary children's fantasy; a kooky mosaic built — as this cover suggests — on the blending of traditional Mother Goose myths with thoroughly modern concerns such as wartime limitations on interstate travel and gas rationing. This was the stuff that kept so many of Eastman Color's young readers interested on a bi-monthly basis for forty-two issues between 1942 and 1949, yet Gelman's fairy-tale barnstormers may have been consigned to oblivion, except for the almost accidental rediscovery of George Leonard Carlson. Decades after *Jingle Jangle Comics* and the world that produced it ceased to be, critics, scholars, and comic aficionados have recovered this unassuming maestro of absurdity who conceived of a comic book wherein dreams and fairy tales would become culturally and aesthetically risky business.[1]

In general, *Jingle Jangle Comics* rates "at best an obscure footnote in most 'versions' of comics history" (Calhoun, 32). As Martin Gardner noted in 1994, "the only tributes to Carlson have been in histories of comic books ... [which] have yet to discover his much more important and prolific contributions" to popular children's media (Gardner 1994, vi). Since then, comics scholars have begun to explore Carlson's interdisciplinary influence as a children's illustrator, riddle maker, crossword designer, art instructor, and "a puzzle maker for the very young" — a skill at which Gardner claims "Carlson had no equal" (ibid.).[2] Beginning in the early 1900s and continuing well into the 1950s, Carlson was a frequent contributor to national magazines and newspapers, but his most impressive early works include the multitude of puzzles, riddles, cut-outs, and visual games he produced for *John Martin's Book: The Child's Magazine* from 1913 to 1933. Carlson also developed an excitingly interactive idiom for children's anthologies and magazines, which included word games, puzzles, and cartoons. These interactive media brought fresh life to early reading, art instruction, periodical cartooning, and comic book design. As Gardner has observed, a complete list of his works "would run to almost a hundred titles," including not only book jackets, political campaign stamps, transportation and advertising premiums, comic strips, and comic books, but also "novelty paperbacks [like] coloring books, paint-with-water books, connect-the-dots books, maze books, how-to-draw books, a series about Uncle Wiggily, and books of riddles, games, and crossword puzzles" (Gardner 1990, 153).

As Gardner himself has reminisced, "a few thousand Americans from middle and upper income families" fondly recall Carlson's signature character of the 1920s, Peter Puzzlemaker; his vivid portrayal of Howard R. Garis' Uncle Wiggily in the 1930s; and the Pie-face Prince Dimwitty of Pretzelberg of the 1940s. These characters could challenge and entice a reader's sense of logic and curiosity by mixing words and images in clever, often confounding ways. In most of his creations, Carlson establishes an enjoyably cheeky multivalent address that toys with conventions of word, image, and sequence, and which still fascinates both children and adults (Gardner 1990, 145). Today, the lucky few who encounter Carlson's peculiar mixture of interrogative address with comic art and juvenile literature find his work among the most intriguingly reflexive in comics history:

> Carlson brought a sophisticated approach to fairy tales, turning out multileveled material in which the visual and verbal worked together. The dialogue in his work demonstrated his fascination with language; it contained left-handed puns, and

stock phrases twisted into new and unexpected shapes. Quite obviously he was amusing himself first and foremost with conscientious dedication [Goulart 2001, 152].

With his more than 30 years as a children's illustrator, puzzle designer, and commercial artist, Carlson developed the Jingle Jangle concept and shopped it to various publishers as both a children's book and a Sunday newspaper feature with no success (N. B. Wright, 124). In the meantime, he worked as a ghost artist on Gene Byrnes' popular newspaper "kid strip" *Reg'lar Fellas*, from the "early 1920s onward" into the 1940s (Goulart 2003, 22). Ironically, Carlson's anonymous work on the strip was widely praised for its fresh humor and dynamic design.[3] In 1947, Coulton Waugh's homage to *The Comics* unknowingly saluted the wrong man for *Reg'lar Fellas'* quality cartooning:

> There is an artistic quality about this strip also, especially in the big color Sunday pages of the old days. Gene Byrnes knew how to spot lively and decorative blacks through his page, and he took full advantage of the set of comic conventions which had been established. So we will find a fine assortment of comic stars and whirligigs, plenty of *Pows* and *Bams*. It is a tribute to Byrnes that his readers' interest is sustained without the lurid accoutrements employed by the average comic artist [Waugh, 116].

The "inventive, furiously alive" technique that Waugh so admires — not to mention the lively blacking and whimsical sound effects — all confirm that Carlson's silent presence lent the strip a uniquely engaging type of "healthy, heartening steam" (Waugh, 116).[4] When *Reg'lar Fellas* was later developed into a comic book, Carlson's association with Byrnes probably put him in contact with Steve Douglas, a shrewd editor at Eastern Color, publishers of the long-running newspaper strip anthology series, *Famous Funnies* (Goulart 2003, 24). Later, Carlson sold Douglas his Jingle Jangle concept and worked "in close harmony" with him to develop an anthology title much like *Famous Funnies* that could be "aimed at the very young" in order to exploit the growing markets in comic-books for pre-literate or early readers (N. Wright, 122).

When the series debuted in the early 1940s with Carlson as a sort of artistic director and "star cartoonist," he was already an "old hand" at designing for children's media (Goulart 2001, 152). As Ron Goulart has observed, "Carlson was a one-man band of a cartoonist who did scripting, penciling, inking — the works. Apparently dedicated to these stories, Carlson always submitted a one-page synopsis of each one to Steve Douglas. After getting the okay, he would prepare a detailed outline that mixed typed copy and handsome full-color pencil sketches" (ibid.). However, the most engaging and personal material of Carlson's career would appear in *Jingle Jangle Comics'* hip mixture of old and new. In fact, the sometimes dissonant fusion of fairy tales with modern life probably helped to distinguish Eastern Color's young readers title from the surging wave of humor and funny animal books that came to "assault the kiddie market" in the mid–1940s (Goulart 2001, 144).

Around this time, industry marketing reports "found that the comic book audience comprised approximately ninety-five percent of all boys and ninety-one percent of all girls between the ages of six and eleven" and that "superheroes alone would no longer be able to carry the industry" (B. Wright, 57). Between the previous vogue for the "paternalistic, imperialistic, and racist" dynamics of violence-driven jungle comics and wartime super-hero fantasies, and just slightly before the rise of EC Comics' scandalous horror, crime, and science fiction titles in the mid–1950s, funny animal and related humorous comic books would balloon in popularity and diversity (B. Wright, 37). In fact, by the mid–1950s, the funny animal book had become one of the most popular and resilient genres in post-war American comics:

> In the 1930s and 1940s there was a good deal more to be found in comic books than just superheroes and costumed crime-fighters. During those years, when the comic book market was still expanding, quite a few comic books really were comic. All sorts of funny animal stuff was available, from relatively sophisticated satire to knockabout burlesque to the kind of bunny-rabbit whimsy that produced giggles in the nursery. The decade of the forties, especially, was a period when publishers sought to expand their audience in both directions, luring older readers with such things as true crime and sexy women and enticing younger readers with more wholesome fare. Most of the material for titles aimed at tots was humorous, and a great many of them featured funny animals [Goulart 2001, 139].

In a sense, funny animal and humor anthologies were throwbacks to the "ludicrous nonsense and way-out slapstick" of early newspaper funnies, but also stylish upgrades of popular mass-market characters and scenarios (Reitberger and Fuchs, 29). Dell's anthology series, *Walt Disney's Comics and Stories*, featured Carl Barks and his inimitable duck adventures, and *Animal Comics* featuring Walt Kelly's Pogo the Possum comprised the most enduring and celebrated of these humor series. Spurred on by the phenomenal success of the "Whitman-Dell Coalition" that developed the best-selling Disney comic books, as well as series based on Warner Brothers and MGM properties, other publishers launched similarly juvenile anthropomorphic titles like Marvel's *Krazy Comics*, DC's *Funny Stuff*, or ACG's *Giggle* and *Ha Ha Comics* (Goulart 2001, 144).

With fanciful material like Gelman's Bingo and Glum, Ben Levin's supersenior citizen Aunty Spry, and Dave Tendlar's quirky bird buddies Chauncy Chirp and Johnny Jay, *Jingle Jangle Comics* helped Eastern Color compete within the young readers' slapstick humor market. Still, buyers could tell immediately that "*Jingle Jangle Comics* was different" in some unexpected ways (N. Wright, 122). Nearly every issue's "mixture of funny animals and humans" was set off by two recurring Carlson features: the ever-quixotic misadventures of Prince Dimwitty the Pie-face Prince of Pretzelberg, and the titular *Jingle Jangle Tales*, which were outrageously original dismantlings of the principal contrivances of nursery rhymes and fairy tales (ibid.). Considering how few covers actually advertised either of Carlson's series, we might assume that Chauncy Chirp and his ilk were probably more popular, and that Carlson's own innovations were hardly appreciated in their time:

> *Jingle Jangle Comics* was never an outstanding success during the Golden Age, and is even more obscure in retrospect. [...] It was, to all outward evidence, just one more commercial periodical introduced to meet a market and discontinued when that market ceased to sustain it [Lupoff and Thompson, 240].

Similarly, Harlan Ellison eulogizes the disappearance of George Carlson's series as something more than a minor commercial tragedy:

> And save for the few who could obtain those old comics, to marvel and chuckle at the product of a rare and febrile imagination, a wit as rich as any in American Humor, he dwindled into the realm of the forgotten [...] swept away with the silt and persiflage of a world whose attention is constantly being diverted to wrest a buck from its grasp [Ellison 1990, 3].

Considering Carlson's substantial achievements in so many fields of art, design, and leisure, Ellison's melancholy tone seems appropriate and merits, perhaps, a brief assessment of how the fields of comics and comics criticism have evolved.

The Secret Origins and Infinite Crises of Comics Theory and Criticism

As Nancy Goldstein observes in her exhaustive study *Jackie Ormes: The First African American Woman Cartoonist*: "We are in the midst of a significant revaluation of the importance of cartoons and comic strips to American commerce, culture, and politics" (Goldstein, 1). In the new century, comic art in all its forms continues to gain aesthetic and historical credibility with prestige museum exhibitions; *New York Times* feature articles, *NPR* interviews, and *New Yorker* special issues; Pulitzer, Booker, and Nebula awards; further refereed journals and academic anthologies; and, of course, record-breaking box-office success in crossover films, computer games, TV series, and multimedia franchises. Critics assessing the production, consumption, and remediation of comics have also expanded their interests to recover past masters who were either too good, too poor, or too unlucky to remain in vogue or in print. Recent comics scholarship has made a trenchant effort to look backwards into the dusty corners of comics lore, recouping and re-assessing the mainstream narrative of popular publishing, graphic design, and creative influence in American cartooning.[5] As the search for obscure mavericks and idiosyncratic outsiders continues, the creations of George Carlson have come to light among the more disheartening oversights in the history of American children's art.

As often as we now celebrate the genius, success, or celebrity of pioneers like Winsor McCay or Will Eisner; absurdists like George Herriman and Rube Goldberg; entrepreneurial *auteurs* like Milton Caniff or Al Capp; or international phenomena like Charles Schulz and, more recently, Frank Miller, we are just now coming to understand the stories of those who struggled for their craft. Most creators worked desperately and anonymously within or outside of the established systems of labor, distribution, and consumption that controlled and defined the history of comics for much of the last century. Even those devoted critics, fans, and scholars who thought they knew the story well for so many years have come to question their own conceptions of comics history. The recovery of marginalized or nearly forgotten talents like Nell Brinkley, Tarpe Mills, Henry Kiyama, Mine Okubo, Jackie Ormes, and Brumsic Brandon Jr. confirms the need for further vigorous plumbing of the medium, its past, and its practices. The recapitulation of an unsung and under-appreciated artist like George Carlson brings a certain sobriety or sadness to comics studies. As Ellison observed in the 1970 essay that almost single-handedly restored Carlson's reputation:

> I find it not strange at all that Carlson should have managed to spin his fantasy webs for so short a time. He was too far in advance of himself. What he did was miraculous and happens only once in a particular art-form. We will never see his like again. Thank God he passed this way at least once. It was a richer world for George Carlson from '43 to '49. And have you noticed [...] it's been a lot sadder since? [Ellison 1970, 247–8].

As Ellison suggests, recovering George Carlson more than 40 years after his death betrays certain limitations in our understanding of how comics, cartoons, and the mechanisms that disseminate them have been studied and scrutinized. Balanced rather precariously between the somewhat divergent interests of creators, publishers, collectors, and now, academics, comic art has remained a troublesome property that cries out for richer, more intrepid analysis, especially in American contexts. The parsing of its histories, the exploration of its influences, the plumbing of its origins, and the investigation of its narrative powers are all somewhat limited by the medium's perpetual struggle for legitimacy and recognition within larger systems of scholarship and appreciation in the U.S. The bulk of the mainstream comics industry and its specialized back issue market continue to revolve around superhero material and remediated manga franchises like Pokemon or Dragon-Ball Z. The resulting critical discourse surrounding such material has only recently expanded to the point where it can accurately explore the idiosyncrasies of rare voices like George Carlson, whose biography has remained even more obscure than his vibrant and inventive comics. Luckily, some substantive ties to the past have endured to help produce a more complete picture of the reserved artist who devised some of America's most unrestrained comic book art.

The Rara Avis Redefined

Critics since Ellison have observed that Carlson's comics exude a peculiar personal edge — an almost perverse delight in composing wild dreamscapes and fanciful companions in the manner of Alice's many adventures through Lewis Carroll's Wonderland. But new evidence suggests that George Carlson's personal life was as sedate and unassuming as his creations were outrageous and exuberant. Beginning his professional career as a commercial artist with a comic drawing of a Native-American baseball player for the *Whitley County News* in 1903, Carlson's relatively unsung but prodigious output in both juvenile and adult publishing and advertising ranks among the most inventive achievements in American children's media. Recent examinations of his interdisciplinary fusion of picture books and cartoon art have helped, and more are in production, but many details concerning Carlson's life remain obscure to comics studies, children's literature, and advertising history. Even with the renewed interest in his creations, only a fraction of Carlson's output as a cartoonist and illustrator remains in print.[6]

In his 1970 exhumation of Carlson's comics, wherein Ellison took comfort in assuming that though the old artist "doesn't do that anymore," he might have had some inkling of the developing enthusiasm about his Jingle Jangle stories:

> He is Santa Claus and Peter Pan and the Great Pumpkin and the Genie in the Jug and what Walt Disney started out to be and never quite made. George Carlson is [...] Or, rather, he was. He's still alive. I have it on good authority, though I've been unable to track him down [Ellison 1970, 241].

In fact, Carlson had died in 1962, and did not live to see his comics and puzzles develop a following.

If Ellison, then *enfant terrible* of psychedelic Science Fiction, had actually met Carlson, he might have been very surprised at the staid lifestyle of this "Samuel Beckett in clever plastic disguise" (Ellison 1970, 241). Interviews with Carlson's surviving daughter June and his grandson Henry Bishop have confirmed a number of details about the man who polished his designs, comics, and drawings in his home studios in Fairfield and later Bridgeport, Connecticut, and peddled them from an office in New York. He was a reportedly kind, reserved and fastidious husband and father whose time as an army cartographer in Washington D.C. earned him a military funeral. Carlson also dressed up regularly for dinner and enjoyed (ironically for Ellison) numerous Disney entertainments with his children and grandchildren, including *Mickey Mouse Magazine* and *The Wonderful World of Disney*. Like many fastidious cartoonists, Carlson kept voluminous files for research and tended to regularly excuse himself from company and family gatherings to work alone upstairs. However, like so many aging artists, Carlson eventually found his unique brand of humor out of step with contemporary styles. By the early 1950s, he seemed unable to produce the type of material the market required. At the urging of his wife, he abandoned cartooning to work as a catalogue designer for Apex Tools, now in Farmington, CT. Though he continued to compile the occasional anthology of jokes, riddles, or crosswords, few of his children's projects saw print after the cancellation of *Jingle Jangle Comics*.

Recent insights into Carlson's life also engender several compelling enigmas that the artist himself might well have appreciated. For example, he spent more than fifty years drawing and designing for children in various formats, yet neither his daughter nor his grandchildren can recall him ever showing, sharing, or testing his material with them. Even more strangely, Carlson's work exudes a continuous affinity with Lewis Carroll's *Alice in Wonderland*, after which he named his second daughter Alice and nicknamed his wife "the Duchess." Carlson's lifelong interest in Carroll's Wonderland also led to several full-length, unpublished comics-inspired adaptations of the Alice books and a short-lived serial "Alec in Fumbleland," which appeared in *Puzzle Fun Comics* in 1943 — an abortive attempt to fuse his two loves of cartooning and puzzle design into a single equitable series. Like Carroll, Carlson seems to retreat again and again into nonsensical scenarios that speak to a furious creativity which, by the mid–1940s, could find no viable commercial outlet.

Though his world was filled with games, riddles, and cartoons, he only read his own children the Sunday comics under duress. Nicknamed "Gookel" since childhood, he often "retired from reality" in order to create, and rarely interacted in the diverse communities that circulated around comic book or comic strip production. He never took on assistants or ghost artists, and sometimes neglected to sign some of his best work in *Jingle Jangle Comics*.[7] Though hardly a recluse, Carlson apparently preferred foreign language textbooks on Swedish and German to movies and TV. The legacy of this last quirk is evidenced in some of the hyper-extended wordplay of Carlson's comics and the occasional joke involving Swedish sound effects.

So how is it then that a teetotaling Baptist who raised two daughters and played with his grandchildren outside his modest Connecticut home ended up delving so deeply into almost psychedelically absurd comic worlds? And more importantly: why has Carlson remained such a marginalized figure in spite of his influence in so many different fields of publishing and children's entertainment?

Nefarious Narrative Strategies and Chaotically Comic Worlds

Perhaps the tardiness in recovering and re-assessing Carlson's importance stems from his proficiency at combining and subverting established codes of word and image narrative. Carlson's knack for dismantling language — which so amused children and adults alike — also exudes something beautifully convulsive and potentially disturbing through its insistence on nonsensical pairings, shocking literalisms, and anarchic explosions of doubled, tripled, or otherwise overburdened signifiers. Like his great influence Lewis Carroll, Carlson's whimsical works tend to critique and condemn conventional systems of order and control. To more fully appreciate how deeply Carlson's comics mobilized and antagonized written and visual literacies, one must begin with an examination of the mediating potential of the comics page itself.

Recent advances in narrative theory and comics mediation have provided valuable critical frameworks for appraising Carlson's beguiling puzzles. Because his word-image games can be quite confounding, Carlson's comics present an especially valuable narratological guide for examining what Thierry Groensteen calls the "iconic solidarity" which drives the semiotic linkages of "iconotexts" like picture books and comic art (Groensteen 2007, 18). Carlson's zany creations are really more about mixing the "iconotext" of children's picture-books with the didactic nature of what Groensteen has called comics' "fragmentary system of proliferation" (ibid., 5). The more furiously Carlson repurposes or parodies iconotextual codes of cooperative instruction and literacy, the more his works exhibit a uniquely "relational play" that toys self-consciously with previously established modes of cognitive engagement. Though different schools of comics poetics continue to debate as to exactly what kinds of engagement drive our reading of cartoons, comic strips, and comic books, McCloud, Wolk, and Groensteen tend to agree that the reader's experience hinges on progressive self-propelled inferences about line, space, direction, plot, and timing (Wolk, 133). At its most basic level, Carlson's work, like that of many comics and children's book creators, builds uniquely on the reassuring yet coercive cues that drive and define our experience of reading and combining signs and spaces in sequence. As much as any sequential framework of verbal and visual signs encourages, instructs, or rewards a reader's engagement with the plots, contexts, or concepts it conveys, the same text also insists that we follow certain mediated pathways of continuity and control. In short, the comic strip, picture book page, or comic-book layout each provides an intrinsically interactive and individually appealing but ultimately insistent set of narrative codes to guide reading groups of varying sizes, ages, and literacy levels through numerous lessons, stories, or situations.

The tensions behind Carlson's best "Jingle Jangle" and "Pie Face Prince" stories grow out of what French comics scholar Benoît Peeters calls the "quasi-encyclopedic possibilities of the comic strip" (Peeters par. 36). In other words, the weird "paradoxical spaces" and narrative confluences that distinguish Carlson's comics arise from a shrewd blending of iconotextual picture book literacies with the loose intuitive "adjacencies" on which comic-book *mise-en-page* relies (Peeters par. 38). Carlson's quasi-absurdist use of "word play, double takes, puzzles, and puns" in comic-book tales finds its origins in the cognitive slippage that takes place within the iconic codes of imagetic texts (Duin and Richardson, 78).

Consider the opening page from one of Carlson's more bizarre comics stories, "The Extra-stylish Ostrich and the Sugar-lined Neck-tie" from *Jingle Jangle Comics* #15 (1944).

Here, the layout is playful but surprisingly conventional and indeed, the bulk of his *Jingle Jangle* work rarely deviates from five and six-panel pages. Likewise, Carlson's opening layouts nearly always begin with half-page panels, followed by a two or three-frame strip to establish the parameters of what Groensteen would call the story's spatio-topical multiframe. As each story continues, Carlson adds exuberant decorative variety to what Benoît Peeters classifies as a "typically rhetorical" page concept, meant to accentuate linear continuity and allow the expressive capabilities of the page to reflect the mood and tone of the story:

> The dimensions of the panel conform to the action being described, the whole page layout is placed at the service of a pre-existing narrative for which it serves to accentuate the effects. Such principles are hardly adapted to the overall graphic effects — unless those do not appear likely to effectively underline the contents of a sequence [Peters par. 23].

Fig. 1, "The Extra-Stylish Ostrich and the Sugar-Lined Necktie," page 1

A typically rhetorical page concept will help readers organize the meaning, movement, and emotion of the progressing story. It need not be completely seamless or invisible in its transitions, but it does strengthen the crucial mediating function of the transitions — pushing actions and events further along as we process the logical progressions that each gutter delineates.

Carlson's "pre-existing narrative" is, however, more opaque than most, and his rhetorical designs privilege neither story nor order. Instead, his fairly standard six-frame layouts emphasize a continuing disregard for order, unity, or purpose within the narrative contexts of his comics. His gutters, transitions, and sequential assumptions simply do not matter. We slip recklessly from one random moment to the next with the express purpose of losing our way and lingering confusedly over random gags, double entendres, wisecracks, and happenstances. Thus, Carlson's jingle-jangled compositions establish a rhetorical *mise-en-page* meant to amplify a reader's sense of distanced futility. The results are consistently ridiculous and amusing, but their nonsensical nature also hints at more complex truths concerning the limitations and redundancies of both visual and prosaic language. Carlson's stories are similarly anemic in their use of conflict and progressing tension, and his plots usually dissolve before the end of the first page. Settings leap back and forth between seasons, years, times of day, or days of the week with schizophrenic frequency. The established relationships and physical motions of characters are usually ignored, elided, or contradicted — occasionally several times per page. Perhaps most importantly, the lines that define Carlson's panel borders are themselves generally as unpredictably volatile or potentially colloidal as the creatures, contraptions, and scenarios they attempt to contain.

Though Carlson's actual layouts were hardly extraordinary for their time, his loose, viscous borderlines swoop, drip, and congeal along the margins, defining a doughy *mise-en-page* quite unique to 1940s children's comics. In short, Carlson's borders are underdone and amorphous, and though they may be conventionally rectangular or circular at given moments within the multiframe, they exude a rare and telling rhetorical concept of spontaneous lunacy and playful chaos. Where most comics base their narrative drive on what readers induce about the transitions from one panel to the next, Carlson eschews the importance of sequential closure altogether and mines the humorous or fantastical qualities of missed connections, aborted actions, and nonsensical slippages across a set of double-crossing visual cues.

"The Extra-Stylish Ostrich and the Sugar-lined Neck-Tie" offers a fairly frenetic example of "iconic solidarity" where canted frames, color schemes, and repeated shapes forge a tightly conceived but graphically wobbly *mise-en-page*. Here, Carlson employs jarring circle-square panel pairings for emphatic effect during his pseudo-transitions, but his sly matching or braiding of colors and shapes actually tightens the "Tilt-a-Whirl composition" (Nadel, 251). Note how Carlson's circular motif begins with the smug cigar-chewing sun, mocking the panache of the dandified ostrich, who also sports a decidedly ovular torso. Soon, a round-headed dumbwaiter and plate continue the circular references, which are, in turn, matched on the facing page by an actual circular panel, the literally spherical rounder Cousin Tuffnut, the puffy zip lines describing the ostrich's pacing, and finally, the round face of a clock happily "beating out" the seconds like an old rug. Observe too how the supposedly random assortment of moments in the *mise-en-page* are given some contiguous arrangement through Carlson's matching lime and pink backgrounds, a technique reminiscent of the four-color funny-animal stories of Carl Barks, Walt Kelly, and Floyd Gottfredson with which Eastern Color hoped *Jingle Jangle Comics* could compete.

Carlson's texts also initiate another mode of reader engagement, which parallels the systemic interplay of braided hints and incongruous panels. Within the holistic space of each individual frame, Carlson's texts deploy their most amusing and occasionally shocking remediations of established narrative frameworks. Consider an excerpt from Carlson's "The Very Royal Lion and the Sun-burnt Cheesecake" from *Jingle Jangle Comics* #9, (1943).

From the opening titles, Carlson's nonsensical wordplay and *mise-en-page* wryly revise familiar fable and nursery rhyme rhetoric. Carlson's anthropomorphic lion is not just noble, but "Very Royal," and despite the presence of a fairly interesting monkey perched between the masthead and the title sign, the king of this hectic cartoon jungle's preferred companion is not the furry burrowing mammalian "mole" we may expect, but rather a personified version of the word's homonym, a dark and squishy, but no less friendly, congenital skin growth. The introduction of other seemingly paradoxical details like the "sun-burnt cheesecake," the mole's "pale suspenders," the clothespinned linens on the lion's tail, and the boots and hat that partially animate the tale's rustic title also predict the random absurdities that will proliferate across Carlson's fantasy world.

In a single panel, Carlson introduces the three signifying techniques that will drive the bulk of his narrative, namely shocking or amusing reversals of our assumptions concerning image-text pairings like lions that befriend talking blemishes; parades of randomly inserted details like 9th birthdays or be-hatted signs that produce their own contradictory or resistant nodes of meaning within the larger linear plot; and perhaps most importantly, the initiation of the sequential linking techniques that will visually and rhetorically interweave or "braid" this collection of juxtaposed frames into what Groensteen calls a

Fig. 3: "The Very Royal Lion and the Sun-Burnt Cheesecake," page 1

comprehensible "panoptic field" of sequentially subversive continuity (Groensteen 2007, 19).

As before, Carlson's irregular panel designs and inverted sequential switchbacks add a seemingly free-spirited whimsy to his creations, but the anti-narrative explosions of contradiction and confusion that lurk within these fantastic iconotexts impart a somewhat more subversive theme to his work. In a sense, Carlson deconstructs the mediating logic of the comic-book framework by deploying the richest puns and paradoxes chaotically and without warning across an otherwise facile and straightforward *mise-en-page*. His overlapping, incongruous frames are predominantly big, colorful, and inviting, but their actual sequence is largely organized through braided hints involving capitalized red letters and arrows. This connective motif begins with the red capital Js and T in the story's masthead, continuing throughout with emphatic "Buts," "Ands," and "At lasts." Most of the incumbent humor arises from unexpected sight gags and nonsensical responses to familiar situations within separate panels that have very little to do with these connective directions. Cartoonists and their readers often place the bulk of their attention on what happens in the borders or "gutters" between panels, but Carlson deprives the gutters of any real logic or reason. His concerns about closure and continuity are invested instead in sudden, startling word-image pairings that insist upon, but often test, a reader's capacity to comprehend the situation, solve the puzzle, or unravel the paradox.

At first glance, the readerly promise of Carlson's panels could not seem simpler. We soon discover, however, that his loud arrows and obvious cues force us into another form of continuity that is nearly devoid of logical progressions, suspenseful developments, or anticipated closure. Instead, the events described within Carlson's *mise-en-page* actually work against or perversely defy the overarching narrative order and abuse the readerly contract initiated by our assumptions about the braided cues of iconotexts. Rather than providing representations of discrete actions or events that advance the story as a whole, Carlson peppers each frame with non-sequential gags, double entendres, and curious slippages of meanings built on unexpected or unusual differences between visual and written signs. For example, in just the first page of Carlson's "Sunburnt Cheesecake" episode, red mittens somehow protect you from getting burnt by "red hot promises," cakes become lighter with the promise of more candles, hot letters "blow off spare steam for a fire sale," bargain basements are housed on a non-existent top floor, and the Very Royal Lion wisely declares, "There's not a minute to lose, so why hurry?" Other comic texts like George Herriman's *Krazy Kat*, Bill Holman's *Smoky Stover*, Fontaine Fox's *Toonerville Folks*, the tongue-in-cheek satires of *Mad Magazine*, and the ironic asides of Robert Crumb or Harvey Pekar develop similarly self-conscious nodes of sly punning. In Carlson's case, however, these moments of what Nikolajeva and Scott have dubbed intra-iconic signification represent the primary force of the narrative rather than a scattering of subtle alternative commentaries meant to debunk or subvert the principal continuity of the plot, characters, or setting.

In Carlson's work, the accepted hierarchies of narrative strands are comprehensively reversed and his basic design relies on a sort of arthrological or manual alphabet, which serves and organizes his intra-panel conundrums, rather than the other way around. Instead of facilitating the "iconic solidarity" of comic strip narrative with meaningful transitions between frames, Carlson deploys zany or preposterous moments of static iconotextual confusion that explode surprisingly out of the otherwise mundane corners of his panel designs. Words and images cooperate to beguile and confound readers by creating "uncertain iconotexts" that frequently "remain ambiguous" despite the reader's best attempts to decode them (Nikolajeva and Scott, 260). The resulting conundrums not only delight juvenile readers with their composite silliness, they also speak to more mature themes of linguistic disconnection, dreamlike condensation of symbols, and the collapsing frameworks of communication, classification, and understanding. If most comic strips strive to further refine the medium's expressive potential, Carlson's unconventional manipulation of lingual codes and generic frameworks produces an entirely different mode of ridiculous, and potentially rebellious, nonsense that was, until fairly recently, too risky for readers to appreciate.

Notes

1. To be fair, Woodrow "Woody" Gelman's influence has also been greatly underestimated. As a publisher, animator, designer, and cartoonist, Gelman would help to develop a number of influential children's products, including DC Comics' "Dodo and the Frog" and Nutsy Squirrel, the advertising characters Bazooka Joe and Popsicle Pete, and the original Topps Mars Attacks! and Wacky Packages series. His Bingo and Glum stories for *Jingle Jangle Comics* remain among the more obscure and outlandish of his creations.

2. For a more detailed discussion of Carlson's influence in children's media, see Daniel Yezbick, "Riddles of Engagement: Narrative Play in the Children's Media and Comic Art of George Carlson." *ImageTexT: Interdisciplinary Comics Studies*. 3.3 (2007). Department of English, University of Florida. 29 May 2008. http://www.english.ufl.edu/imagetext/archives/v3_3/yezbick/.

3. Carlson's most famous creation exists completely outside of comics and is not juvenile. In 1935, he developed the original book jacket for Margaret Mitchell's best-selling blockbuster *Gone with the Wind*. Though Carlson's concept lacks any trance of his characteristic interest in visual and verbal punning, it does exemplify his proficiency as a designer for both young readers and adults. Soon after the book's phenomenal success, Carlson seems to have enjoyed a brief reputation for producing nostalgic representations of the Old South. A more complete account of Carlson's interactions with MacMillan and Margaret Mead during the development of the book jacket is currently in development as part of Ellen Firsching Brown's exhaustive study of *Gone with the Wind*'s publishing history.

4. Many sources also observe that because Byrnes knew his limitations as an artist, he employed other ghost cartoonists alongside George Carlson, including Tack Knight and Burr Inwood.

5. For some examples of the dynamic recovery efforts in comics scholarship, see recent issues of the industry's two stalwart organs of comics news and criticism, *The Comics Journal* and *Hogan's Alley*. *The Comics Journal* has also initiated a regular archival section which features anywhere from 10–20 pages of reprinted material by under-represented artists. The short-lived but seminal Ohio State University journal *Inks,* also broke new ground in its meticulous attention to cartooning and comics history and practice, and remains readily available to scholars and researchers.

6. At the time of writing, a complete reprint of Carlson's *Jingle Jangle Tales* and *Pie-face Prince* stories is planned through Fantagraphics Press of Seattle, Washington. Samplings of these comics can be found in Blackbeard and Martin Williams' 1981 *Smithsonian Book of Comic-Book Comics*, Dan Nadel's 2006 *Art Out of Time: Unknown Comics Visionaries 1900–1969*, and the October/November 2004 edition of *The Comics Journal*. A 2007 edition of his mid–1930s Funtime Library for Platt & Munk is now available through Green Tiger Press also of Seattle. Dale Seymour's 1991 and 1997 compilations of Carlson's Peter Puzzlemaker games of the 1920s are also readily available through online retailers, but these editions alter many illustrations to make the puzzles more politically correct for use in classrooms and daycare environments. His most enduring guide to cartooning, *Draw Comics: Here's How!* is available as Dover Thrift Edition under the title *Learn to Draw Comics*. No adequate reprint of Carlson's prodigious book illustration, magazine art, advertising or design work for *John Martin's Book* yet exists, nor has his role as a ghost artist for Gene Byrnes' *Reg'lar Fellas* been adequately considered.

7. Related by Carlson's surviving daughter and grandson in interviews with the author.

3

Suspended in Mid-Month
Serialized Storytelling in Comics

Daniel Wüllner

The collected trade paperback of *Batman: The Long Halloween* highlights an interesting yet unexplored issue that challenges the seemingly convincing term "graphic novel." Jeph Loeb and Tim Sale's story portrays Batman, in battle with his most famous enemies on major holidays, from one year's Halloween to the next. While the collected version of the comic offers the reader the complete year in one volume, the story-arc was originally published by DC Comics as a thirteen-issue monthly series in 1996 and 1997. Readers could thus follow their superhero in real time. The collected trade paperback is now being sold as a graphic novel, and many readers might agree that the term is used in this case as a mere marketing-tool to justify reprinting the comic. The use of the term "graphic novel" to indicate a closed text harbors considerable risks because this new scholarly focus tends to neglect the original format of the comic book and its narrative form, namely the serial. Issues congregate around the concept of serialized fiction, such as readers' response to cliffhangers as well as authors' use of intended breaks as a narrative tool. Rather than legitimating the graphic novel as a consistent critical category, would it not make more sense to analyze the original serial publication format? The question I will address in this article may be summed up as follows: How may we define the scholarly import of the words "to be continued," which postpone closure, leaving the reader suspended?

In order to answer this question, Scott McCloud's *Understanding Comics* offers a good point of departure. What happens when the last panel of one issue and the first panel of the next issue are divided by a time-span of one month? While McCloud defines six different kinds of transition from panel to panel, his critical vocabulary does not include any mention of serial publication (McCloud 1994, 70–2). Given that McCloud's aim was to provide a comprehensive overview of the formal structure of the medium, his work does not take into account the historical development of the industry. His refusal to link formal structure to historical developments in comics' history should be addressed, given that the rise of the graphic novel highlights the need for such research. Scholars like Christopher Couch are meticulously reconstructing the history of the medium in order to investigate comics' narrative form because any "reading must be accompanied by a review of the historical and journalistic context in which these cartoons appeared" (Couch 1994, 60). Couch describes comics traditions of Japan, the U.S.A., and Franco-Belgium, to provide further insights into the birth of the graphic novel, concluding his essay with the turn to larger works of sequential art.

Following in the footsteps of Will Eisner, comics scholars, creators, and publishers have employed the term "graphic novel" as a synonym for serious comics, originally conceived as a form that promotes "worthwhile themes and the innovation of exposition" (Eisner, 141). This description is currently used for every large collection of panels, perhaps in response to Thierry Groensteen's question: "Why are comics still in search of cultural legitimization?" (Eisner, 12). But while the concept of the graphic novel opens up new possibilities for the medium, other aspects of its narrative form are inexcusably neglected, especially its serialization.

A History of the Serialized Form

Reviewing the history of serialized fiction, one can easily trace the path the form followed over time in the fashion of McCloud's brief historical overview. Just as McCloud draws on examples from Egyptian hieroglyphics to the Bayeux Tapestry, one could likewise cite numerous instances of narratives delivered serially, such as Homer's *Odyssey* or the tales that comprise *The Book of the Thousand and One Nights*. Yet like McCloud's journey through history, such an approach fails to reveal anything significant about serialization itself.

It might be more helpful to take a step back from the history of serialized fiction in order to take a closer look at the predecessors of early comics, and especially at their serial form. In writing that "[t]he birth of serial fiction [...] closely parallels the growth of the information industry," literary scholar Barros-Lémez emphasizes the effect of the industrially printed page and its high circulation, as it effectively turned serialized fiction into a mass-medium (Barros-Lémez, 106). The earliest examples of the merging of serialized fiction and publication practices of the Industrial Age, are European models such as Eugene Sue's famous feuilleton-novel *The Secrets of Paris*, or Charles Dickens' *The Pickwick Papers*. The close relation between the American and European literary markets in the 19th century, led to the adaptation of this publication pattern overseas.

Influenced by the European model of serialized fiction, continuous storytelling was introduced to the American magazine market in the early 19th century (Lund, 13). Famous authors such as Mark Twain, Harriet Beecher Stowe, and Herman Melville wrote their manuscripts in segmented parts and even extended their stories for *Harper's Magazine* or *The Atlantic* (Couch 1994, 62). Literary scholar Michael Lund has published meticulous research on serialized narratives, in which he points out the origin of *Uncle Tom's Cabin* as a serial work of fiction, and proposes a new interpretation of Melville's *Bartleby the Scrivener* by reading the mysterious change in the clerk's behavior as a consequence of the fact that the story was published in two parts. What happened to the clerk while the story was suspended for one month, and why the radical change thereafter? While such considerations are of the utmost importance, one must also keep in mind that the literary market for inexpensive entertainment was rapidly expanding as Melville was writing.

The 19th century witnessed the birth of the comic strip and the comic book in their predecessor the dime novel, which explored new literary territory (E. Smith, 124). The first dime novel, *Malaeska, the Indian Wife of the White Hunter*, was published in 1860 (DeForest, 15). Inexpensive means of distribution kept prices low by linking postal rates to the ongoing distribution of new issues. At this point stories were not yet serialized, although wrappers and numberings did give that impression. While low postal rates paved the way to success for the medium, these very same rates spelled out the medium's end:

> A change in postal regulations delivered the most devastating blow to the format. Dime novels no longer qualified for 2nd Class postal rates, forcing publishers to pay another one or two cents per issue to ship them. For an item that sold for a nickel or a dime, this was a ruinous rise in overhead [DeForest, 26].

At the turn of the century the dime novel was replaced by two successors: the pulp magazine and the comic strip. Although only the latter prevailed in this uneven contest, the prominence of pulp magazines highlights an important issue in the creation of comic books. Pulp magazines, so named because they were printed on low-quality paper, usurped the role of the dime novel because they were an economically superior product (N. Wright, 2; DeForest, 25). This was not the only change: the content of the new format differed as well. Pulp magazines tried to fill thematic niches such as horror and science fiction previously neglected by the "slick magazines." In contrast to the dime novel, stories in pulp magazines were not only sold but told serially. Even the appearance of a pulp magazine was different from its predecessors because publishers hired illustrators to give their publications added graphic appeal.

Authors and publishers readily adopted this new format. Although Frank A. Munsey's *The Golden Argosy* was first published in 1882 as a dime novel, he published it from 1896 onwards as the first serialized story in a pulp magazine. Munsey changed the publication later even further, always with his readership and his finances in mind (DeForest, 26–28). But even the pulp magazine encountered problems: due to a paper shortage during the Second World War publishers suffered financial losses. In 1954, pulp magazines made way for the dime novel's other successor, the comic strip. Although pulp magazines did not succeed economically, their content and themes were responsible, in large part, for the first serial comic narratives.

Serial Form in Comics

With the demise of dime novels and pulp magazines, and due to the "demand for more graphical storytelling," the comic strip was introduced into the pages of humor magazines and newspapers (DeForest, 108). While the pulp magazine was a stand-alone publication, the comic strip, a short collection of two to four panels, was always bound to other publications such as newspapers or humor magazines and could thus adapt to the ever-changing market. DeForest praises the medium for its "regular flow of gradually unfolding plot twists, characterizations and cliffhangers, presented in a seamless melding of words and images, [with] its own unique and valuable appeal" (DeForest, 146–47). As we will see, the serialized form of the comic strip led to various changes in comics' history.

The sequential ordering of comic panels — a technique introduced by European immigrants — led to the birth of the comic book. Two 19th-century pioneers of these stories were the Swiss doctor Rudolphe Töpffer and the German Wilhelm Busch. These two authors added words to continuous stories, thereby establishing the practice of telling stories only through images. By the early 20th century, artists such as the immigrant Rudolf Dirks (*Katzenjammer Kids*) and second-generation immigrant and painter Lyonel Feininger (*Kind-Der-Kids*) were producing comic strips that resembled the work of Töpffer and Busch.

Newspaper mogul Philip Randolph Hearst and his rival John Pulitzer soon recognized the appeal of comic strips and began acquiring new artists as early the close of the 19th century. One such artist was Richard F. Outcault, who invented the character Mickey Dugan, later known as *The Yellow Kid*. While Mickey Dugan was initially a minor character in Outcault's comic strip *Hogan's Alley*, which "appeared in a variety of sizes and formats" in Pulitzer's *New York World*, he soon appeared in his own strip in Hearst's *New York Journal* (Couch 1994, 60). Although the continuous struggle between the two newspapers is another story, *The Yellow Kid* adds an interesting twist to the debate surrounding the first comics and their serial form. For many scholars, the word and image combination was the deciding feature that distinguished comics from other publications at that time.

According to Couch, the introduction of comic strips in newspapers was made possible by Pulitzer, who included supplement magazines in the Sunday issue of *New York World* (62). Later he added a humor magazine in which installments of *Hogan's Alley* ran as "full-page compositions usually described as single-panel cartoons" (Couch 1994, 60). Couch locates the beginnings of the comic strip in the "plate tectonics" of the comic page made up of images alongside text columns (ibid., 64). Outcault merged these two for the first time in the medium's history, and placed the comic strip on the newspaper page:

> Rather than arguing from the contemporary comic strip and searching for antecedents that appear to mirror its formal properties, the importance of the *Yellow Kid* can only be understood when the history [...] is examined without preconceptions formed from subsequent developments [Couch 1994, 65].

The question remains as to how serialization may have influenced comics form and publication? The complete cast of *Hogan's Alley* was present in large, single panels. Although most of the early strips featured such large sets of figures, serialization connected the idea of a continued reading and the introduction of text into action. As readers became familiar with the adventures of the *Yellow Kid*, they learned to absorb the included text-passages more readily. It was only through the serialization of comic strips that readers were introduced to notion that words and images could work together on the printed page.

As we have seen, the inception of early comic strips was intertwined with their serial format. However, this is not the only occasion when changes in the history of comics coincide with different forms of serialized storytelling. While *Action Comics* issue 1 is generally remembered as the first comic book, the Eastern Color Printing Company had released the first collected comic strips in a book-format five years previously, in 1933. This work, entitled *Funnies on Parade*, was intended as advertising for companies like *Procter &*

Gamble, and presented as a collection of serialized comic strips, bound and printed on "seven-by-nine-inch printing plates" (N. Wright, 3). Although the new medium was a useful tool in the advertising business, publishers soon realized that the new format alone would not attract readers and that its content would have to change as well. This juncture in history saw the return of pulp magazines, with authors and publishers exploring new themes, thus creating new niche markets. Cleveland-based writer and artist team Jerry Siegel and Joe Shuster implemented a significant subject change that was to affect the medium on a larger scale.

Their creation of Superman single-handedly conquered comic book culture in less than a year. Siegel and Shuster tried to sell the superhero to comic strip syndicates but their idea of the *Übermensch*—inspired by the science-fiction stories in pulp magazines — was repeatedly rejected (Wright, 7). As their last-ditch effort to see their superhero in print, the authors accepted an offer for a comic book in which Superman was featured alongside Tex Thomson and Zatara the Magician. The prototype for every subsequent superhero first appeared on the cover of *Action Comics*, issue 1 in 1938. Within a year Superman had become so popular that an entire comic book was devoted to stories exclusively about him. At the same time the introduction of *Superman* led to a change of a completely different nature, namely the growing importance of episodic structures in comics.

Although it would be difficult to find any sort of "to be continued" in the first *Superman* comics, Umberto Eco has argued that their narrative structure differed from the serialized form of cartoon strips that came before them. While newspaper audiences followed the adventures of Milton Caniff's *Terry and the Pirates* with every new day, readers accompanied their hero into each new episode. Eco describes "The Myth of Superman" as being without history (Eco 1972, 15). We know that he works in Metropolis as a 30-year-old reporter for the *Daily Planet* after he was saved from the planet Krypton and raised by the Kents. Surprisingly, he is still 30 years old and works for the *Planet* after 70 years of adventures. In order to be able to tell the stories of *Superman* over and over again, the authors decided not to construct a linear evolution of the Man of Steel, so that every single story was placed next to each other, rather than sequentially. Eco vividly describes how audiences accept the never-ending story with scant narrative change. He terms the justification for this repetition as "neobaroque aesthetics," or the pure pleasure of knowing the outcome of the story, while the search for microscopic differences in identical stories keeps the audience interested (Eco 2005, 205). This form of episodic narration became the model for nearly every superhero narrative as well as many other comic stories.

The Direct Market System

The next important change in the serial form of comics occurred at the end of the 1970s. Since their birth in 1933, comics had been sold at newsstands (McCloud 1994, 66). Every newsstand owner had the right to return unsold issues to the publisher. Comics could therefore only be published in small or very stable lots because publishers could not afford to take them back. These financial circumstances changed with the introduction of the Direct Market system because "Direct" refers to the direct sales of non-returnable comic books to comic specialty stores (McCloud 2005, 66). New modes of distribution led to the opening of new, specialized comic shops, which bought a certain numbers of comics that could not be returned. This made it possible for small publishers to calculate with stable figures.

Comics scholar Matthew Pustz judges the effects of the Direct Market principle not only from the economic point of view but also in terms of the changing content of comic books. In *Comic Book Culture*, he illustrates how changes in distribution offered new possibilities for narration as well (Pustz 1999, 131–132). While newsstand sales made it difficult for readers to find specific titles, publishers produced only comics that were episodic in structure. These comics could be read even if the consumer missed an issue because the status quo was re-established at the end of every story causing the percentage of linear, continuous storylines to decline. The new comic shops offered readers a subscription service for each single comic; publishers were thus interested in different forms of narration. Readers were forced to buy every issue in fear of missing an important issue; thus: "[p]ublishers have found monetary concerns at least as important as aesthetic ones in the emphasis on continuity" (ibid.). Again, the economic factor seems to prevail, yet publishers of independent comics used this renewed interest in continuous storytelling to their own advantage.

In terms of ongoing storytelling, one name stands out: Canadian author Dave Sim and his comic book *Cerebus*. In 2003, Dave Sim finished a 300-issue run of his uncategorizable epic *Cerebus*. His complete narrative is made up of 6000 comics pages published on a monthly basis. Over the course of several years, Sim frequently changed his serial narrative mode. Starting out in an episodic fashion, he soon went on to write unusually long story arcs covering up to 30 issues (600 pages). While some of these collected story arcs, such as *Jaka's Story,* are often classified as "graphic novels," others were treated as mere collected versions of a confused monologue (e.g. Sim's discussion on the Torah in *Latter Days*). Although Sim himself refers to his larger works ironically as telephone books, this example shows the problems and especially the restrictions that the term graphic novel poses for any academic discussion of sequential art.

Even today when graphic novels are readily available from most major booksellers, we still have to ask ourselves how to categorize certain comics, such as those of Chris Ware. Over the course of the last years, he has not only published a diverse selection of ever-changing formats for his *Acme Novelty Library* series, but he also added this peculiar sense of nostalgia to his works that keeps us spinning between past and present. Here the term "graphic novel" ignores this concept of nostalgia, and turns comics culture into a world without history.

Alison Bechdel's *Funhome* was celebrated as the year's best work of fiction by *Time Magazine* in 2007. Critics have unexplainably referred to the book in question as a "graphic memoir" rather than a comic book or graphic novel. By categorizing her work in this way, critics once again define the medium based on content and genre, which Scott McCloud attacked with his concept of "aesthetic surgery" (McCloud 1994, 5). Bechdel tells the story of her dead father, without a doubt a memoir with clear literary ambitions. She includes intertextual references to literature and literary constructs by framing her chapters in the tradition of the novel, which would seem to make "graphic novel" a far more appropriate term than "graphic memoir."

Serialized Fiction: A Modus Operandi

I have undertaken this survey of the serial form as a means of highlighting the problems we encounter if we blindly embrace the term "graphic novel" and neglect comics' traditional serial form. As I have shown, the publishers of serialized fiction often use this term for its marketing potential, but at the same time serialization remains an important narrative tool. While most authors have relied on cliffhangers, others have followed the lead of Charles Dickens, a pioneer of serialized storytelling, here quoted by Richard Patten: "we shall keep perpetually going on beginning again, regularly, until the end of the fair" (Patten, 126). It is equally the case that incidents, chapters and segments repeatedly wind down and stop, so that the "end of the fair comes early and often" (ibid.). But exactly what kind of mechanisms work in a serialized form such as continuing comics? In this section, I will provided a more detailed description of how comics function and what is specific to how they function.

When discussing serialized fiction, we encounter a problem similar to the one McCloud came up against when he attempted to separate the "comics" medium from its content and genre. Instead, I would like to offer a structural approach to a theory of serialized fiction. In a move directly opposed to McCloud's, I will try to separate this narrative model from any medium. Before explaining the mechanisms involved in this form, I cite the following general definition of the term "serial:"

> A serial is, by definition, an ongoing narrative released in successive parts. In addition to these defining qualities, serial narratives share elements that might be termed, after Wittgenstein, "family resemblances." These include refusal of closure; intertwined subplots; large casts of characters (incorporating a diverse range of age, gender, class, and, increasingly, race representation to attract a similarly diverse audience); interaction with current political, social, or cultural issues; dependence on profit; and acknowledgement of audience response (this has become increasingly explicit, even institutionalized within the form, over time) [Hayward, 3].

At first glance this lengthy definition ranges from a short survey of the subject to a lengthy description of the serialized form. Hayward's definition however clearly highlights the essence of the term, while adding a list of "family resemblances." Hayward succeeds in presenting a general overview of all the aspects of the serial form, but in an effort to sharpen her definition, I would like to take up some of the problems mentioned in my historical overview of serial comics.

To begin, there are problems involved with my presentation of the *Yellow Kid* as the first comic strip that employed narrative serialization. For while Outcault chose to work for Hearst, Pulitzer hired the artist George B. Luks who continued *Hogan's Alley*, so two *Yellow Kids* appeared in newspapers of this era (Frahm, 2003). This raised questions concerning notions of original and copy, while the comic strip's continuity was threatened. The co-existence of the two characters also led to intertextual references on a meta-level. Comics scholar Ole Frahm described the situation as follows:

> In such cases it is hard to keep up. This may be the reason why it is often stated that everyone who has read one comic book knows them all, that all series are one and the same, that only the brains of infants are apt for the monotony of the jokes. But as I have shown, the signs of the comics materialize a historical signature on every new page with a specific singularity that is never simple. In their topicality the transitory comics remind us through many details of long-forgotten stories of the twentieth century [*sic*]. This is another reason to reread them again and again. In comics, it's the little things that matter, an "incorrectly" written, overdetermined sign, a single line, their historical materiality [Frahm, 2003].

Only with the use of an in-depth analysis of a single comic book history are we able to interpret its "historical materiality." Results of such an analysis have to be judged according to various standards of serialized fiction. One of these standards determines the difference between two models, namely episodic repetition and linear continuous narration.

In the discourse of serialization, the terms repetition and continuation seem to be opposites, yet they are two sides of the same coin. Repetition and continuation are illustrated by the episodic structure of each issue of *Superman* on the one hand, and *Cerebus* on the other. Both methods of storytelling can be termed "serial," because, according to Hayward, their "narrative [is] released in successive parts" (Hayward, 3). In order to demonstrate how these two narrative modes operate, I will turn to Richard Patten's analysis of Dickens' most prominent serialized work, *The Pickwick Papers*.

Patten sees the key to understanding Dickens' serial mode in his complex temporal system, which includes three different aspects of temporality: the "forward-looking serial," the "representation of the *mentalité* of the day," and "looking backwards" (Patten 1994, 122–131). The first type of temporality is naturally included in any serialized form of fiction when closure is postponed with three simple words: "to be continued." In this respect, every form of serial, be it episodic or linear, is a "forward-looking serial." When applying these categories to the two previously cited examples of *Superman* and *Cerebus*, we find that linear narration has various options at its disposal to keep readers involved. While most *Superman* stories begin anew with each issue, Sim plays with the expectations of his readers over a month and offers a whole array of narrative solutions to his own cliffhangers.

Patten's second form of temporality can also be observed in both comics. In contrast to the author of a novel, the serial form permits the authors of *Superman* and *Cerebus* to interact with current political issues and to respond to contemporary trends. Moreover, the temporal mode of the episodic form offers other advantages, such as the ability to adapt comic book figures like *Superman* to keep pace with the *Zeitgeist* in every new embodiment of the superhero. While Sim intended to let his protagonist age over the course of his narration, Superman has yet to age in his 70 years of existence.

Interestingly, the third form of temporality unites both repetition and continuation. In his analysis of *The Pickwick Papers*, Patten recognizes a third mode, which he terms "looking backwards" (Patten, 124). This mode should not be mistaken for a simple synopsis of events that have taken place earlier in a serial storyline, but should rather be seen as a self-reflective mode of narration, as a "nostalgia for previous modes of discursive practice, feeling, and social organization" (ibid.). Patten gives a further description for "looking backwards" in a serial:

> The serial instalments that reconsider their own material, and in doing so grow up, change from an assemblage of disconnected documents, like the monthly parts themselves, into a story, one marked always by the same wrapper design yet continuously re-examining its initial alphabet in the light of the experience of reading [Patten 1994, 1].

While repetition and continuation are common aspects of serialized fiction, this third mode can only be recognized as the conscious aesthetics of the serial, yet in a much more general way than Eco's "neobaroque aesthetics." Only through the idea of "nostalgia for previous modes of discursive practice" are we are able to fully grasp the work of Chris Ware.

Returning to my key example of Loeb and Sale's *Batman: The Long Halloween*, Patten's last mode of temporality presents a key argument against misguided applications of the term "graphic novel." As I have been arguing, narrative production and the reader's response to serial comics differ from the production of and response to the graphic novel. While *Batman: The Long Halloween* was created in a serial fashion, the reception of the same text as a graphic novel gives rise to a different effect and a different aesthetics of reception. The contrast between the closed form of a graphic novel and the open text presented in serial form divide the consideration of comics as such. Yet some scholars of comics have already tried to address this discrepancy. For example, in *Alternative comics: An emerging literature* Charles Hatfield tries to reconcile the two seemingly opposed notions of the never-ending serial and the closed narrative form. Although he recognizes "that too exclusive an emphasis on the 'graphic novel' can impoverish or obstruct appreciation of the art form," Hatfield argues that "graphic novels are created serially" (Hatfield, 153).

Like Couch, Hatfield reviews the serial form of the medium and even praises its discontinuities in terms of narration with numerous examples. In a sub-chapter entitled "The Devil of Serialization," Hatfield openly criticizes serialization and does not accept it as a genuine form of storytelling. As an example he describes the serial narration in Alan Moore's *Watchmen*: "Moore and Gibbons cannily exploit the 'wait time' between the penultimate and the final chapter by ending chapter 11 with a terrible disclosure" (Hatfield, 155). Although the villain reveals his evil schemes to the heroes, they are helpless to avoid it because the plan has already been carried out. Yet this "wait time" does not exist in a collected graphic novel. His conclusion that "[s]erialization, then, can allow graphic novels to comment on the terms of their own reception" not only confuses both terms, but also degrades serialization as a mere tool of the graphic novel (Hatfield, 159).

Conclusion

We are currently witnessing an age wherein comics intersect with other media, establishing cross-references with literary texts and breaking with their own narrative traditions. As I have shown there is one narrative concept in comics that has been neglected in favor of the idea of a closed text, namely serialized storytelling. Loeb and Sale's *Batman: The Long Halloween* is but one striking example of how the appreciation of serialized storytelling goes along unnoticed. Even academic secondary texts concerning comics, such as McCloud's *Understanding Comics* or Hatfield's *Alternative Comics: An Emerging Literature*, do not recognize this concept of storytelling as a genuine form of narration in comics.

In an effort to uncover this largely overlooked term, I started out by giving an overview of serialized storytelling in general fiction and afterwards its special effect on the mode of narration in American comics, from early cartoon strips to today's graphic novels. This brief overview offered an insight into the narrative processes that began with the earliest narrative forms and continue to adapt to the reading behaviors of the present day. Although often used as a tool to keep readers hanging on, the resulting cliffhangers or cesuras created a unique mode of narration that even produced such literary landmarks as Harriet Beecher Stowe's *Uncle Tom's Cabin*.

This broad evaluation of serialized storytelling can only briefly suggest the importance of the serial narrative mode in comics. Being a direct successor of the serialized fiction of pulp magazines, the medium adapted relatively easy to always changing market environments. Yet authors also applied this narrative concept inventively beginning with the first cartoon strips, and it has been in use ever since. From the recurrent appearance of characters in the *Yellow Kid* to the never-ending cycle of *Superman* adventures, repetitions and continuing stories have constructed types of narration that can only be analyszd correctly if one takes into account their serialized origins. Although highlighting completely different editorial decisions, my third primary text, Dave Sim's *Cerebus*, is of special interest here. It displays quite strikingly a whole palette of methods and makes use of various narrative modes in comics. While shifting between episodic and continued structure, Sim always tries to fragment perception, leaving the reader suspended.

In order to analyze these issues more methodically, I adapted a literary approach to the field of comics. In Patten's analysis of Dickens' serial mode of narration, the literary scholar defines three different types of temporality that can easily be applied to serialized narration in comics: the "forward-looking serial," the "representation of the *mentalité* of the day," and "looking backwards" (Patten 1994, 122–31). Although the complex serial structure of comics cannot be completely explained, these three terms offer a formal outline that can be seen as a starting point for the analysis of serialized storytelling in comics.

As comics scholars like Ole Frahm and Christopher Couch have already proclaimed, we are in need of an approach that takes into account the "historical materiality" of comics. Serialized storytelling in comics not only offers a method to highlight this "historical materiality," it also presents comics as a narrative mode that stands in contrast to the amorphous term "graphic novel."

PART TWO

What We Talk About When We Talk About Comics: Theory and Terminolog

4

Balloonics

The Visuals of Balloons in Comics

Charles Forceville, Tony Veale, *and* Kurt Feyaerts

The tailed balloon is one of the most defining visual conventions of the comics medium. One need only insert a stereotypical balloon-with-tail into an image — whether an advert, a photograph, a film still, or even a piece of high art — to turn that image into a comics panel. In this chapter we will examine the conventions of the balloon in more detail. Our main goal is to present a provisional blueprint of the visual variables governing balloonic information, and thus contribute to comics scholarship. Such a blueprint will be a useful tool in the analysis of comics, allowing for a comparison of styles and the identification of idiosyncrasies. More generally, quantifying variation among balloons sheds light on how visual elements can be meaningful at all. We will also hypothesize that at least some balloon variables display "natural" processes of representation rather than being governed by arbitrary convention. Finally, the approach adopted here allows us to discuss some instances of how the "standard" balloon can be adapted in the service of creative play.[1]

The presence of balloons is not a defining element of comics: one can conceive of comics without balloons, while balloons only signify comics when they occur in a linear sequence of images. Nonetheless, the balloon — a visual element of a scene depiction that does not actually correspond to anything visual in the scene — is probably the most characteristic aspect of comics. Eisner (1985, 26) describes speech balloons as a "desperation device" in comics, noting that they are an artificial means of capturing that which does not have visual form — i.e., sound. Eisner (1985) and McCloud (1994) describe the rudimentary form and function of balloons, and suggest how form conventionally encodes function. Eisner notes that balloons can communicate meaning in a number of ways: by the shape of the balloon; by the text contained in the balloon; and by the formal characteristics of the text. The most informative part of a balloon is, as a rule, the content expressed within: usually a character's utterances or thoughts. Yet balloons also communicate a great deal of ancillary meaning via their shape, color, location, size, and the orientation of their tails or thought bubbles. Moreover, balloons do not always contain wholly verbal or textual information. They may contain pictograms, complex images, stand-alone punctuation marks, or non-mimetic flourishes.[2] Finally, balloons may also convey information via the use of atypical or exotic fonts for the letters, words, or punctuation marks occurring in them.

Our data come from European and American sources that exemplify mainstream comics from these continents. The sources are: (i) *Tintin et les Picaros* [*Tintin and the Picaros*] (Hergé 1976); (ii) *Les Lauriers de César* [*Asterix and the Laurel Wreath*] (Uderzo and Goscinny 1972); (iii) *Le Bandit Manchot* [*The One-Armed Bandit*] (Morris and De Groot 1981); (iv) *New Avengers: Civil War* (vol. 21–25) and *Avengers: Disassembled* (vol. 500–503 and "Finale"), two trade-paperback collections of Marvel comic book installments by Brian Michael Bendis (2006); and (v) *Pirates of the Caribbean Part 3: At World's End* (Disney/Hoofddorp: Sanoma [Dutch edition] 2007). We believe that a systematic examination of the balloon use in these comics can serve as a basis for identifying variables and formulating tentative generalizations that can subsequently be tested and refined by comparisons with other works. We even consider the development of analytical tools and the demonstration of their applicability of greater import than interpretations of the findings, since our limited and relatively arbitrary selection of works does not allow for sweeping generalizations.

	Picaros (Tintin)	César (Asterix)	Bandit (Lucky Luke)	Avengers (Marvel)	Pirates (Disney)
Number of pages	62	44	44	262	50
Number of panels	755	410	387	1281	280
Number of balloons	1079	563	540	1581	256

Table 1. Number of pages, panels and balloons in the corpus per source

Table 1 demonstrates that the American comics have fewer panels per page than the European comics. This may be partly due to the smaller size of the Marvel comics pages; closer inspection reveals that panel distribution on the page is also freer than the strict grid pattern of the European comics in our data. *Pirates* averages less than one balloon per panel, which could be indicative of this comic's strongly action-oriented content.

Variables in Balloonic Information

In this section we present quantitative information about visual balloon variables that have the potential to be narratively significant.

Balloon Form: Arguably, the most salient balloon variable is its form. We submit that deviations in balloon form within a single work are, in most cases, significant. Deviant balloon-forms usually convey information about the emotions and states of mind of the persons to which they are tailed. Only occasionally are there variations in balloon form for purely practical purposes, such as leaving room for important visual features such as a character's head.

The popular software application *Comic Life*, developed by PLASQ.com and distributed with most new Apple computers, exploits intuitions about typical comic strip balloons, allowing non-professionals to create documents that have the look and feel of a comic (see Table 2, Column 1). Defining *Comic Life*'s eight subtypes as "standard" allows us to chart how the balloons in our data relate to this stylized norm, as well as to assess and compare the idiosyncrasies of each artist's balloon use. For this purpose we add a ninth category ("other") to catalogue deviations from the norm.

Since comics balloons often fail to conform completely to the stylized specimens of *Comic Life*, we performed both a "strict" and an "extended" categorization. Balloons are classified as "strict" only if they are virtually identical with the standard, and as "extended" if they display the most salient features of the category, but vary freely in one or more clearly defined aspects. Balloons that deviate most significantly from *Comic Life*'s standards are therefore classified as "extended other."

Type	*Name*	*Definition*
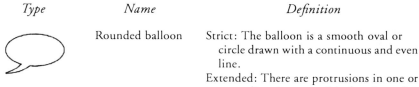	Rounded balloon	Strict: The balloon is a smooth oval or circle drawn with a continuous and even line. Extended: There are protrusions in one or more directions, possibly forming sub–balloons or connected sub–balloons; and/or there is no tail, or more than one tail.

Type	*Name*	*Definition*
	Thought balloon	Strict: The balloon has a fluffy cloud-form and a tail consisting of a sequence of bubbles.
		Extended: There are protrusions in one or more directions, possibly forming sub–balloons or connected sub–balloons; the balloon is non–rounded; and/or there is no bubble-tail, or more than one bubble-tail.
	Interrupted contour balloon	Strict: The balloon is a smooth oval or circle drawn with a broken or dashed outline.
		Extended: There are protrusions in one or more directions, possibly forming sub–balloons or connected balloons; the balloon is non–rounded; and/or there is no tail, or more than one tail.
	Serrated contour balloon	Strict: The balloon is an oval with a regular and serrated edge.
		Extended: There are protrusions in one or more directions, possibly forming sub–balloons or connected balloons; the balloon is non–rounded; and/or there is no tail, or more than one tail.
	Jagged contour balloon	Strict: The balloon has sharp-edged protrusions to form a regular or irregular contour.
		Extended: Multiple balloons are partially merged, or connected, to form a complex multi–balloon shape; and/or there is no tail, or more than one tail
	Rectangular rounded balloon	Strict: The balloon is rectangular or square, with slightly bulging edges and rounded corners.
		Extended: There are protrusions in one or more directions, possibly forming sub–balloons or connected balloons; and/or there is no tail, or more than one tail.
	Balloons with protruding edges	Strict: The balloon is a smooth oval or circle with four symmetrically placed angular protruding edges.
		Extended: There are protrusions in one or more directions, possibly forming sub–balloons or connected balloons; the balloon is non–rounded; or there are more

Type	Name	Definition
		or less than four angular protrusions; and/or there is no tail, or more than one tail.
	Rectangular straight balloon	Strict: The balloon is rectangular or square, with straight edges and rounded corners. Extended: There are protrusions in one or more directions, possibly forming sub–balloons or connected balloons; the edges bulge inward or outward; and/or there is no tail or more than one tail.
OTHER	Anything else	Strict: Whatever is scored in any of the first eight categories as "extended" is here counted as "strict." Extended: All balloon manifestations that were too deviant to be attributed to the "extended" varieties in any of the above categories.

Table 2.

Table 2. The standard range of text balloons, as codified in the *Comic Life* application. Notes: (i) The tail or bubble extension can point up, down, left, or right; this does not prevent categorization as "strict;" (ii) the fact that balloons may have been flattened because they are located against one of the panel's four sides, or are partially "blocked" does not affect their categorization.

Table 3 gives the percentages for balloon form for each of the albums both on a "strict" and an "extended" count.

		Picaros	César	Bandit	Avengers	Pirates
	Strict	9.1%	95.7%	95.2%	47%	—
	Extended	9.3%	99.1%	99.6%	75%	—
	Strict	0.1%	0.4%	0.2%	0.2%	—
	Extended	2.7%	0.4%	0.2%	0.2%	0.8%
	Strict	—	—	—	0.1%	—
	Extended	—	—	—	0.1%	—
	Strict	—	—	—	—	—
	Extended	3.9%	—	—	—	—
	Strict	0.8%	—	—	0.6%	0.4%
	Extended	0.9%	—	—	1.5%	0.8%
	Strict	—	—	—	—	—
	Extended	—	—	—	—	—
	Strict	—	—	—	—	—
	Extended	—	—	—	0.4%	2.2%

		Picaros	*César*	*Bandit*	*Avengers*	*Pirates*
	Strict	79.9%	—	0.2%	2%	62.1%
	Extended	82.2%	—	0.2%	3%	96.2%
OTHER	Strict	10.1%	3.9%	4.4%	50%	37.5%
	Extended	1%	0.5%	—	20%	—

Table 3. Frequency of different balloon forms according to the criteria in Table 2.

Comments: Table 3 demonstrates that different comics have different "standard" balloons. Whereas oval balloons with a tail account for more than 95% of all balloons in the *Lucky Luke* and *Asterix* albums, the standard in *Tintin* is the rectangular balloon with rounded corners.[3]

Avengers uses its standard much less frequently than the others, especially on a strict count (47%). But even on an extended count only 75% of the balloons conform to this standard, which means that Marvel uses far more balloons with protrusions. Because the Marvel sample of 1581 balloons has been drawn from a vast series involving many artists, we should avoid generalizing about a whole genre. The score for *Avengers* in the "extended other" category indicates that 20% of the balloons have such deviant designs that they do not fit in the extended categories of *Comic Life*'s ontology; they are thus the most unusual, at least by *Comic Life*'s standards. The European comics are far more normative by comparison. However, the "other" category of the table does show that of the three European albums considered here, Hergé's *Picaros* makes the most original use of balloon form, while the fact that the balloons occur in five of the eight standard categories (as opposed to two in *César* and three in *Bandit*) demonstrates that Hergé here draws on a wider range of opportunities afforded by balloon form than his fellow European artists.

Balloon color. A balloon can have a different color than the standard (white) to convey salient information.

	Picaros	*César*	*Bandit*	*Avengers*	*Pirates*
White	95.9%	100%	100%	81.1%	100%
Red	0.4%	—	—	0%	—
Yellow	3.4%	—	—	2.4%	—
Blue	0.1%	—	—	0%	—
Multicolored	16.5%				
Other	0.2%	—	—	—	—

Table 4. Variation in balloon color.

Comments: For the most part, non-white balloons in our data provide information about the emotional states and sensory experiences of characters. Usually, there is additional information to reinforce this, such as non-standard balloon form (see Table 3), the presence of non-verbal information (see Table 5), and/or non-standard fonts or orthography (see Table 6). An exception is *Picaros'* use of yellow, in combination with serrated balloon contours, whose function is the signaling of electronically relayed text and sound (via TV, radio, walkie-talkies). Again, we can gauge from Table 4 that both *Avengers* and *Picaros* make the broadest use of the spectrum available on this variable.

A variable not registered in Table 4 is the use of colored elements *within* balloons, such as pictograms or punctuation marks. *Bandit* has colored pictograms in the running gag of the curses (e.g. 3.2.1),[4] while *César* has colored flowers in 45.3.1. and 45.3.2, to convey the insincere or ironic nature of the verbal message. *Picaros* occasionally has colored punctuation marks (e.g. 1.4.3, 6.2.3a). In the "Finale" section of *Avengers Assembled*, the heroes, about to disband, reminisce about the favorite moment in their shared history; here (tailless) balloons have a "shadow" in a color that differs per Avenger.

Contents of balloons. In addition to or instead of verbal text, balloons can contain one or more of the following:

(i)   Stand-alone punctuation marks, typically question marks and exclamation marks, indicating a character's surprise, shock, or confusion;

(ii) Pictograms (visual representations with a fixed, context-independent meaning, e.g. $ ♫ ☂; for more examples see Gasca and Gubern 2001, 312–411; Cohn 2007, 49–50) and pictorial runes (flourishes such as speed lines, droplets, and spirals to indicate emotion; for discussion, see Forceville 2005);

(iii) Non-speech vocalizations and onomatopoeias, which differ across languages (see Fresnault-Deruelle 1977). The former are involuntary utterances produced rather than said by characters (e.g. "Pfouah!," "Hic!," "Snif"); the latter refer to words imitating sounds by non–human agents (e.g. "Grrrr," "Clic!," "Toot").

Table 5 charts the frequencies of these in our data.

	Picaros	César	Bandit	Avengers	Pirates
Verbal text	87.4%	94.1%	88.8%	94%	92.6%
Stand-alone punctuation mark(s)	7.5%	3.6%	6.3%	—	2.7%
Pictograms and runes	0.5%	2%	2.6%	1.5%	1.6%
Non-speech vocalizations and onomatopoeia	5.7%	3.6%	6.1%	4.5%	4.7%

Table 5: **Balloon contents. If a balloon features elements in more than one category, it is counted in each of these.**

Comments: *Avengers* does not use stand-alone question and exclamation marks — a standard resource in the other works. The Marvel sample arguably strives for a cinematic feel, in which every utterance is a precise vocalization, as in a movie script. Alternatively, stand-alone punctuation marks may belong primarily to comics striving for humorous effects. As for pictograms, *César* has one panel (39.3.2) in which black flowers in a balloon indicate the insincerity of what is said (cf. 45.3.1 and 45.3.2). *Bandit* has pictograms for snoring, cursing, and musical notes for singing and whistling, the latter also found in *Picaros*, *César*, and *Pirates*. Pictograms and in-balloon pictorial runes may be related to humor. Pictograms and punctuation marks are often colored. Note that it is sometimes a difficult (and even sensitive) issue to decide whether something is a "non-speech vocalization" (e.g. the Indians' "Ugh!" and "woulouwoulou!" battle cry in *Bandit* — here *not* counted as belonging to this category).

Fonts and styles in balloons. Each comic has a standard balloon typeface. Deviations from the standard typeface comprise (i) various degrees of bold font; (ii) non-standard italics; (iii) different styles, fonts and/or sizes for different words within a balloon; (iv) letter contours that are angular, curved, compressed, or otherwise deviant. Large-sized bold face generally connotes loudness. The use of more than one style for different words in one balloon may suggest that only *part* of an utterance is spoken loudly or emphatically, while a sustained font-shift in mid-utterance can communicate a change in spoken delivery (e.g. *Picaros* 9.2.1).

	Picaros	*César*	*Bandit*	*Avengers*	*Pirates*
Plain-style	0.3%	84.9%	84.4%	95%	62.9%
Bold-style	12%	14.7%	16.1%	26.5%	35.2%
Italics-style	87.6%	3%	10%	31%	32.4%
Deviant typography	3.2%	2.7%	—	5%	—
Mixed styles	0.7%	2%	1.7%	27%	20.3%

Table 6: Variations in font and style within a single balloon. If a balloon features elements in more than one category, it is counted in each of these.

Comments: One panel of *César* (1.3.1) displays different translations used by a Roman tour guide at the Circus Maximus, rendered in mixed styles.[5] Deviant typography in *César* includes "dancing" letters in text balloons emanating from drunk persons (e.g. 13.4.3; 43.1.2), while this style is in *Avengers* used for transcribing the speech of alien characters or magical incantations. Note that when avenger Tony Stark speaks as Iron Man, he has his "own" font, and his speech is generally rendered (in *The New Avengers*; not in *Avengers Assembled!*) in red print in a beige balloon.

Location of balloon source. The balloon's tail points to the person or agent vocalizing or thinking. We here chart the following varieties:

(i)   The balloon's tail points to a visible source within the panel: a face, other body part, or apparatus (e.g. TV, radio). This is the standard situation.

(ii) The balloon's tail points to a non-visible source within the panel. Here the source is supposed to be present in the panel's frame, but is either invisible because s/he is too far away to be identifiable or because his/her presence is visually blocked.

(iii) The balloon's tail points to a source outside the panel, and may be cropped by its border. As readers we have to guess (or remember) who might be the source of the balloon's information. However, the balloon's intended producer is unidentifiable on the basis of visual balloon information within the panel.

(iv) The balloon's tail crosses the gutter to point to an identifiable source in another panel.

	Picaros	César	Bandit	Avengers	Pirates
Tail/bubbles point to visible source in panel	91%	91.6%	90.7%	93.1%	88.3%
Tail/bubbles point to non-visible source in panel	6%	2.7%	1.5%	1%	4.3%
Tail/bubbles point to source outside panel, ending or curtailed within panel	3%	5.7%	7.6%	4.7%	7.4%
Tail/bubbles point to source outside of panel, crossing the gutter	—	—	0.2%	1.2%	—

Table 7: Location of source of the utterance in a balloon. Reported frequencies are for balloons with tails/thought bubbles only.

Comments: In mainstream narrative comics, it is generally clear who is the source of ballonic information. A tail pointing to a source outside of the panel may be used to provoke momentary surprise. Cases of tails crossing gutters are rare, occurring exclusively in *Avengers*, where this creates a dynamic, cinematic effect: voices emanate from "off-screen," overlap, and maintain a functional ambiguity, whereby an utterance could be attributed to a plurality of characters. A feature not registered in Table 7 is the situation wherein a balloon "bursts" and extrudes beyond the panels in which it belongs. This device, when combined with other visual features such as non-standard balloon form or bold face, tends to suggest excessive emotion. In the *Avengers* sample, where balloons frequently straddle the gutter between different panels, the bridging effect reinforces and paces the coherence of the narrative.

Paraballoonic Features

We will now address various paraballoonic phenomena, whose only shared characteristic with balloons is that they have a tail or, alternatively, display onomatopoeia in quasi-balloonic, non-bordered zones in the picture. We will also address two other sources of verbal information: (i) narrator text ("*récitatif*" in Fresnault-Deruelles [1972] and "caption" in Saraceni [2003]); and (ii) written texts that are relayed via a medium in the story world itself, such as newspaper headings, graffiti, letters, and notices (Lefèvre and Baetens 1998, 18), which we will call "inscriptions."

Onomatopoeia outside balloons. Onomatopoeia is the device *par excellence* to convey non-verbal sounds in comics.[6] While onomatopoeia often occurs in balloons, it may also appear in white paraballoons without tails (*Picaros* 13.2.2; *César* 39.4.2; *Bandit* 9.2.1), or as a physical aspect of the scene itself. However, even in these cases onomatopoeia is often framed within a kind of border that lends it a quasi-balloonic status. This border-effect may be achieved by placing the onomatopoeia in the middle of an explosive cloud (*Picaros* 44.3.3, *Bandit* 36.4.1, *Pirates* 22.1.1), or by surrounding it by wavy sound lines (*Picaros* 35.4.1; *César* 21.3.1; *Bandit* 31.1.2). Alternatively, the onomatopoeia may be surrounded by a circle of short spiky lines (see Figure 1). In this latter case, because of the absence of a tail, there must be additional information making clear where the sound comes from, for instance the onomatopoeia being located physically close to its source.

Tails designating sound effects. A tail is sometimes used to indicate the source of a non-verbal event. In *Picaros*, little gray clouds have a tail pointing towards a pipe or cigar (21.1.3a, 31.4.2) to suggest a puffing sound or the source of the smoke, while white-tailed clouds are used in combination with onomatopoeia to convey slammed doors (*Picaros* 19.2.3; *César* 19.4.2) or to indicate other varieties of literal or figurative "friction" (*Picaros* 19.4.2, *César* 7.3.1).

Captions. Captions are usually distinguished from balloons by visual means. This is important, because they convey the discourse of an agency at a different narrative level; that of a narrator that is not a character in the

Fig. 1: **Sound-enhancing straight lines (schematic)**

story world (see e.g. Bal 1997, Bordwell and Thompson 2008).[7] But since, like balloons, captions are containers filled with verbal text, it is useful to briefly compare captions to balloons. In mainstream comics, captions are formally distinguished from balloons by occurring, usually in boxes, at the top or bottom of panels, and by having no tails or thought bubbles, the latter being a logical consequence of the fact that they communicate information from an agency outside the story world. Presumably for the same reason, no pictograms or runes occur in captions in our data; pictograms and runes suggest emotions and humor, while non-diegetic narrators are taken to be neutral, "invisible" agents. Remarkably, however, several captions in *Pirates* feature exclamation marks (e.g. in 8.3.1; 10.3.1) and question marks (e.g. 18.1.1; 39.2.1), suggesting a degree of emotional involvement on the non-diegetic narrator's part.

Picaros, *César*, and *Pirates* make systematic use of a distinctive color for captions which in *César* are also used to provide translations of Latin words. *Bandit* uses mostly white captions, while the four yellow captions (8.1.1, 9.1.1, 10.3.2, 41.3.1) all indicate the passing of time (but cf. 19.1.2). In *Picaros*, narrator text in captions is, moreover, rendered in a different font, and in *Pirates* captions resemble tattered scrolls. The external narrator texts in *Avengers* consist of bold-face colored words that often appear directly on background visuals.

Diegetic, non-balloonic verbal inscriptions as part of pictures. Inscriptions are non-onomatopoeic verbal texts that are part of the visuals (street names, headlines, labels, graffiti, etc.). Like captions, but unlike onomatopoeia, inscriptions are meant to be silently read rather than mentally vocalized. Their status is primarily cued by *where* they occur, but font choice may also reveal something about the material or cultural dimensions of the object on which they appear. Thus *Picaros* uses a "print" font for newspaper text (e.g. 5.1.2 and 9.2.4), and an irregular font for Alcazar's hand-written letter (53.4.2), while the name of a slave trader's shop appears in "angular" print in *César* (15.3.2). *Bandit* uses a very different type of font than *Picaros* and *César* for the (painted) names of saloons and other prairie town buildings (e.g. 8.2.2, 16.1.1, 23.1.1).

Ontology of the Balloon

Balloons and paraballoons are *containers* of verbal and non-verbal information. Furthermore, because of the orientation of the tail or line of thought bubbles, balloons indicate the *source* of salient information, and imply a *des-*

tination. Moreover, non-standard varieties of balloons qualify the *manner* in which this information is to be understood. According to Lakoff and Johnson (e.g. Lakoff and Johnson 1980, Johnson 1987, Lakoff 1993), containment is a central human schema, enabling us to make sense of numerous phenomena. Balloons contain information and can be seen as a visualization of Michael Reddy's (1979) *conduit* metaphor. Reddy points out that our ideas about language are modeled and constrained by the consideration that we understand meaning as residing *in* words and sentences. Communication is typically understood as a process in which a speaker puts meaning into words, which are then sent to the listener who extracts the meaning from them.[8] The balloon appears to be a visual variety of the conduit metaphor: it is a "bag" of words (or other signals) with a more or less specific meaning that is transmitted from a source to a destination.

While the source of balloonic information typically emanates from a human being or anthropomorphized entity, the destination of information is twofold. In most cases information is provided for the benefit of fellow characters, but it is *always* provided for the benefit of the reader, who has privileged access to balloonic information that may not be available to other characters in the story world. Thought balloons are a good example because they are often the equivalent of interior monologue, conveying information that a character may suppress, or depicting dreams and hallucinations. We speculate that, owing to the conduit metaphor, any visual signs occurring in balloons acquire objective status. While iconic information in panels, such as gestures and facial expressions, may be ambiguous, visual signals in balloons have the same objectively explicit status as words.

"Manner" usually pertains either to the sound quality with which the information is conveyed (where "loudness" is the most dynamic variable), or to the emotional state of the character from which the balloon emanates.

Embodiment or Arbitrary Convention?

An intriguing question is whether the various dimensions of (para)balloons should be considered as completely arbitrary conventions whose use seems natural only because we have become so used to them, or whether they are motivated. If we are to look for possible forms of motivation we may take our cue from what is known in cognitive linguistics as the theory of "embodied realism" (e.g. Lakoff and Johnson 1980, 1999). Embodied realism, or experientialism, refers to the ways humans make sense of their lives, as reflected in their use of language, which can be explained by the human body's reliance on sensory facilities and motor skills. This leads for instance to the dominance of the "source-path-goal" schema, which does not only govern literal movement but also helps structure goal-directed behavior, as in expressions such as "we are making *progress* on this project," or "she is *ahead* of me."[9] Here we will consider whether it makes sense to detect any embodied features in the balloon parameters identified above.

Typography. The choice of typeface is a visual feature of increasing importance, as computer programs provide users with a wide range of fonts. There does not appear to be anything "embodied" in the choice of most standard typefaces or sizes for different sources of verbal information, with the exception of large, bold typeface to indicate loudness. This latter can be seen as a manifestation of the general notion that big equals more and, more specifically, size indicates volume. A "cultural" motivation (as opposed to an embodied one) can be found in the fonts chosen for the Roman tour guide's multilingual translations in *César* (1.3.1).

Balloon color. There appears to be no embodied motivation for the use of balloon color other than white. Of course, in some albums there is internal color consistency once an (arbitrary) convention has been established, as holds for the yellow serrated balloons in *Picaros* indicating electronically relayed text. Onomatopoeic gunshots (*Picaros* and *Bandit*) and punches (*César*) occur in (para)balloons of varying colors, as do expressions of pain. A more extensive study might lead to the conclusion that the color red (see e.g. *Picaros* 11.2.2, 42.2.2) is preferred for situations associated with violence, strong negative emotion, and pain. As "red" is associated with blood and heat, there might be an embodied motivation for its use in non-iconic signs.

Balloon contours. The *Picaros, Pirates* and *Avengers* samples recurrently deploy deviant balloon contours to mark special communicative circumstances. When contours are asymmetrical they are also often "jagged." Contours with irregular round, droplet-like edges are found in *Picaros* whenever a character drinks the whisky that professor Calculus has made unpalatable, causing the character to spit out the whisky. Here one can assume that the splashy contour iconically imitates the expelled liquid. A variant occurs in panel 3.3.2, where Haddock, after drinking, suddenly worries whether there may be poison in the whisky. Here the contour suggests dripping rather than centrifugally-dispersing droplets, perhaps mimicking "breaking out in a sweat" or suggesting that the balloon falls apart or melts. Hergé is highly consistent in his use of irregular contours to suggest a negative emotion or experience. It is moreover noteworthy that in most cases, Hergé's irregularly contoured balloons also break the frame, adding to the impression of abnormality and excess. In *Pirates*, speech balloons with a deviant or jagged tail indicate a sudden increase of narrative tension or unexpected danger (9.3.2), accusations (15.3.3; 25.2.1), or sudden rage (26.1.1).

We hypothesize that the above is not an arbitrary convention. As far as *form* is concerned, we can roughly distinguish between, on the one hand, "angularity" or "jaggedness" and, on the other, "roundness" and "smoothness." As far as *contour* is concerned, there is a rough dichotomy between symmetry and asymmetry. Other things being equal, angularity and asymmetry have more negative connotations than roundness and symmetry. Sharp, angular things are dangerous and potentially harmful, unlike rounded, smooth things. In addition, humans have a strong preference for balance and symmetry (Arnheim 1969: chapter 1; Ramachandran and Hirstein 1999: 27). The idea that asymmetry in balloon-contour connotes "bad" things may therefore be rooted in embodied cognition. Moreover, these phenomena also play a role on the level of elements *within* (para)balloons: the "rule" that angularity and asymmetry evoke negative connotations appears to be borne out in letters, pictograms, and runes as well.

Balloon contents. As indicated, pictograms have clear denotations and, in many cases, unambiguous connotations. In *Picaros,* the pictorial runes found in balloons and paraballoons are restricted to the expression of music, in *César* to droplets surrounding drunken "hiccups," and in *Bandit* to curses — although in the latter case the distinction between runes and pictograms is sometimes unclear. Whether all, some, or none of these elements are motivated signs is an issue that cannot be resolved here.[10]

Location of source of balloons. The convention of the balloon tail pointing to the mouth of the speaker makes sense if we see the tail as a variation of an "arrow" (Lefèvre and Baetens [1993] use the Dutch word for "arrow," *pijl,* for the tail), but this may be the result of a cultural rather than an embodied motivation. In contrast, the convention of a tail pointing outside of a panel to denote the speech of somebody who is not yet, or no longer, in the field of vision or attention of the person(s) represented in that panel does seem to reflect our everyday embodied experience.

Convention and Creativity in Comic Balloons

On the basis of the comics we have investigated, we propose the following description of the prototypical balloon. It is (i) a symmetrically formed (ii) white-colored (iii) oval or rectangular container (iv) with a continuous contour (v) located above or to the side of the character's head (vi) and linked by a tail (or thought bubbles) to a visible character, who thereby is designated to be the source of the information represented in the balloon (vii) which information is verbal text.

If we compare the balloon forms discussed in our data with the Comic Life inventory, it is noticeable that artists often vary freely from the stylized norms proposed there. Furthermore, in *Picaros*, *Avengers*, and *Pirates*, the basic balloon form differs in minor respects from the stylized norm (beveled corners, multiple protrusions, and variations on the round-edged rectangle). Balloon form thus provides an opportunity to help create a specific visual style for specific works.

The possibilities for creative play with balloonic norms are substantial, not least because the variables can be combined in many permutations. For instance, although pictograms have almost completely fixed meanings, making them functionally equivalent to what in other arts are called "symbols," it is possible to vary pictograms.[11] Moreover, one occasionally comes across unique iconic visuals in balloons, for instance depictions of people or events that a character is speaking or thinking about, and across deliberately unreadable text (Figure 3a). Another source of creative play pertains to exposing the balloon as artifice. One way of doing this is by turning balloons into literal containers (Figure 3b) or objects (Figure 3c); or letting characters somehow interfere with their own or another character's text or thought balloon. An interesting example of this is Figure 3d, in which a young man either is in the process of putting a real heart (his own?) in his thought balloon, in between an "I" and a "U"—or of removing it. The balloon use is daring on three counts: it allows a character to manually add something to (or detract from) a layer of text that ordinarily can only be manipulated at the level of narration; the (bleeding) heart is possibly ripped from his own body; and the "real" heart grimly plays with the convention of the pictogram that one might have expected to see instead.

Concluding Remarks

In this chapter we have offered the first version of a "blueprint" of the comics balloon by identifying a number of its crucial variables in five different comics sources. This is only a modest beginning. Examples of significant phenomena encountered but not counted in our data include balloons "breaking the frame," letters "breaking the balloon," and untranslated foreign/alien balloon text, while the current formulation of the norms and variables themselves requires extensive comparison with many other comics, and is in need of further extension and refinement. Moreover, calculating *correlations* between

Fig. 3a-d. Creative balloon use, examples a-c thanks to Gert Meesters. *3a:* Francois Ayroles (2001). [s.n.] Lapin 28. Paris: L'Association, p. 67. *3b:* Willy Vandersteen (1995) Suske en Wiske: De Tamtamkloppers. Antwerpen: Standaard, p. 4. *3c:* Merho [Robert Merhottein] (1994) Kiekeboe 26 Antwerpen: Standaard, p. 14. *3d:* Found on internet; source and provenance irretrievable.

variables will be necessary to fully reap the fruits of the laborious counting work exemplified here; as we have informally noted, many deviations from the norm occur in specific combinations (e.g. bold face *and* angular jagged balloon form *and* the balloon breaking the frame). Finally, we have only hinted at the subject of creative balloon use. Nonetheless we hope the current chapter offers a starting point for further analyses. Let us summarize what we see as the merits of our approach:

  • *Charting and analyzing balloon variables aids in the characterization of stylistic features.* Clearly, the somewhat arbitrary choice of comics in this chapter does not allow for sweeping or conclusive generalizations.

But at least cautious claims can now be formulated as hypotheses and, more importantly, they suggest how, in the interest of comics scholarship, further comparisons can be conducted within and across oeuvres, styles, and cultural traditions.

• *Recurring deviations from a balloonic norm invite theorization of and experimentation with the ways in which pertinent information is conveyed visually.* Just as designers in other genres and professions, comics authors strive for new and creative ways to make form meaningful and concise. Balloons are a crucial element of comics, demonstrating substantial variation but ultimately governed by conventions. The analytic approach adopted in this chapter also provides the basis for experimental research, since balloon variables can be combined in many different permutations and their effect on viewers tested under controlled conditions.

• *Balloon variables can be studied for their place on the "embodied-accultured" continuum.* We have suggested that features such as "symmetry" versus "asymmetry" and "jaggedness" versus "roundness," both in balloon form and in elements occurring within balloons, suggest deeply rooted, embodied and hence possibly universal features of human perception. Other variables may be more culturally or idiosyncratically determined. Investigations of balloons in comics are thus highly germane to discussions about the continuum between embodied and accultured meaning, as argued by cognitive linguists (e.g. Lakoff and Johnson 1980, 1999; Kövecses 2002, 2005; Gibbs 1994; 2006; Yu 1998).[12]

Notes

1. Balloonic information acquires its meaning only in combination with iconic (mimetic) visuals, language, and extra-balloonic pictograms, pictorial runes, and panel composition on the page. We will refer to these sources of information only inasmuch as they are necessary for characterizing balloons.

2. Kennedy (1982) and Forceville (2005) discuss these latter in terms of "pictorial runes." Walker (2000) uses "indicia" while McCloud (1993) prefers "cartoon symbols" (see particularly 127–131).

3. We have ignored the fact that the typical balloon in *Tintin* has beveled corners, and scored this type as "strict"; in *Pirates*, the standard speech balloon is also rectangular but with four sharp corners; this, too, has been counted as "strict."

4. To facilitate identification of panels, the following three-number code is adhered to: the first number refers to the page, the second to the row, the third to the number in the row. Where necessary, the third number is further subdivided via letters (a,b,c).

5. Since in *Bandit* and *Pirates* all instances of bold fonts are also instances of italics, the latter category does not carry independent meaning (differences between the scores in both categories are the result of the fact that bold-faced stand alone punctuation marks were not counted as italics, since it was impossible to assess this criterion). The high percentage of mixed styles in *Pirates* may be due to a preference to make clausal stress and intonation patterns systematically explicit visually.

6. See Fresnault-Deruelle (1977: 195–196) for a discussion of various types of onomatopoeic words in European and American comics.

7. First-person character text in some comics occurs in boxes that are visually indistinguishable from those used for non-diegetic narrator text (e.g. in Marjane Satrapi's *Persepolis* and in some sections of Manu Larcenet's *Le Combat Ordinaire*). It is thus necessary to distinguish between boxes' *visual form* and their *narrative function*.

8. Reddy discusses as a serious danger of this *conduit* metaphor, so deeply embedded in language itself, that meaning is understood as something that is objectively there, packaged into words by a sender and unpackaged, identically, by a receiver. In fact, meaning is construed with considerable effort by both sender and receiver, with the ever-present risk of misunderstandings.

9. See Johnson (1987), Lakoff (1993), Turner (1996), Kövecses (2002), Forceville (2006), Forceville and Jeulink (2007).

10. For a tentatively affirmative answer for runes, see Kennedy et al. (1993), Forceville (2005), Shinohara and Matsunaka (forthcoming) and Eerden (forthcoming).

11. Examples in our data are *Bandit* 21.3.1 and *César* 5.3.3, 39.3.2; for many more see Gasca and Gubern's (2001) richly illustrated book.

12. This chapter was written in 2008 during the authors' fellowship at the VLAC (Vlaamse Academie), the Centre for Advanced Studies of the Royal Flemish Academy of Belgium for Science and the Arts in Brussels, where they worked on the project *The Agile Mind: Creativity in Models and Multimodal Discourse*. The first author has gratefully used the library of the *Centre Belge de la Bande Dessinée* in Brussels. We warmly thank Gert Meesters (University of Liège) and Lisa El Refaie (University of Cardiff) for their insightful comments on, and corrections in, an earlier draft of this paper.

5

Remediation and the Sense of Time in Graphic Narratives

Kai Mikkonen

My premise in this chapter is that graphic storytelling enables us to pose some fundamental questions about the temporal conditions of narrativity. By narrativity, I mean what is generally understood by this term in narrative studies, that being the set of formal and contextual properties that characterize any narrative as narrative (Prince 2003, 65). Graphic narratives and comics[1] help us raise questions about the dynamics of narrative time differently from literary narratives because they manipulate the relation between the visual and verbal means of conveying a sense of time, and do so particularly well when they "think with their medium," i.e. when they reflect on the affordances that affect the construction of narrative time in this medium.[2] What is more, and what makes graphic narratives different from many other forms of visual narrative, are the specific uses of graphic drawing and showing, involving not only the spaces seen in the images, but the frame and the gutter, and the visual space of the page, in creating a sense of time.

The relationship between images and a sense of time is often complex, specifically in relation to so-called narrative images. One of the most central questions of narrativity in the study of graphic narrative has been the ways in which graphic *images* participate in the making of a story: How does a single image or frame participate in the narrative continuum? What is it that makes a collection of panel pictures a narrative text, and how is a series of images processed as a story? Here I wish to examine more specifically, by look-ing at references to other visual media in a recent graphic travel book, the way images in comics enable or, in some cases, inhibit "cognitive mapping" of temporal sequences and the process of mentally locating things and events at a moment in time.[3]

A single fixed image always poses the question of how to spatialize a sense of time (or how to narrativize things seen in the image). Narrative images have a range of visual resources for suggesting chronology and causality, for instance by depicting body language or gestures, in particular when they have a visible effect on other characters. A "monophase image," which represents only one phase of an event, can also suggest temporal progression and narrative by arresting movement at a significant moment in the action. However, the status of a single image or single panel always remains ambiguous as to its dependence or independence within a sequence of images, being at once a separate framed unit and an element that is connected to other surrounding panels both verbally and visually.

In this essay, I will approach the question of the sense of time in panel images by examining the ways in which the representation of other visual media invites questions about the temporal conditions of narrativity in the graphic narrative medium. This is, therefore, a study in remediation where the interest lies in the process of embedding other visual media that produces some of the effects of the medium in question in order to imitate it or revive it. As Jay David Bolter and Richard Grusin define the function of remediation, it is "the formal logic by which new media refashion prior media forms" (273). Both the embedding and the embedded medium seem to be affected by this transposition in such a way as to produce a doubly coded discourse. Semiotician Yuri Lotman and, more recently, literary scholar Emma Kafalenos have defined doubly coded discourse as a text within a text structure where the included section "is encoded in the same way as the remaining text and thus is doubly coded" (Lotman 381) What makes doubly coded artworks particularly interesting is that they, as Kafalenos argues, "invite questions of interpretation about the relations between the embedding and the embedded section" (30).

Two Visual Citations and the Question of the Key Frame

As my main example, I will take *Pyongyang: A Journey in North Korea* (2003), a documentary graphic narrative by French Canadian cartoonist Guy Delisle. *Pyongyang* is a travel story that describes the author's experiences during a two-month period of overseeing the production of an animated work at a film studio in the North Korean capital of Pyongyang. The story revolves around the question of remediation in two basic ways: the story comments ironically on the conditions of animation production — the use of cheap subcontracting in a totalitarian regime — while it also borrows from and refashions North Korean propaganda art in several panels.

I would like to begin with a visual citation in Delisle's narrative, taken from Hugo Pratt's Corto Maltese story "L'ange à la fenêtre d'orient," originally included in a collection entitled *La Lagune des mystères*. In *Pyongyang*, where the panel is marked with a copyright sign at the edge of the panel frame, the image is made to appear in more than one medium at a time.

On the one hand, the citation functions as a unit in a sequence of other panels, while on the other hand, the panel is also the potential key frame of an animation adaptation, as well as a monument to the comic book as an art form. This double function is revealed by its caption, "Corto Maltese — Monument of the 9th Art ," and the conversation within which the image is embedded.

The image shows the hero, Corto, about to shoot a revolver into the air. This example succinctly demonstrates the kinds of questions concerning interpretation that embedding raises, especially with regard to the temporal function of the panel. First, this panel is reframed, and within this new frame there are two pieces of additional verbal information: the words "Corto Maltese" above the image and, below it, the phrase "Monument of the 9th Art," referring to the prevalent distinction of comics as the ninth art form, especially in Francophone comics culture and scholarship on the medium. These statements do not belong to the direct discourse of the conversation, nor do they belong to the narrator's self-narration. Corto's name appears as a kind of title to the image, while the statement below functions as a dedication or declaration of the artistic value of the image.

The narrative context of this embedding ironically draws attention to how graphic heroes are adapted in animated films. The citation is placed within a scene containing a conversation, set in a Pyongyang café, where

OUR COLLEAGUE HAS COME TO WORK ON CORTO MALTESE.

Fig. 1 *Pyongyang: A Journey in North Korea*

one of Delisle's colleagues explains that he is currently working on a Corto adaptation. In the subsequent panels, the author-narrator explains that in order to minimize the expenses of the production, the key frames of the animation are drawn by animators in Paris, while the in-between frames are drawn by assistants in North Korea. The idea of a key frame is also illustrated on the bottom of the page by a series of figures and the accompanying quiz-style question, "which of these are key frames?"

At the end of the conversation, we "hear" Delisle's character commenting disparagingly on the Corto project, saying "Great, that way kids don't have to bother reading books. They'll just think everything started on the TV, like Tintin."

The notion of a key frame is important here, as it has a different meaning in comics than in animated films. In graphic narratives, some panels may carry more visual information, or propel the story forward more forcefully, than others. Key moments can also be emphasized visually, for instance by different types of frames or double frames. All frames in graphic narratives are, however, in some sense key frames. Normally panel pictures represent clearly distinct moments of an ongoing event that cannot be fully seen. It is crucial to narrativity in graphic narratives, therefore, that the reader-spectator recognize the possibility of alternative consequences between the panels. The space in between, also known as the gutter, is the manifestation of the simultaneous discontinuities of space and time. As a symptom of the spatialized illusion of time, the gutter requires the spectator-viewer to conceive of the meaning of the transition and possibly imagine actions that are not drawn,

Fig. 2 *Pyongyang: A Journey in North Korea*

but which must necessarily take place between the images. Film narratives can approximate a similar effect, for instance by using a "montage-sequence": a collection of shots that show selected segments of a given event.[4] In the graphic form, however, there is no equivalent to ongoing screen time. As Philippe Marion has argued, the idea of a string of images in comics is not a metaphor to describe the succession of images in time, as in cinema, but a literal string of images that materializes in space (184).

This Corto citation foregrounds the seminal issue here, namely that the device of the frame separating the panels also functions as a mechanism that breaks the narrative down into its constituent parts. The Hugo Pratt panel is taken from a narrative sequence of images, where it depicts a central moment in the action. In contrast, the panel as a citation serves to arrest the narrative flow. To illustrate the point further, we can look at the original panel sequence from which the given picture is borrowed. In this passage, we see adventuress Venexiana Stevenson escaping in an airplane from the hands of Venetian guards and of Corto himself.

What is further presented is the dramatic effect of Corto's mental process. The manipulation of a time lapse between the panels, and the changes in perspective from one panel to another, reveal Corto's spur-of-the-moment decision to not shoot at the plane at which he is aiming.

Delisle's reframing of the panel emphasizes the distance of this picture from the unfolding narrative in which it is embedded, as well as the function of the image as a separate image that is potentially meaningful in its own right. We must, however, also note that there is a small figure next to the Corto panel sitting on his haunches in the space between the panels, which seems to be a gutter, a narrative box, or both, placed below the explanation, "Our colleague has come to work on Corto Maltese." The figure is in effect another citation from *Les Ethiopiques*, another Corto Maltese adventure, portraying an Abyssinian rebel soldier name Kuš, who befriends Corto Maltese during his visit to East Africa. What I would like to point out here is the function of the Kuš figure as a kind of symbol of the graphic style of the Corto series. Here, Kuš presents another citation, the Corto panel, to the viewer, thus reminding the viewer of the importance of the frame from his space outside the frame. In other words, this segment demonstrates how the shape and size of panels, frames, or gutters can be given expressive value, unlike the space of an animation film, which is delineated by the screen on which it is projected.

The passage in which the citation occurs prompts the question of what may transfer from a comic book to an animated film. The recent Corto Maltese animation films are a case in point, in that the artist who created the series

Fig. 3 Hugo Pratt, *La Lagune des mystères*

has made an exhaustive attempt to create an impression of fidelity to the graphic style in Pratt's work.[5] However, similar visual styles may function differently in various media. For example, despite the stylistic fidelity of the animated versions, the Corto stories shed a good deal of their reliance on the representation of discontinuous time and space when transferred to the screen. It is characteristic of the Corto comics that most of their movement takes place in between the images. It is also typical of Pratt's panel-to-panel transitions to suggest the effect of not moving too much, if at all. Animation can manipulate temporal rhythm through various techniques, such as cutting, establishing shots, shot-reverse-shot sequences, fade-out images, or immobile figures stationed in front of a moving background.

But the expressive use of panels, frames, and graphic writing is not amenable to the relentless movement of film projection. Even if the animated adaptation focuses on immobile figures, the image is restricted by the necessity of showing at least some things that are moving, such as moving lips in speech, or the wind blowing through a character's hair. In contrast, each panel in graphic storytelling is framed and registered as a discrete entity. Similarly, the expressive function of graphic letters, which interact with the graphic line of the image, is lost in animated adaptations, and replaced by a soundtrack. Still another aspect of this doubly coded panel that lets us pose questions about the construction of a sense of time in graphic storytelling is the juxtaposition between the citation in the segment I have been discussing, and a poster. This includes the remediation of propaganda art featured on the next double spread. This is one of the North Korean propaganda images included in Delisle's book that often spread over a whole page and invite the reader-spectator to "stand back" and take time to contemplate the monument.

Various visual and narrative means suggest a link between the poster remediation and the Corto citation, given that both have a double frame around them, and both images are accompanied by a caption that creates a rupture in the ongoing verbal self-narration. For example, the translated propagandistic caption of the poster slogan reads, "Forging ahead into the 21st century!" prompting the viewer to imagine forward movement in the picture, and this contrasts with the Corto citation that emphasizes the colonial adventurer's status as a monument of the art form. Furthermore, the poster image repeats the gesture of a hand pointing a gun in the air. The North Korean soldier's hand is elevated at a sharper angle than in the Corto image, and the soldier seems to be brandishing the gun menacingly rather than directing it at anything specific. But the position of the missiles in the background equally recalls Corto's hand. Turning the page therefore leads the viewer's eye from the Corto reproduction to the poster image, emphasizing the monumentality of each image.

All visual media transfigured in this passage, including the graphic narrative itself, appear to be affected by trans-semiotic, intermedial "contamination." The narrative transfigures the animated key frame and the monumental poster into its graphic form, thereby challenging the presumed symbolic value and sense of immediacy of both within Delisle's (seemingly) much more spontaneous graphic style. At the same time, this juxtaposition reveals yet another important aspect of narrativity that is typical of graphic sequential art. Besides the linear sequence of images, single panels have the potential to interact across a narrative continuum. Graphic narrative can play on a network of spatially arranged visual connections between different panels on the same page; on subsequent double spreads; or even on more distant parts of the story.

Fig. 4 *Pyongyang: A Journey in North Korea*

Graphic Showing

Let us now move on to a more theoretical discussion concerning the temporality of graphic images in narrative sequences. What does the double-codedness of the two citations in *Pyongyang* imply about the construction of a sense of time in graphic narratives?

There are two characteristics of graphic storytelling that I would like to focus on here: the act of *graphic showing* and the *picture function* of the panel. First, whereas the act of showing is minimal, ancillary or non-existent in verbal narratives, it is crucial in graphic storytelling, since that which is shown and seen often elicits a narrativizing response from the spectator.[6] Showing can add to the degree of narrativity as, for example, by implying that there is a difference between what is shown and how something is shown, or that there is a difference between what can be seen in the image and what is left out of its field of representation. Delisle's narrative builds on such contradictions on many levels because so much of the author's experience involves the limitations put on his movements in Pyongyang, and how much can be shown of North Korea. On the visual plane, differences between what is shown and how something is shown are frequent. For instance, the realistic visual style of the two citations constitute graphic gestures that differ greatly from Delisle's habitual simplified graphic style, with the result that the citations seem more realistic yet also less spontaneous than the story around them. The viewer's perception of such contradictions between images necessarily contributes to the degree of narrativity since such observations can only be evaluated in relation to a sequence of images, their fields of vision and centers of perception.

Visual signs in graphic storytelling are different from many other forms of visual narrative, because whatever is presented in graphic narratives is always drawn, not shown in the same sense as in a live-action film or a photograph. Philippe Marion, who has developed a theory of graphic narration following André Gaudreault's notion of showing, or *monstration*, in cinema, has claimed that the graphic trace is always an opaque sign.[7] The opaque graphic sign, more or less realistic or stereotypical, lets us see the trace of the graphic act, the graphic performance, as if it were occurring before our eyes. Generally speaking, the graphic image also constitutes the material that it presents. Therefore, we may be able to differentiate not only between what is shown in the image and how it is shown, but also the graphic act of showing, as distinct from both what and how something is shown.

With regard to the visibility of the graphic trace, there is perhaps no crucial difference between graphic storytelling and animated films, except that the trace is perceived as moving in an animated film. In general, both graphic narratives and animation, no matter how different their graphic styles may be, privilege narrative drawings that feature expressive physical gestures and easily identifiable features of physiognomy, movement and situation. However, despite the similarities between comics and animated films, *graphic* showing has salient, unique elements. Such elements include, perhaps most importantly, the expressive use of panels, frames and gutters. The frame has a twofold function as a structural and expressive device, exerting influence on the narrative process by separating and setting a pattern for reading, while interacting in different ways with the texts and images that they contain.

The Picture Function of the Panel

I would now like to focus briefly on the expressivity of the panel and its frame by way of using Philippe Marion's notion of the picture function of the graphic panel. As Marion argues, inspired by the theories of Pierre Fresnault-Deruelle and Benoît Peeters, the panel can be seen as an expressive fragment traversed by two contradictory dimensions: the story and the picture (1998, 212). Furthermore, he defines these two dimensions as the picture function and the story (or narrative) function:

> I would call the *narrative function* that which guides the viewer in gliding past the frame, and the *panel function* that which, on the contrary, is responsible for illiciting a fixation on the image by isolating — through various means — a continuum.[8]

The picture function of the panel [*fonction-tableau*] is, in other words, that which strives to focus the viewer's attention on a particular image by isolating it from the rest of the story, thus urging the viewer to spend more time with it. The narrative function of the panel [*fonction-récit*], however, is that which makes the spectator glide over the image, viewing it as merely part of the narrative continuum. An extreme case of the picture function is a maximally self-sufficient image, or what could be called a "memorable panel," that risks jamming narrative responses to the image. Such panels appear to refer to no exterior field of vision or other image. A panel may also be made "memorable" by cutting it off from its narrative context, as in the case of posters based on individual Corto Maltese panels cited above, or by turning such panels into autonomous works of art and monuments to the ninth art, as has occurred famously in pop art.[9]

The distinction between the two functions cannot be drawn sharply, since, as I argued above, images that show can always contribute to the act of telling and to narrativity, to say nothing of the viewer's narrativizing responses to the narrative potential in a fixed image, or in two juxtaposed images. However, the principle of the picture function of the panel can help us point out the way images can remind the spectators of their supposed immediacy, and also make evident their incompleteness as part of a series of images.

Both Hugo Pratt and Guy Delisle are relatively conventional graphic artists, in that they employ a regular, fixed grid of panels on each page. In the *Corto Maltese* series, the panels are likewise standardized with regard to their height. As many readers have noted, however, the regularity of Pratt's grid allows for the smallest modifications to have great impact. Such modifications may for instance include changes in the focus and scope of the perspective or subtle changes in the depicted action and the characters' attitude.

Here we see another scene of a man with a gun from the story "L'ange à la fenêtre d'orient," where Corto reacts instinctively to the sudden appearance of a giant marionette by shooting at it. Each panel modifies the perspective, juxtaposing different individual points of view of the same instant, some of which are closer to the character's point of view, while others remain distant from it. The modification of point of view creates a dramatic effect, possibly making Corto's reaction more understandable to the viewer.

Moreover, each panel in the *Corto* story is always off-balance in relation

Fig. 5 Hugo Pratt, *La Lagune des mystères.*

to the other panels surrounding it, requiring the reader-spectator to process the meaning of panel-to-panel transitions. Without knowledge of the other images around it, and without being able to process the time of the spaces in between, it is impossible to say whether the Corto of the citation is about to shoot, is just shooting, or has just shot his gun (see Image 1). The picture function of the panel, which is foregrounded in the citation by the double frame around the image, attempts to arrest the perception of narrative flow. The citation thereby calls the spectator's attention to the division of visual space into frames. In this process a sense of time is also introduced within the monumentality of the propaganda poster as it is incorporated into the story.

Conclusion

I hope that the payoffs in analysing narrative temporality by way of remediation have now become evident. The refashioning of other visual media enables graphic storytelling to explore some of the shaping constraints of the medium that affect the presentation of time. In the remediation of a film image or a poster, one kind of temporality is juxtaposed with another and, further, translated into yet another temporality of graphic storytelling. Remediation thus allows artists to visually encompass and include different temporal spaces — past, present and, future — or histories within one panel, and to produce a multiple layering of time planes, without violating the conventions of plausibility. Similarly, by transfiguring other visual media, graphic narratives can develop complex points of view by multiplying the centers of perception; by making the frames of the image more visible; or by making the image seem more independent and spontaneous.

The *Corto* citation and the remediated poster emphasize the picture function of the panel as they ironically reflect on the isolation of these panels as fragments of the animation industry, as well as monumental art and propaganda. Both images are set apart from the narrative continuum by their double framing and through their accompanying captions. The temporality of these images and their graphic narrative engagement is therefore bracketed to some extent. The more open and spare space of the poster remediation further makes manifest the ways in which images can *show* a world or a situation, concentrate on a moment of action, and incite an emotional response in the viewer. In this juxtaposition, the narrative calls attention to the mediated nature of its visual space and style.

While revealing that the sense of time in an animated film is dependent on a series of key frames that we cannot distinguish as separate images, the graphic narrative suggests that it can rival animation and perhaps even surpass it by openly showing and manipulating the frames that it is made of. At the very least, it shows that graphic storytelling does not pretend, like animated film, that story-time, or the sense of chronology and discourse-time, or the order of presentation, could be equal.

However, my final point is that if we consider the temporal conditions of narrativity in graphic storytelling in relation to individual panels, the inherent instability and heterogeneity of the expressive meanings of the visual form of panels and their frames becomes evident. There is no automatic correspondence, or direct proportionality between the shape or size of the panel frame, or the frequency of panels on a strip of images, and the duration of the action presented in the image. Instead of conveying some general temporal structure through a sequence of panels, the relation between the two is only *suggestive* of temporally organized meaning, or a *condition* of such meaning. A series of multiplying panels, for instance, does not have to create an experience of speed in action. The sense of rhythm and duration in time depends on the given narrative context wherein such changes could suggest various temporal experiences and structures, including repetition, and slow motion. Ultimately, the potential sense of time in each picture panel depends on the local means and aims of narrative breakdown, the relations between the panels, and the viewer's active cognitive mapping of this relation.

Notes

1. By "graphic narrative" I understand a range of types of narrative work in comics. See Chute and DeKoven 2006, 767.
2. I borrow the expression of "thinking with the medium" from Marie-Laure Ryan (2005).
3. The perspective is inspired by Herman's (2002, 285–299) discussion of the functions of spatial reference and the reader's attempt to construct a storyworld in Flann O'Brian's novel *The Third Policeman*.
4. See Chatman, particularly page 69.
5. The French-Italian animated production of *Corto Maltese en Sibérie*, re-titled as *La Cour secrète des arcanes*, screened in the fall of 2002 and was followed by a series of TV adaptations in the two following years.
6. By showing, I simply mean the use of pictures to communicate meaning as if in front of the spectator's eyes. This practice I take to be different from verbal telling. By images, I mean iconic signs that are analogous to their signifieds in some culturally recognizable way.
7. By way of developing Gaudreault's film theory, Marion argues that one should not only consider the role of *monstration* (or showing) in comics but also pay heed to the specific functions of the graphic trace or imprint (or *graphiation*). This is since, Marion argues further, showing in comics never has the same figurative transparency or the same transitivity as in cinema. Due to the graphic trace of the image, "graphic material always resists and is opaque, it impedes monstration's capacity to be fully transtive" [*la matière graphique fait toujours résistance, opacité, et elle empêche la monstration d'être pleinement transitive*] (Marion, 36, translation Joyce Goggin).

8. "J'appellerai *fonction-récit* ou fonction narrative celle qui tend à entraîner le spectateur et à le faire glisser sur la case, et *fonction-tableau*, celle qui, au contraire, s'efforce de susciter une fixation sur l'image en l'isolant — par divers moyens — d'un continuum" (212, translation Joyce Goggin).

9. Most famously in Roy Lichtenstein's enlarged and altered comic strip panels from the early 1960s.

6

Brick by Brick

Chris Ware's Architecture of the Page

ANGELA SZCZEPANIAK

Architecture functions as an organizing mechanism in many of Chris Ware's comics. In *Jimmy Corrigan, the Smartest Kid on Earth*, the construction of the imposing Chicago World's Fair structures not only forms the backdrop for much of the young Jimmy's most resonant adventures, but it also registers the emotional residue of his alienation. Similarly, Ware's more recent *Building Stories* is largely framed by the bricks and mortar of the architectural design space.[1] As the title suggests, not only do the "Stories" take place within the stories of a particular building, the title further puns on the idea of "building" (constructing) a text. As a visual metaphor, architecture calls attention to the self-reflexive *construction* of the comics medium itself and since comics structure is commonly considered at the level of the panel, not the page, the sequencing of individual panels is privileged as the primary strategy for both comics composition and reading. By contrast, an architectural model reinforces the connectedness of panels, rather than their isolation as discrete units.

Each panel therefore, constitutes a brick in the whole construction site that is the page. While each has its individual function, all are integral to form the larger scaffolding, which draws the reader's focus to the overarching infrastructure of the page. In this view, comics do not consist solely of linear sequences of discrete moments of action. Instead, the medium affords a more complex structure — one that is not strictly linear, but almost weblike: a constellation.[2] Ware's running architecture metaphor establishes comics reading as an act of dynamic construction, inviting the reader to assemble the text through active, creative engagement.

As Scott McCloud points out in *Understanding Comics*, the gutters between frames are a visual representation of the space in which readers must connect and interpret the graphic units contained within panels, literally making sense of the fractured text in their minds, frame by frame. This emphasis on the reader's interpretative textual assembly suggests a valuable link to considering comics in literary terms. That said however, it is important to keep in mind that comics are a unique medium and differ from language-only forms, and that exploring the narrative elements of comics helps to make clear the specific interpretative strategies that the medium requires. Ware's work in particular lends itself to a literary reading and demands an acute awareness of the medium's construction and intense readerly work to if one is to unpack his pictorially and textually dense comics.

Comics reading diverges from other literary interpretation since it requires a synthesis of both verbal and pictorial elements. Likewise, comics images often function differently than other image types (like photographs), in that they are positioned in relation to one another, frequently developing narrative sequences. It is important to note though, that even comics containing little or no verbal content require a "literary" interpretative strategy. Lawrence A. Abbott goes "so far as to say that the manner of perception is to a great extent determined by the literary nature of the comic art panel. The perceiver is, after all, termed a "reader"— and the subordination of the pictorial to the literary in comic art is one of the subtlest realities of the medium" (156). While it is a specious gesture to subordonate one element of the medium to another, it is constructive to note the literary nature of reading the comics pictorial. As narrative elements, the pictorial plane in comics is *literary*, whether or not there is actual verbal content present.

Inking the Reader's Voice

Comics can be considered an interactive medium partly because of the artistic devices, such as the frame-gutter "fractured" page layout, that comprise it. However, the magnitude of the reader's role is reinforced through the paratextual letters space, which prints the letters of actual readers. In this way, readers' interpretative work literally becomes a part of the comic book. These direct addresses to a text afford a unique opportunity to observe the relationship between readers and artists. For example, one of Ware's readers raises many concerns regarding Ware's ongoing series, *The ACME Novelty Library*, as well as the position of the reader within the comics medium more broadly[3]:

You are a liar! You are a liar!

What is the matter with you? I was in Chicago for the big game so I walked by the address of ACME which is not really it! It is a regular place with no room for thousands of workers and there are no gardens or pool. What are you doing?

And are you gay? In your third comic book you talk about sweaty messengers and that journal thing in the LETTERS space says the word "gay." I am very unsure if it is what you are doing! Why is the table of contents not accurate?

Is J. Corrigan a little boy or an old man? The guy in number three really looks like a little rock or a cigarette butt. What is it? I tried to put the ROBOT and PICTURE MOTION together and they do not work. I do not think if I sent away for things you offer in the magazine that they would really come to me. What are you doing?

The distress of J. Walker's reading experience is palpable, with its almost obsessive concern over Ware's "lies," and what he may be *doing* in his work. This anguish, though it seems curious and amusing, is a condition that may confront any Ware reader. His work is visually dense; upon first glance it astounds the eye, sometimes stunning it to the point of poster blindness. Readers must consciously make sense of what they encounter. The graphic complexity and saturation of images, combined with Ware's biting irony that often appears in the guise of an "authentic" voice, render the *ACME* experience a challenging one.[4]

But J. Walker's angst also stems from an apparent misconception of how to engage with Ware's text at all. Although the fruitless journey to the fictitious ACME headquarters is unfortunate, J. Walker is, in the end, a victim of his or her own readerly assumptions: in this case, evidently, the expectation of authenticity and truth, for Ware's text to be taken at face value. However, Ware offers no such passive reading opportunities.

It is important, though, to note such a reader's expectations, since reading — especially comics reading — is frequently conceived of as a passive experience.[5] Even the revered comics artist and theorist Will Eisner makes a similar assumption in theorizing his concept of the reader. In *Comics and Sequential Art*, he discusses the "contract" between a reader and artist, essentially arguing that readers are strictly bound to the artist's intentions (Eisner, 40). He insists that the medium calls for "the tacit cooperation of the reader" to fulfill a text by absorbing it, almost as an immutable transmission from the artist (ibid.). In other words, Eisner's comics reader is passive, and he maintains that, "[i]n comics the imagining is done for the reader. An image once drawn becomes a precise statement that brooks little or no further interpretation" (Eisner, 122).

In sharp contrast, Ware does not allow such consumptive, superficial reading: both his page design, and the intensely ironic narratives that permeate his texts, are complex, multi-layered pieces that are only meaningful through active interpretation. Indeed, if Eisner's conception of the reader held true, J. Walker would not be so perplexed. The letter indicates a complete lack of cooperation on the part of the reader — the desire simply to absorb Ware's text is clearly the overriding readerly impulse here, but it is precisely this drive for passivity that leads this reading experience horribly awry. Comics, like any artistic medium, require an active engagement from a willing reader. As W.J.T. Mitchell argues, pictures, although they may appear to be "natural," free of the cultural codes that infuse other signs, must nonetheless be interpreted, not passively received.

Some Assembly Required

> In the limbo of the gutter, human imagination takes two separate images and transforms them into a single idea.
> — Scott McCloud

Part of the reading process that comic books demand is that readers fuse discrete moments of a text in their own minds. Comics artists, according to Scott McCloud, have an "equal partner in crime known as the reader" (1994, 68). That the artist and reader are figured as "*equal* partners" significantly identifies readers' agency within the construction of meaning, licensing them to *read* independently of the artist's possible intentions. McCloud privileges the reader's necessary involvement in assembling the text, gesturing toward reading as an active *process*, even celebrating this readerly engagement: "several times on every page the reader is released — like a trapeze artist — into the open air of imagination" (McCloud 1994, 90). Yet, however liberating McCloud's description seems here, he is also quick to control the reader as much as possible: "In comics the conversation follows a path from mind to hand to paper to eye to mind. Ideally the artist's "message" will run this gauntlet without being affected by it, but in practice this is rarely the case" (McCloud, 195). Although he concedes the impossibility of controlling a reader fully, he betrays a longing for the artist's message to be unaffected by the reader, implying that the interpretative process is apt to result in a failure of communication. In this view, the text is spoiled by the process of reading, given the anxiety that the reader may not absorb it exactly as the artist intended.

But the gap between the artist and reader can be a productive space. Wolfgang Iser exploits this *secondary* gutter between artist and reader, rendering reading as an actively creative process:

The literary text activates our own faculties, enabling us to recreate the world it presents. The product of this creative activity is what we might call the virtual dimension of the text, which endows it with its reality. This virtual dimension is not the text itself, nor is it the imagination of the reader: it is the coming together of the text and imagination [Iser 1974, 279].

Reading as a creative endeavor suits an artist like Ware, whose work demands an acute awareness of the process of reading itself. Ware's readers can never forget that they are holding and reading a book. His texts often require physically turning the book, squinting at the sometimes-miniscule text, or using a finger to literally trace the possible routes through the page. Ware's focus on the reading process is significant, as it shifts the conception of reading as a goal-oriented practice to a processual one, encouraging readers to enjoy the *experience* of reading itself, rather than racing to the finish line. While there is nothing inherently wrong with goal-oriented reading, when applied to visually dense comics like Ware's, readers can often miss the many stunning elements that stand outside the most direct route to the end of the narrative.

Iser further theorizes that the language-only text is equally as fractured as the comics page. Much like McCloud's gutters, Iser sees a series of "gaps" and "blanks" between ideas presented in verbal texts that the reader must bridge in order to find meaning. According to Iser, the blank "is an empty space which both provokes and guides the ideational activity. In this respect, it is a basic element of the interaction between text and reader" (Iser 1978, 194–195). Not only does the reader go about interpreting the text, the text actually demands such activity, and provides the tools to fulfill this engagement.

As much as both Iser and McCloud acknowledge the reader's activity, neither is willing to let control rest primarily with the reader. Iser suggests that the blanks (or gutters) between ideas,

> are the unseen joints of the text, and as they mark off schemata and textual perspectives from one another, they simultaneously trigger acts of ideation on the reader's part. Consequently, when the schemata and perspectives have been linked together the blanks "disappear" [Iser 1978, 182–183].

Of course, the comics page never allows the blanks to "disappear," since they are visually embedded within the text. Although readers supply connections between frames, the actual blank space between them is always present, leaving space for further interpretation. Even once a reader achieves "closure" from one frame to the next, the fixed gutters suggest that the interpretative space is always present, continuously opening up the text to the reader's intervention.

The most pertinent question then, becomes whether it is possible to completely "fill" these textual blanks. Eisner suggests that it is not only possible, but that this is the only goal and activity required of readers. He removes agency from the reader as much as possible:

> The sequential artist "sees" for the reader because it is inherent to narrative art that the requirement on the viewer is not so much analysis as recognition. The task then [for the artist] is to arrange the sequence of events (or pictures) so as to bridge the gaps in action [Eisner, 38].

As much as Eisner may resist relinquishing control of his text, it is futile and unproductive to micromanage the reader's activity — ideas cannot be communicated in unadulterated whole-form, directly into a reader's mind. An artist must, eventually, release a work, giving way to the reader's engagement in order to bring meaning to a text independent of the artist. The comics page and the frame are not so much "unit[s] of containment" (Eisner, 40) as they are open works.[6] Although some texts are less "open" than others, readers must, nonetheless, *interpret* what they see and read. It is difficult to engage passively with Chris Ware's work, as it presents an explicitly open invitation to the reader.

Consider the following *Quimby the Mouse,* which is the second half of a two-page strip. Overall, it is impossible to establish a single, determinate meaning, as it presents several clustered vignettes — a constellation of nonlinear elements left for the reader to assemble and reassemble in the spirit of active play. The establishing panel features the house and environs that form the basis of the thought balloon and memory sequences. This architectural structure unifies the page, in that all the subsequent narrative threads apparently stem from this panel, but it also splinters the narrative. It simultaneously connects and fragments narrative possibilities, leaving no single way of consolidating the page. Reading one panel after the next, following Eisner's notion of sequence, becomes an insurmountable task. Despite the copious arrows, which would normally reveal a clear path through a piece, the sequence becomes a directionally complex network — almost a formal joke, mocking a preoccupation with sequence. These arrows instead lead to multiple narrative threads, never precisely delineating a cohesive structure, so as much as one may follow the arrows, there are always moments when one must backtrack against the indicated direction in order to take in all the elements of the page. The piece becomes a labyrinth of arrows, showing numerous possibilities for navigating meaning from the complicated, polyvalent field of the page.

Even determining what actually "happens" in this piece is difficult, requiring an almost hyperactive reader to plot a course through the clusters

Fig. 3 *Quimby the Mouse*

of vignettes. Simple questions arise, demanding that readers make choices, such as where to begin reading — the top tier frame, which functions as an establishing panel for the piece? Or the bottom tier, with the sequence of the Quimbies in bed? If one begins at the bottom, does one move from the first unframed image to the thought balloon, which encompasses the rest of the page above? If so, at what point does one continue the sequence of the Quimbies in bed? Several sequences of panels circulate around a few key panels, and nearly implode in on themselves. This narratively destructive labyrinth of framed and unframed moments defies Eisner's focus on passive sequence at every turn; readers "graze" the page, "nibbling" brief moments of action as they move from one vignette to the next, making vast logical leaps along the way to connect these discrete sequences (Barthes 1975, 13).

Although arrows in comics typically imply a chronology of events, Ware's strip withholds this linear progression. It makes a hash of sequence, at points relying on linear narratives, then completely breaks loose from those threads. Through this chaotic narrative, readers are instead left with a faint impression of tone, atmosphere, and feeling that cannot be quantified in terms of narrative events. There is a vague aftertaste of confusion and emotional conflict, which mirrors acts of perception and memory, here configured through the younger Quimby's thoughts. The wishing well vignette suggests a sense of loss considering the rapidly aging Quimby, especially as the rest of the piece melds earlier moments of healthful exuberance with the increasingly ailing twin. The tone shifts throughout the memory fragments, ultimately leaving no unified sense of either narrative or emotion. Since time and space are so jumbled, readers must decipher the conflicting emotional state of the thinking Quimby — a challenging task, since there are so many plausible ways to fill the "blanks," inciting countless interpretations. Readers are left to play with all of these elements, to generate multiple closures and meanings, which is especially compounded by the apparent narrative diversions that combine with various sequences. The insect saga in the fourth tier, for instance, is connected to the wishing well vignette, but there are many possible ways in which it may figure in the larger narrative. Meaning is not only fulfilled by the reader's creative assembly of various design elements, but the elaborate connective tissue that the text demands is almost entirely *supplied* by the reader.

Ware's pages are intense, lush spaces. While there are often gestures toward narrative elements that demand a given reading sequence, he also encourages the eye to deviate — to dwell on features that are not necessarily prescribed by the narrative. Ware regularly features images not directly related to the plot, which add to the "distraction" for the eye, encouraging readers to wander through whole pages, rather than anchoring them to a rigid, monolithic sequence. Instead, the saturated page breeds a kind of *reader fatigue* that stunts the ability (and perhaps the desire) to absorb the text. It is a productive exhaustion, though, as the eye is freed to roam through the images, rather than limited by linearity.

Eisner is greatly troubled by the power that this freedom affords the reader, citing that "[t]he most important obstacle to surmount is the tendency of the reader's eye to wander. On any given page, for example, there is absolutely no way in which the artist can prevent the reading of the last panel before the first" (Eisner, 40). However, it is unproductive to dismiss the reader's *reading* as an obstacle. Although Ware attempts to guide readers in certain directions, he also structures the page as an exploratory design space to be pored over. The sequence of panels is an important element of a Ware page, but it does not supersede the experience of the page as an intricate design space.

Gene Kannenberg observes that Ware's *Quimby the Mouse* and some of his other "gag" strips do not attempt a continuous narrative, but instead "recall sonnet sequences, in that each page is a single unit and the aggregate whole is more concerned with communicating mood and feeling than in presenting a narrative" (Kannenberg, 178). The *Quimby* strips are concerned with issues that are not necessarily linked to a linear narrative. As such Ware opens up the text to the reader, which foregrounds a reading strategy that is *processual*, rather than a goal-oriented. While the comics medium in general (the work of Chris Ware included) manipulates sequence as an organizing mechanism, it is limiting to privilege sequence as the only, or even the primary formal element of comics art.[7] Equally fundamental are aspects that stand outside the narrative sequence, such as the atmosphere and tone of a piece, as well as the visual texture of the layout. These aspects can be configured and reconfigured by the reader, to foster an enriching, active reading experience. Although sequence is clearly a part of the comics page, focusing primarily on sequence obscures significant non-narrative details in a rush to reach the finish line. With the singular goal of assembling the narrative passively, the *experience* is elided, disregarding considerable somatic and affective responses.

It is possible to practice narrative tunnel vision, driven only to reach the end of a piece, but readers more commonly scan forward and backward, taking in the page as a whole as much as they read to follow the sequence. Comics scholar Charles Hatfield describes this as a "holistic" reading strategy. As he contends, "[t]he 'page' [...] functions both as a sequence and as object, to be seen and read in both linear and nonlinear, holistic fashion" (Hatfield, 48). For Ware, this "holistic" reading practice is essential. He structures panels to lead the eye in certain directions, or to take clusters of frames together at points, which does create a linear narrative. But at the same time, readers must maneuver multi-directionally through the sequence, to appreciate all the images that permeate the page.

As part of the ideational activity it is constructive to consider the function of elements that are not overtly related to the narrative. They create mood, atmosphere, tone, and texture. The page embraces affective qualities, in addition to pragmatic contributions to narrative threads. In fact, these elements can stand outside the sequence altogether, since they contribute to the overall meaning of the piece, whether in affective or cerebral terms.

Another of Ware's single page strips, "Sparky's Best Comics and Stories, Featuring Carlton the Collapsible Horse" playfully integrates Ware's formal,

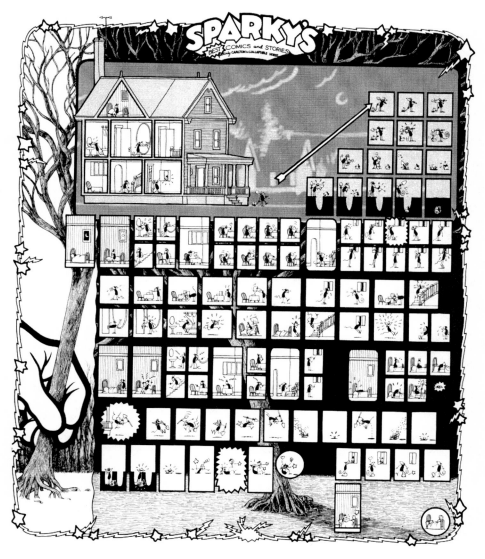

Fig. 2 "Sparky's Best Comics and Stories, Featuring Carlton the Collapsible Horse"

architectural engagement with the page. Similar to the house in the "Quimbies" strip, the house in this piece functions as a splash panel. Through the framework of the cross-sectioned house we see each room within it as a separate panel, again concretizing a visual pun, or analogy to architecture. The integration of the house into the panel structure of the page organizes the narrative according to the formal devices of the medium. Panels, like other graphic and textual details, are dynamic, active elements, fully integrated into the narrative structure of the design space.

The eye is immediately drawn to the marginal details that may be thematically or holistically linked to the narrative, but that do not advance the plot. The left margin features a tree that forms part of the border (or the elaborately designed "frame" that constructs the "meta-panel" of the page). The tree is reinforced as a structural element, as it establishes one layer of the background. Casting an eye over the page, one cannot see the panels in the foreground without also seeing the tree behind them, in which the central panels are nested. Likewise, the night panels create a complex visual texture: readers have the simultaneous condition of seeing each panel within its sequential structure, which develops the plot, while seeing the whole page. The neighborhood and the darkness that envelops it form another layer of background behind the panels and the tree, and to a degree, fill in the "gutters" between frames. When Quimby steps out of the house, he does not enter another panel, nor a conventional gutter, but the background neighborhood. The page becomes a multilayered, polyvalent design space that opens out from the panels, rather than the panels enclosing discrete actions. The meta-panel border and background images visually connect and unify the internal panels, which establishes the page both as the unit of artistic composition, as well as of architectonic readerly construction.

Textual Seesaws: The Playground of the Page

> The constellation is a system, it is a playground with definite boundaries. the poet sets it all up. he designs the play-ground as a field-of-force and suggests its possible workings. the reader, the new reader, accepts it in the spirit of play, then plays with it. [...] the constellation is a challenge, it is also an invitation.
> — Eugen Gomringer, *The Book of Hours and Constellations*

Ostensibly, it is a vast leap to consult a concrete poet about the comics medium; nonetheless, Eugen Gomringer offers an invaluable theory of the reading process that furthers an understanding of the active engagements readers may have with texts. His conception of the poem and the reader's participation in constructing it usefully describe the type of reading enabled by Ware's work, and other comics like it. The text is a fertile space that does not subordinate the reader's crucial interpretative involvement; the text and the reader form an equally active partnership, generating multivalent constellations of meaning. Ware treats the comics page as that "field-of-force," inviting readers to "play" within the construction site of the playground that is the page.

The spirit of play is key here, as readers may create their own interpretive games with a text — a process of ideation that is infused with a sense of enjoyment and pleasure. Reading is an experience to be savored, not an object to be consumed. As Roland Barthes advances, "what I enjoy in a narrative is not directly its content or even its structure, but rather the abrasions I impose upon the fine surface: I read on, I skip, I look up, I dip in again" (Barthes 1975, 11–12). This methodology offers a viable strategy for dealing with constellations within a visual field, much like the "playground" Gomringer envisions. For the "Quimbies" and "Sparky's" strips in particular (though even Ware's longer narrative works benefit from this treatment), it is unproductive to look for an overarching sequence governing the text and reader. Instead, Ware supplies the parameters of the text, but then leaves it open for the reader to enjoy. Readers interested in a more passive experience are often left confused and frustrated as J. Walker's letter catalogues. At best, flaccid narrative-driven reading engenders disappointment. Douglas Wolk criticizes Ware's artistic style as sterile with its clear line technique, intricately detailed panels, and complicated narratives, thus "nearly impossible to enjoy, because it's explicitly meant to write off the kind of 'enjoyment' it flirts with" (Wolk, 358). He analogizes his reading experience to Ware dangling pleasure "like a bunch of grapes," then snatching it away (ibid.). Wolk's position is especially fascinating, because, more than anything, it betrays his own reading experience and expectations as a reader, much like J. Walker's assessment. Wolk clearly does not take pleasure in the work that Ware demands of his readers; he is unwilling to grasp the opportunity to play in Ware's textual playground, which leaves his reading experience unfulfilling.

But let us accept, for a moment, Ware's "invitation," with another of his *Quimby the Mouse* strips. Again, more remarkable than any narrative sequence is the design of the page itself, particularly the way it allows the eye to play within the whole "field-of-force," rather than anchoring it in sequential panels that are devoted solely to propelling a narrative forward. Ware challenges the concept of a linear sequence initially with the entry into the strip. Beginning at the bottom left corner, we literally ascend into the narrative proper with

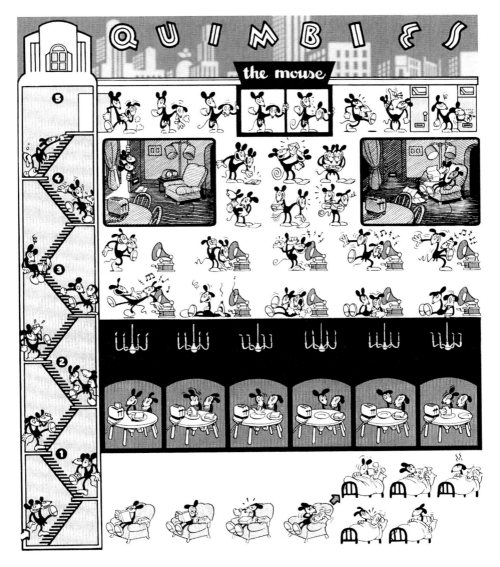

Fig. 1 *Quimby the Mouse*

the Quimbies, the stairs forming a border of marginal images that frame the page, essentially treating it as a larger meta-panel.

The lack of hard frames in the stairwell furthers the fluidity of this structure: as the Quimbies pass from one floor to the next, the landings function as formal divisions, but overall the framing here creates a vertical sub-panel.

Generally, panels are thought of as completely discrete units separated by gutters. This page contains a lot of white space, but minimal proper gutters, as there are very few hard frames that delineate sequences of action. Contrary to the conventional conception of the frame representing isolated moments, freezing each in time, Ware blends space and time, by treating his panels as parts of a larger infrastructure. The whole page becomes a dynamic design space, with many actions, both freezing *and* blending various moments. Sequence is clearly one part of Ware's work — we can follow the Quimbies' movements one moment at a time — but he blurs the distinctions between panels, thus using sequence more freely as an organizing mechanism.

Most of the hard frames in this piece represent actual architectural walls that are structurally relevant to the narrative. The staircase frames the action, again pointing to the architecture of the page. Ware teases the idea of framing as a technical device: the central frame below the title arch is especially compelling, as the figures are aware of it. It is tactile for them — they lean on it, they touch it, walk through it. It becomes part of their physical reality, not merely a formal device required by the medium. Because the Quimbies are aware of the physicality of their borders, as one would be of walls and doors, they draw attention to their artifice as cartoon characters. The Quimbies' cognizance of their own construction invites readers to join their formal puns, making them similarly conscious of the form, as well as their own textual position navigating the page. Playing with their own frame borders as the Quimbies do here, suggests that they are not enclosed by their frames. The frame, for them, is fluid and within their purview to manipulate. They lay the terms of their own construction bare, thwarting submissive reading strategies. Rather than becoming absorbed in the story, the reader is invited to diverge from the narrative sequence — as freely as the Quimbies are frameless — to take in the whole design space, rather than arriving at the punch line as directly as possible.

The implications of Ware's innovative design structure, particularly given his allusions to architecture, significantly re-conceptualize the comics medium. Through his intense exploration of the formal possibilities of the page, Ware creates opportunities for generative engagements with texts. In contrast to goal-oriented, passive reading practices, such as those Eisner advances, Ware resists the assumption that the reader's involvement is simply to arrive at the end of a piece, harvesting and consuming information conveyed by the artist. Because his design structure compels readers to "play" more actively in the space, Ware instead enables a *processual* reading strategy — one that encourages readers to appreciate the *experience* of reading itself.

Notes

1. Segments of *Building Stories* have appeared in a number of publications, including *Nest Magazine*, and have been serialized in *The New Yorker*.

2. The term "constellation," taken from Eugen Gomringer's *The Book of Hours and Constellations*, describes the playful interaction of various disparate design elements of a page that readers must assemble. I return to this poetics of constellation later in this essay.

3. J. Walker, *New York City, New York* (*ACME* vol. 3), I would be remiss in not pointing out that Ware has occasionally been accused of writing the cited letter himself, or that it is simply a joke perpetrated upon Ware by a more self-aware reader than J. Walker is here, although Ware has denied these allegations ("Panel Discussion." Harbourfront Festival, Toronto, Ontario, October 29, 2005). In the context of this essay, determining the authenticity of this particular reader is irrelevant, since the letter raises pertinent issues concerning (mis)reading, through representing a potentially "real" engagement with Ware's text, whether stemming from an actual or mock reader's pen.

4. The tiny, intricate paratextual advertisements for nonexistent products which readers are encouraged to mail order, like "six-packs of happy memories," demand fairly vigorous decoding from the reader, especially because they often function as satirical vehicles that critique consumerism.

5. See Charles Hatfield (*Alternative Comics*, 32–36) for a more detailed history of comics reception and various perceived effects of the medium on reading processes and general literacy.

6. I define "open work" according to Umberto Eco's theory in *The Open Work*, particularly for the freedom given to readers, through a "controlled disorder": "[t]he *possibilities* which the work's openness make available always work within a given *field of relations*," but the works remain, nonetheless, "open" and dependent upon a reader's active interpretation for meaning (19).

7. Both Will Eisner and Scott McCloud term comics "sequential art," a title that, especially when associated with these seminal theorists, tends to privilege sequence over any of the other significant elements of the medium.

PART THREE

Out of the Gutter: Comics and Adaptations

It Was the Best of Two Worlds, It Was the Worst of Two Worlds

The Adaptation of Novels in Comics and Graphic Novels

DIRK VANDERBEKE

I

The history of comics is also a history of adaptation: movies were adapted to the comic book format, and comics have increasingly been adapted to the screen. Less popular, but nevertheless equally interesting, are comic book adaptations of novels.[1] The last decades have seen a few courageous projects like the adaptations of Marcel Proust's *A la recherche du temps perdu*, J.R.R. Tolkien's *The Hobbit*, and Paul Auster's *City of Glass* alongside less bold endeavors as, for example, numerous rather simplistic adaptations of Western novels, science fiction and other adventure tales. Moreover, there are whole series of short comic book adaptations of literary texts, like for example *Classics Illustrated*, which also include artistically ambitious works like Bill Sienkiewicz's rendering of *Moby Dick*. Of course, comic book adaptations of novels pose theoretical questions and aesthetic problems, and this paper will explore some of these aspects and the solutions offered by different artists.

Adaptation theory has not yet dealt satisfactorily with this topic, and comics and graphic novels are frequently neglected. Linda Hutcheon opens the preface to her *Theory of Adaptation* with the assertion that adaptation has always been a phenomenon that could not be restricted to a few media only, but included every possible form of artistic expression:

> The Victorians had a habit of adapting just about everything — and in just about every possible direction; the stories of poems, novels, plays, operas, paintings, songs, dances, and *tableaux vivants*, were constantly being adapted from one medium to another and then back again. We postmoderns have clearly inherited the same habit, but now we have even more materials at our disposal — not only film, television, radio and the various electronic media, of course, but also theme parks, historical enactments, and virtual reality experiments. The result? Adaptation has run amok. That's why we can't understand its appeal and even its nature if we only consider novels and films [Hutcheon, xi].

However, one cannot fail to notice that the list does not include comics and graphic novels, and in the course of Hutcheon's analysis, they only receive a few cursory nods. Moreover, the rare examples she provides deal almost exclusively with the relationship between graphic novels and the movies, while the adaptation of literary texts is only mentioned twice.[2] It seems that the author's "perverse de-hierarchizing impulse" or the "often radically egalitarian approach to stories (in all media) by both narratology or cultural studies" still turn a blind eye to sequential art, favoring media that have by now gained acknowledged status (xii, xiii). It will therefore be necessary to perform some adapting of my own, using more exhaustive theories of film adaptation for my purposes.

When we discuss adaptations of literary works to comics or graphic novels, we first face the usual resistance to the process as such. In the context of the movies, received wisdom holds that adaptations will usually be measured against the quality of the source text and may approximate or — at best — match the standard set by the original work. However, it will usually fail to do so:

> The language of criticism dealing with film adaptation of novels has often been profoundly moralistic, awash in terms such as *infidelity, betrayal, deformation, violation, vulgarization*, and *desecration*, each accusation carrying its specific charge of outraged negativity [Stam, 54].

Similarly, Robert B. Ray has argued that the appreciation of adaptation follows the traditional Western hierarchy that favors the original over the copy (Ray, 45). However, this evaluation is not a given and could well be replaced by alternative views, as for example adaptation as citation, as artistic transformation, as commentary, as elaboration, as encounter, as subjective reading, as artistic vision or, as Linda Hutcheon called it, as "extended revisitations of prior works" (Hutcheon, xiv).

Of course, the critics' disregard is chiefly directed against adaptations that dare to tread where only literary genius may walk freely, i.e. when canonical texts are adapted to the new medium. We would otherwise be forced to concede that a considerable part of all films and the vast majority of Oscar-winning movies are necessarily failures.[3] But then, no critic would seriously debate whether John Ford's *Stagecoach* (1939) actually managed to capture the style and meaning of Ernest Haycox's "Stage to Lordsburg," whether Stanley Kubrick's *Dr. Strangelove* (1964) is faithful to Peter George's *Red Alert*, or even whether Jean-Luc Godard's *Le Mépris* (1963) measures up to Alberto Moravia's *Il disprezzo*. In these cases, the idea that the movie was based on another source is either simply ignored, or the literary text is treated as no more than the germ from which the artistically superior work has taken its departure.

Things are, again, different when other media like paintings or the opera are scrutinized. Dudley Andrew points out that there "is no question of the replication of the original in Strauss's *Don Quixote*. Instead the audience is expected to enjoy basking in a certain pre-established presence and to call up new or especially powerful aspects of a cherished work" (Andrew 30).[4] As comics and graphic novels have been generally regarded as one of the lowest forms of artistic expression, one might expect that adaptations would be met with the same mistrust as the movies, and that they would be measured against the achievements of the novel's written word and judged in respect to their fidelity. And indeed, this perspective seems to inform at least some of the criticism on comic adaptations of literary works. Cari Keebaugh, for example, in her essay on various adaptations of Mark Twain's *A Conneticut Yankee at King Arthur's Court*, comments favorably on some panels in the King's Classics version, because "Hank is portrayed with notable complexity and fidelity to the novel," or "Merlin's character is beautifully rendered, aesthetically and faithfully to Twain's original intentions," a bold claim indeed if one keeps in mind that intentionalism was discredited long ago in literary criticism by Monroe and Beardsley.

However, it sometimes pays to be regarded as the village idiot, and as the good shepherd will take more delight in the one lost sheep that returns to the fold than in the ninety-nine that never left it, critics have begun to celebrate comics and graphic novels if they present serious topics or demonstrate artistic sophistication. In consequence, comics are now discussed more frequently in prestigious journals and newspapers. And as it seems impossible for sequential art to provide a faithful rendering of major literary works like, say, Proust's *Recherche* or Melville's *Moby Dick*, the critics' demands seem to have changed. Subjective readings, individual visions and occasional glimpses of some "essential" aspect or artistic "truth" now meet with approval. These works could thus pave the way for the appreciation of adaptation as a form of dialogue with the original, as variants, as comments or as "revisitations."

The evaluation of a comic book adaptation of a literary work will hover between two poles: on the one hand, it will be impossible to ignore the fact that it is an adaptation, and thus the relation with the source must be explored. This does not only include direct adaptations, but also revisions that interfere with the source texts and occasionally offer radically different perspectives or narrators, as for example Will Eisner's *Fagin the Jew*. The natal cord that links the work to its source cannot be cut successfully without dismissing some of the important aspects of the adaptation, so that it does indeed refer to its source and offers some commentary on it. In consequence, the question of whether certain artistic approaches are suitable to their subject — and possibly more or less suitable than a cinematic adaptation — can still be valid, even if the notion of fidelity is challenged.

On the other hand, the adaptation's novelty and originality requires the critic's attention, since the creative departure from the source is significant in the new work. Aspects of visualization, illustration, metaphorization, defamiliarization, and individual vision come into play, and as some metaphors, styles, and revisions are particularly striking or powerful, some adaptations can be assessed as more successful than others, even if the emphasis on subjective approaches seems to preclude any recourse to "objective" standards.

II

Comics are frequently regarded as an intermediate form or hybrid between the written text and the movies. Combining text and image, they negotiate between these two worlds and their specific ways of presenting information. In his book on *The Language of Comics*, Mario Saraceni points out that the illustrations of children's books usually demonstrate a strict correlation between the pictures and the words in the style of "See Spot jump." He then adds:

> In comics things are very different: words and pictures are far from being redundant. In comics, that is, words and pictures don't just mirror one another, but interact in many different ways, and each of the two contributes its own share for the interpretation of the text [Saraceni, 29].

This prescriptive view to the difference between children's books and comics or graphic novels becomes problematic when we deal with the adaptation of a literary work. For example, each adaptation of Melville's *Moby Dick*,

Tolkien's *The Hobbit*, Auster's *City of Glass* or Proust's *Recherche* will almost necessarily try to maintain the famed first lines ("Call me Ishmael," "In a hole in the ground there lived a hobbit," "It was a wrong number that started it," and "For a long time I would go to bed early") that the audience associates with the novel almost as much as its title. However, each of the sentences creates specific problems.

In The Hobbit and City of Glass, any attempt to maintain the first line will probably lead to a redundancy of text and picture, and this is precisely what happens on the first page of Wenzel's and Dixon's adaptation of Tolkien's book. The attempt to preserve as much as possible of the original text and the wish to accommodate their intended young audience on the one hand, and Tolkien fans on the other, forces them constantly to repeat what the text tells us in the images. As a result, the pictures are overloaded with Tolkien's words, which they only illustrate. The implicit questions presented to the reader in the first line — "In what kind of hole does what exactly live" — are answered before they are even posed, as we see the hole and the hobbit on the first page before we read the words. The artists seem to mistrust their own ability to transform the information into pictures. Moreover, the high volume of text requires an equally high volume of pictures. Thus the first page not only tells us in Tolkien's words that hobbits "are inclined to be fat in the stomach; they dress in bright colors, wear no shoes, because their feet grow natural leathery soles and thick warm brown hair," it also shows us three almost identical pictures of a fat, and unshod Bilbo with hairy feet and colorful clothes to provide enough space for all the sentences taken verbatim from the first pages of the novel. The very attempt at fidelity is thus transformed into artistic failure as we are presented with the worst of two worlds. In cases like this, one might diagnose one of the most dangerous stumbling blocks for the adaptation of novels: treating the text as sacrosanct will diminish the artistic opportunities to fully exploit the potential of the new medium.

This problem is hardly unique to Wenzel and Dixon: it can be felt in almost every adaptation of literature, whether the authors have succumbed to the desire to maintain big chunks of the original text or whether they have tried to shed the fetters of faithfulness. In the movies, the voice-over which is frequently employed to maintain the narrator's persona can similarly produce a redundancy between the spoken text and the images, and the captions of the panels in the graphic novel may tell us what we have already seen. Texts are linear, but while the comic is, of course, also read in a deliberate sequence, one can hardly fail to see all the panels on a page at once. Moments of narrative surprise are, therefore, often introduced with the turning of a page, and so the respective "rhythms" of the original text and the comic would have to be synchronized and adjusted to the space on the page.

A possible way out of this dilemma is a stronger trust in the new medium and its ability not only to illustrate but also to create meaningful information. Karasik's and Mazzucchelli's adaptation of *City of Glass* preserves a lot of the original text, but frequently divorces the words from the images, or at least creates a productive tension between text and picture. The very first panel is completely black, presenting only the first line: "It was a wrong number that started it all." The first association is, of course, a dark room, but the panels on the next page show that it is the black surface of a telephone in extreme close-up. The next panels then zoom out and reveal it to be only an image on a telephone directory. The reader thus has to readjust twice, first from empty space to a three-dimensional object and then to a two-dimensional icon. The subsequent text, providing information about the main character, is accompanied by fragmented images.

The ratio of text and images is far more balanced than in *The Hobbit*, and the pictures do not quite match the information provided by the words. For example, we see the image of a mystery book by William Wilson some panels before we are told that Quinn writes under this pen name, and the face that comes with this information is certainly not Quinn, but rather the detective from the novels he writes. The graphic novel thus dissolves the seemingly coherent text by the juxtaposition of disjunctive images; instead of a cinematic approach that follows the action, the book offers disconnected pictures with subjective associations and idiosyncratic associations. Here the narrative is not transformed into pictures; the images move around the text and add information. In consequence, the pictures do not make sense unless the reader relates them to the text. A first look at the page produces questions that will later be answered — or not — over the course of the book. In an interview, Mazzucchelli commented on this approach:

> Most of the comics I made before *City of Glass* have cinematic tendencies — and by "cinematic" I'm referring to the way each panel creates a kind of *mise-en-scène*; and the way the sequence of panels — often without narration — evokes a linear progression of time. [...] Paul [Karasik] thinks of comics in much more graphic terms — drawing as symbol, cipher, icon ... cartoon! [Kartalopoulos, Mazzucchelli].

In the adaptation of *City of Glass*, the images are almost always unexpected, and thus the graphic novel indeed offers more than merely an illustration of the original. It is not faithful to the novel, but to its own reading of the novel, and it affirms that sequential art can not only join the discourse on Auster's text, but also take its position as a work of art in its own right.

III

Things grow even more complicated when the original text does not present us with the comparatively simple external view of the action, but with a first-person narrative.

> [A] text narrated in the first person is inevitably drawn towards a third person point of view in the adaptation [...]. This is due to the almost unavoidable graphic depiction of protagonists referred to as "I," which widens the gap between reader and narrator and makes identification and the classical perception through the eyes of the first person narrator more difficult [Ferstl].

The movies face the same problem, as it is almost impossible not to show the main character in adaptations of *Moby Dick* or *David Copperfield* and thus to depart from the narrative point of view in the novel. Attempts at introducing a strictly subjective camera, as for example in the adaptation of Raymond Chandler's *The Lady in the Lake*, have not met with success. Showing the narrator does indeed pose a new problem, as the time of action is supposedly not the time of narration. For example, it is not easy to define the time in which the words "Call me Ishmael" are spoken or written by the fictional narrator. We may read the narrative parts of the novel as Ishmael's story told after he has been saved by the Rachel, but also as a kind of sailor's yarn spun in an inn, or as a recollection of adventures of yore, or even as direct communication of the action while it takes place.

This ambivalence tends to disappear when we are presented with the protagonist in the first panel. The Pocket Classics adaptation, for example, shows a young man waving at the reader and speaking the famed first line, thus making the time of narration coincide with the action. In the first panel of his adaptation, Bill Sienkiewicz presents a man with white hair looking distractedly upon a street, probably Nantucket, where a younger man has just arrived. The first line is not in a speech balloon, but in a banner, and so the times of experience and narration are clearly divorced, and it even remains questionable whether the elderly man is, actually, Ishmael. And as this figure is clearly an external element in the panel, the time and location of narration remain uncertain. Moreover, the graphic novel only contains four panels in which Ishmael can be clearly identified, one of which is the last one with Ishmael floating on Queequeg's coffin. We therefore recognize a subjective perspective or, in later passages, the possibility of some kind of disembodied narrator to be present even in situations where Ishmael cannot.

Memories and temporal distance offer interesting possibilities to approach first-person narratives, and what appeared to be a dilemma may turn out to be an asset. In Stéphane Heuet's *Remembrance of Things Past*, the first panel with the famed first line "For a long time I would go to bed early" does not show us the narrator, but the window shutters of his room from the outside. A double perspective divorces the experiencing subject from the remembering subject, and the graphic novel then switches frequently from an external perspective on Marcel to the subjective view through his eyes. In addition, many panels only present text, most often very condensed passages that offer far more information than could be covered by a series of panels.

The actual comic's art is reserved for aspects of the text that either lend themselves to the adaptation or even allow for some creative response within the new medium. For example, Proust's novel contains the famed passage in which Swann humorously compares the pregnant housemaid to Giotto's fresco of *Charity*. It is, of course, questionable whether the readers of the book were actually able to recall the image immediately. Heuet created a pregnant maid that slightly resembles Giotto's *Charity*, but he also presents us with a comic book version of the fresco, the face of which is now rendered as somewhere between the original and the maid. The imagery thus offers the background information required to make sense of a complex allusion, but nevertheless maintains the perspective of the young Marcel who tries to understand Swann's joke.

IV

In the last volume of his *Recherche*, Marcel Proust reflects on the appropriate subject for literary creation:

> The reality that must be expressed resides, I now realized, not in the appearance of the subject but in the degree of penetration of that intuition to a depth where that appearance matters little, as symbolized by the sound of the spoon upon the plate, the stiffness of the table-napkin, which were more precious for my spiritual renewal than many humanitarian, patriotic, international conversations. [...] Some [...] wanted the novel to be a sort of cinematographic procession. This conception was absurd. Nothing removes us further from the reality we perceive within ourselves than such a cinematographic vision.

The development of new technologies for the representation of external reality had quite obviously left their mark, and photography and film offered possibilities that could not be matched by the traditional arts, such as literature and painting. Moreover, epistemological doubts in modern philosophy challenged the notion of a direct access to an unmediated external reality and stressed the importance of the experiencing subject and the internal construction of reality. In consequence, Proust turns from the external world to internal experience as the reality that literature is best suited to explore, while still including the surface of things.[5]

This turn in the concept of literary realism has, of course, an impact on the problem of intermediality. If literature rejects a cinematographic approach, this necessarily poses the question of whether the movies can be a suitable medium for adaptation. Indeed movie versions of *Ulysses* (Joseph Strick's *Ulysses* and Sean Walsh's *Bloom*) as well as Volker Schlöndorff's *Un amour de Swann* focus on the "objective" tale of the respective works far more than on the subjective experience of the characters or the literary innovations. At this point, the potential of the comic book may come into play, as it is, like literature, in no position to compete with photography or film in the representation of external reality, but particularly well suited to present individual subjective experience that includes distortions and internal deviations.[6] Especially the internal constructions of non-standard focalizers, such as madmen, drug addicts, religious fanatics, and children in the magical stage of their psychological development, are frequently investigated in modern and postmodern literature and may meet with a host of fascinating artistic possibilities. The aggressive colors used in Mattotti's and Kramski's expressionist rendering of *Dr. Jekyll and Mr. Hyde* transmit the violence in the subjective perception of external reality, and the strange world of Peter Stillman's mind is wonderfully captured in the disjunctive imagery of Karasik's and Mazzucchelli's adaptation of *City of Glass.*

This potential of comics seems to have been acknowledged by the movie adaptation of Philip K. Dick's *A Scanner Darkly*, which introduces comics' visual characteristics for the depiction of a world as experienced by drug addicts.[7] Similarly, the matter-of-fact introduction of the supernatural in magical realism may lend itself to the adaptation into a medium which by its very nature constantly works in the field of the "not quite real." One may even ask whether comics may not have had some kind of influence on a literary genre or mode that interweaves realism with elements of the fantastic and frequently employs "ex-centric focalizers" (Hegerfeldt 115). Be that as it may, the grotesque caricatures in the adaptation of Kafka's *Metamorphosis* present the reader with an absurd world, in which Gregor Samsa's transformation is certainly not the only abnormal element, while it is hard to imagine that a movie could successfully adapt that particular work.[8]

V

One of the most celebrated aspects of modern literature is the construction of time, in particular the difference between the time of our experience and mechanical time as measured by clocks. Bergson's distinction between time and duration had an enormous impact on modern literature, but then the necessity to come to terms with the subjective experience of time had been a topos for authors long before. Literature is perfectly able to slow down or speed up time, as there is no external clock controlling the pace of the narrative. Adaptations of literary passages that present the reader with the difference between external mechanical time and internal experienced time face the problem that film is controlled by the regularity of external time, and experimental films that lean heavily on slow and fast motion will necessarily clash with aesthetic conventions as well as anatomical and neurological factors that determine our vision. The passage in Virginia Woolf's *To the Lighthouse* in which Mrs. Ramsay measures the brown sock against the leg of her son is almost unfilmable, as her thoughts over the course of this miniscule action require several pages. The transitions between the external action and the internal monologue are so smooth that readers frequently fail to notice the clash between time and duration. The attempt to render this passage in a movie would require a constant shifting between an almost imperceptibly developing external action — the measuring of the sock — and a multitude of hard cuts to the various ideas, memories or plans that engage Mrs. Ramsay's thoughts. A similar problem in the filming of the "Proteus" episode of *Ulysses* has in both adaptations led to a conspicuous voice-over accompanying Stephen on the beach, and only a few cuts to specific memories and associations.

While twenty-four frames make up a second of cinematic time, and either slow or fast motion will appear unnatural to the observer, comics do not share the resultant impediment to the adaptation of variable temporal experiences. The temporal gap between panels is far less strictly defined, and may be a fraction of a second or several years, depending on the context. A moment can thus be stretched out over several panels or even pages, while an entire sequence of events can be compressed into a single panel. In Heuet's *Recherche*, this potential comes into focus when the adult Marcel suddenly feels transported back into his childhood by the fragrance of a piece of Madeleine dipped into his tea. This tiny event is stretched out over eleven panels, but redundancy is avoided by offering various fragmented images of the scene. Blue, translucent waves extend from one panel to the next, indicating the aroma, and also forming a link with the memories of the past — first the room and situation in which the boy tasted the Madeleine, then the village square, and finally the whole town. The sequence thus shows how the *mémoire involuntaire* not only evokes a specific moment of the past, but rather creates an extra-temporal experience in which "all the flowers of our garden and those of Mr. Swann's park, and the water lilies of the Vivonne, and the good folk of the village and their little dwellings and the church and all Combray and its surroundings, everything taking form and solidity, [...] emerged, city and gardens, from my cup of tea" (Heuet, 17).[9]

In contrast to this fragmentation of a moment over several panels or even pages, Karasik and Mazzucchelli's *City of Glass* compresses a long period of time into only three panels, showing how Quinn literally becomes part of the wall he is leaning against. The caption, "it was as though he had melted into the walls of the city" actually proves redundant here, as the visual image fully communicates the message (Mazzucchelli, 111).

These examples show the successful adaptation of literary devices to the comics medium and thus seem to indicate the idea of "fidelity" that was challenged earlier in this paper. It is not the objective of this argument to revive this notion; I rather wish to point out that the medium's malleability offers possibilities for the artist to transform a specific element of fiction into a different but analogous form.

VI

It is a truism that works of art not only communicate with their intended and actual audiences, but also with their past. Consequently, adaptations have to come to terms, in one way or another, with the problem of influence and intertexuality in the broadest sense. Quotes, allusions, comments and borrowings from other works are an integral part of artistic expression, but do not always translate well from one medium to another. The maintenance of intertextual references almost necessarily requires that the adaptation revert strongly to the original, to preserve more text than the new medium usually allows for. In addition, allusions and references will show at least some resistance to a transfer into the new medium and, while movies make use of quotes as well as literature does, they will rarely follow similar paths of signification. A series of literary quotes or semi-quotes, metaphors and references can easily present the reader with a convincing line of associations within a stream of consciousness, but the attempt to capture the same process in a movie or a graphic novel would almost certainly be bound to fail.

However, as the example of Giotto's fresco in Heuet's Proust adaptation shows, pictorial arts may try to make up for their lack of linguistic depth by digging into an equally complex system of imagery, borrowed from any kind of visual art, including advertising, films and sequential arts. Occasionally, the original work already suggests some possibilities for quotes and allusions, and Mazzucchelli and Karasik's *City of Glass* includes a comic book version of Breughel's *Tower of Babel*. In other cases, the allusions serve as interpretations or comments on the original. Lorenzo Mattotti and Jerry Kramsky's adaptation of Stephenson's *Dr Jekyll and Mr. Hyde* is stylistically reminiscent of expressionist painting; moreover, it includes not only an allusion to Edvard Munch's *The Scream*, but also prominent references to the satirical sketches and paintings of Otto Dix and George Grosz. The story is thus implicitly moved from the *fin de siècle* to the decadence of the 1920s, and instead of the moral ambivalence and double standard of late Victorianism, it is now suggestive of the close link between bourgeois capitalism and the rise of fascist violence.

However, potentials for allusions and quotes are also occasionally neglected or dismissed and, once more, *The Hobbit* may serve as an example of missed opportunities. Famously, Tolkien preferred the scoop to the spoon when he dipped into the cauldron of stories, and he borrowed extensively from Nordic mythology and medieval literature. In consequence, one might have expected some references to medieval art or allusions to early visualizations of mythical tales. However, the style of the graphic novel is unimaginative and occasionally even influenced by works that Tolkien would have rejected. The dwarves' hoods have been replaced by the more stereotypical pointed caps, making Thorin and his companions resemble Walt Disney characters. Nor do the goblins seem to fit Tolkien's description very well: they are green and definitely not humanoid, bearing some resemblance to the Badoon or the Skrull of the Marvel universe, possibly owing to the fact that David Wenzel had previously worked on *The Avengers*.[10]

This is not intended as a critique of allusions to works of "low culture." In the adaptation of *City of Glass*, the information that Quinn writes mystery novels is accompanied by the image of a stereotypical private eye in the tradition of Dick Tracy, and this serves as a beautiful commentary on the particular kind of books that the protagonist produces. Moreover, it also foreshadows Quinn's own somewhat grotesque attempts at soft-shoeing. Peter Kuper's adaptation of Kafka's *Metamorphosis* is reminiscent of crude woodcuts, and of caricatures and political cartoons of the early 20th century, but it also bears some stylistic similarities to various underground comics of the sixties, thus self-reflexively projecting Gregor Samsa's problems with his highly authoritarian father onto a time when the counterculture was occasionally compared to vermin by the bourgeois establishment.

VII

When we read a text, we construct time, space and action from the necessarily disjunctive information we receive, but adaptations into movies or graphic novels frequently have to show what is only implied in the text. Famously, every text contains innumerable gaps that need to be filled in by the reader's imagination. Reception theory has taught us that descriptions, no matter how detailed, can never fully present the object, landscape or person in question to the reader, and when Leopold Bloom fondly thinks of Molly in her new violet garters, the reader will have to use his or her imagination — and the difference between *his* and *her* may be considerable. Any adaptation to a visual art must present the audience with completed images. A room that is only vaguely described in the book is filled up with furniture or, alternatively, left deliberately empty, but in both cases a decision has been made that the author of the novel could evade. A creative handling of close-ups or the focus on details may, of course, leave a room as undefined as it was in the text, but our response to the respective scene will be altered in ways that may be undesirable to the artist.

But because of its sequential nature, the comics medium will necessarily employ its own "poetics of absence," leaving a considerable part of the action in the gutter, and occasionally omitting some of the possible images either to kowtow to the censor's stern gaze, or to demand that the readers take over some of the imaginative work. Scott McCloud's example of an "invisible" axe-murder may well fit both aspects, as the image would probably be rather lurid on the one hand, but on the other hand, as Lessing taught us long ago in his *Laokoon*, no fixed image can match the potential for horror lurking in our imagination.[11]

The graphic novel can also simply refuse to comply with the seemingly inevitable demands of the written word. When the beginning of *City of Glass* only shows Quinn's foot instead of some image of the rooms he inhabits, the authors obviously have decided to forego the expectations of the audience, and the many disjunctive details on the first pages certainly force us to "mind the gap" even more radically than the novel does. Similarly, the expressionist style in Mattotti's and Kramsky's *Dr Jekyll and Mr. Hyde* allows for some departure from "realism," as the coloring frequently takes priority over the depiction of external reality.

In addition, the usual comics format may restrict the possibilities for an "adequate" or "faithful" rendering of the original, and what often leads to an absurd reduction of a complex novel to its most basic outline may also offer some artists the chance to work on those elements that he or she finds inspiring. Sienkiewicz's *Moby Dick* is a mere forty pages long and thus offers a supremely abbreviated version of the original narration at best. However, this does not seem to bother the author, as he even includes some of the non-narrative passages like the taxonomy of whales into his work. The focus is thus not on the novel's plot, which is in all probability sufficiently familiar to most readers of this particular adaptation anyway, but on the style in which it could be visually rendered. The specific light shed on the novel by the new and striking images may then spread, and it may well be the task for the reader now to "adapt" this artistic form to the rest of the novel in his or her imagination.

The necessity for abbreviation may thus be seen as an opportunity rather than a restriction. The very impossibility of adapting the whole text to the new medium may force the artist to search for some elements that can be used as a synecdoche for the individual approach, as the part that offers an artistic perspective on the whole, as the fragment that embraces the totality of the text.[12]

VIII

An article of this scope can only address some of the theoretical and practical problems involved in the "adaptation" of novels by comics and graphic novels. However, the points raised here indicate that the attempt at "fidelity" to the "original" may well prove detrimental to the endeavor. A comic cannot substitute for the "original," just as no film can take the place of the text it is based on. The potential for an artistic comment, a creative dialogue with the text, or a subjective and imaginative perspective on the original does not lie in the aspiration to match the work in its own field. Instead, the very difference between the original and the adaptation allows for a new encounter, a tension that leads to an interaction between the two works of art. Each adaptation is also a metaphorization, and in the perennial discussion of the deliberate falsehood or potential truth of metaphors, Don Swanson argued for the importance of difference:

> My guess is that a metaphor, because it is an erroneous statement, conflicts with our expectations. It releases, triggers, and stimulates our predisposition to detect error and to take corrective action [...]. It preempts our attention and propels us on a quest for the underlying truth [Swanson, 162].

If a comic or graphic novel could indeed reproduce a novel faithfully and adequately, it would implicitly support the traditional hierarchy of the arts and undermine its own legitimacy and potential as a creative response to an aesthetic experience. Moreover, there would not really be any need for this enterprise, or, as Caesar points out to his envoy Noxius Vapus in *Asterix and the Chieftain's Shield*, "bis repetita don't always placent:" repetitions are not always pleasant (Goscinni and Uderzo, 42).

But one cannot fail to notice that few adaptations live up to the hopes for artistic and imaginative encounters. It may be in the nature of all media that only a fraction of their products successfully explore their respective possibilities and potentials. But then there is a peculiar potential in adaptations to transgress the already dissolving borders between high and low culture. Of course, "great books" can all too easily be turned into trashy movies or comics, while texts of little artistic merit can be transformed into major aesthetic accomplishments. The achievement is not in the source, but in the mind, the pen, the crayon, the ink, or the graphic tablet of the artist, and this is what a theory and critique of comic adaptations has to deal with.

Notes

1. For a brief survey of the main traditions see Ferstl. I want to thank the author for a preprint of his article.

2. Art Spiegelman is quoted on Paul Karasik's and David Mazzucchelli's adaptation of Paul Auster's *City of Glass*, and *Classics Illustrated* are mentioned as one of the earliest introductions of canonical literature to children.

3. According to Linda Hutcheon, 85 percent of all Oscar-winning movies and 95 percent of all mini–series are adaptations (Hutcheon, 4). Other accounts hold that half of all commercial movies are adaptations or that thirty percent of all narrative films in the classic era of Hollywood were based on literary works (cf. Ray, 42 and 50).

4. Cf. Hutcheon, 3.

5. Similar programmatic statements can be found in the writings of Joyce, in particular in his concept of the epiphany, or in the essays of Virginia Woolf, notably in "Mr. Bennett and Mrs. Brown."

6. This argument can be extended to all literature that departs from realism and uses caricatures, stereotypes, fantastic elements or aspects of the grotesque. Texts like Jonathan Swift's *Gulliver's Travels*, Nikolai Gogol's *The Nose* or François Rabelais' *Gargantua et Pantagruel* would suggest themselves to creative and imaginative adaptation as comics or graphic novels far more than to the movies.

7. In this respect one might well argue that the use of computer-generated pictures in movies in general indicates the introduction of elements from the animated movies and ultimately from the comics.

8. Kafka is frequently seen as a European ancestor of magical realism (cf. Hegerfeldt, 26).

9. The translation differs only slightly from C. K. Scott-Moncrieff's and Terence Kilmartin's, published by Penguin, 1981.

10. Tolkien suggested George McDonald's depiction of goblins as his source (Tolkien, 108). While McDonald in *The Princess and the Goblin* offers a hideous image of these creatures, he adds that they "were not so far removed from the human as such a description would imply" (McDonald).

11. Lessing writes about Timomachus' painting of Medea: "He did not paint Medea at the instant when she was actually murdering her children, but a few moments before, whilst her motherly love was still struggling with her jealousy. We see the end of the contest beforehand; we tremble in the anticipation of soon recognising her as simply cruel, and our imagination carries us far beyond anything, which the painter could have portrayed in that terrible moment itself" (Lessing, 19). Even though Lessing famously objected to the combination of language (poetry) and the visual arts, the passage above with its focus on anticipation and absence shows that this text could be particularly interesting for theoretical problems in the "gutter" art of comics (ibid. 101).

12. This impossibility also often makes itself felt in movie adaptations that rush through complex novels in order to capture most of the action but in consequence completely dismiss the pace of the text, the individual sense of duration and the rhythm between fast and slow passages. Peter Jackson's *Lord of the Rings* may serve as an example, but also both movie adaptations of *Ulysses*.

8

The *300* Controversy

A Case Study in the Politics of Adaptation

DAN HASSLER-FOREST

Since its release in March 2007, Zack Snyder's film adaptation of Frank Miller's graphic novel *300* has been the subject of heated debate. Not only have most American critics from both sides of the political divide focused on the film's political subtext, it has even prompted the Iranian government to voice complaints against the film's portrayal of the barbaric Persian hordes. It is unusual for an escapist blockbuster action film to attract this kind of debate, especially one that is based on a comic book. But as with last year's *V for Vendetta* (James McTeigue, 2006), viewers and critics alike have viewed the film first and foremost as a political allegory, and have based their judgments of the film in large part on their political/ideological interpretation of it. As the following analysis aims to show, the debate surrounding the film raises issues that reveal a great deal about public views of literary adaptations, and in this case more specifically: comic book adaptations.

A Question of Fidelity

Critical, academic and public debates on the quality (or lack thereof) of a film adaptation of a work of literature have traditionally focused on the degree to which the film version is faithful to the source text. Besides the trimming down of narrative information from lengthy novels to accommodate commercial films' conventional two-hour running time, a major area of contention has always concerned the visualization of characters, locations and events that are arguably more abstract on the page. A case in point is the most recent film adaptation of Jane Austen's *Pride and Prejudice*, in which actors Keira Knightley and Donald Sutherland were attacked in the film's public and critical reception for departing too strongly from many viewers' ideas of those characters. One reviewer describes Knightley's Lizzie as "chronically unable to conceal an emotion or deliver a sarcastic quip without a giveaway twinkle in her eye and puckering of her cheeks," while Sutherland is lambasted for having been "bizarrely charged with playing Mr. Bennet as some kind of neo–Victorian hippie" (Dorr).

These debates on literary adaptations are generally the result of inherently medium-specific differences between traditional literature and the cinema: whereas film is a visual medium, most literature is not. The reader's visual imagination is called upon to construct the images the author is attempting to conjure up, thereby leaving room for individual variation and interpretation. The idea that "the word is only a partial expression of a more total representation that requires incarnation for its fulfillment," is what Kamilla Elliott has identified in her article on literary film adaptation as the "incarnational concept of adaptation" (Elliott, 234–5). According to this notion, the book's more abstract signifiers are elevated by their materialization on the screen into "word made flesh" (ibid.).

For adaptations of comic books or graphic novels, a large part of the debate is usually, once again, focused on fidelity. But as comic books are made up of both images and words, visual faithfulness is targeted much more specifically. The publicity surrounding *Spider-Man 2* (Sam Raimi, 2004), for instance, often included side-by-side comparisons of well-known comic book panels and shots from the film that copied them faithfully. A more recent film that took fidelity to visual source material to extremes was the film adaptation of Frank Miller's *Sin City* (Robert Rodriguez and Frank Miller, 2005). A deluge of publicity consisting of interviews with Rodriguez and Miller, who was famously granted a co-director credit on the film, surrounded its release. Since then, the tale of how Miller refused to sell the film rights until Rodriguez showed him a demo reel that demonstrated how faithful his adaptation would be to Miller's visual style has become a well-known Hollywood legend. As with Peter Jackson's *The Lord of the Rings* trilogy (2001–2003), much of *Sin City*'s promotional campaign, as well as the extra features on the DVD release, continually stressed aspects of visual fidelity to the source material, with leading actors from the film repeatedly emphasizing their dedication to the source text in interviews. On the DVD's audio commentary, director Robert Rodriguez even goes so far as to reject the very term "adaptation," explaining that the film constitutes a "translation" to another — similar — medium that leaves the original work entirely intact (Miller and Rodriguez 2006).

Following the success of this much-hyped Frank Miller film, it came as no surprise that the publicity around *300*, the next film to be based on this graphic artist's work, should again emphasize visual fidelity first and foremost. The movie's website was launched by producer/distributor Warner Bros. in December 2005, a good fifteen months before the film's theatrical release. The first images to appear on the website were instances of "conceptual art" that illustrated, often through side-by-side comparisons, how closely the film's visual style would adhere to the comic book. Throughout 2006, video journals were added to the website that documented the film's development, each of which continuously pointed out that this was not to be "a Hollywood version" of Miller's book, but that it was their intention to make it "real." Through these specific marketing strategies, the studio and the filmmakers clearly drew on the popular discourse and seal of approval that had been granted the *Sin City* film two years previously, not just in the strong emphasis on visual fidelity, but also on the similar production process, shooting actors in a warehouse before a green screen and creating digital environments and lighting effects in post-production.[1]

This sustained emphasis on the film's visual fidelity to the graphic novel successfully defused any negative feedback from the fan community, which was also actively encouraged to contribute to the film's online publicity campaign through its strong presence on Myspace.com. Instead, the controversy the film has more recently generated was focused almost entirely on the film's political and ideological message. The campaign to legitimize the film's fidelity to its source material has in fact been so successful that much of the negative criticism it has received has been directed squarely at Frank Miller, whose only credit on the film is that of executive producer. The film, which quickly became an international box office phenomenon that has broken records in the U.S., Greece, Japan, and many other countries, has clearly been embraced by moviegoers, even as it became a serious point of contention amongst critics. Reviews in the mainstream media once again reflect today's intensely polarized political climate: critics from the left have lambasted the film for its reductionist East-versus-West conflict, some even going so far as to define it as "fascist art" (Roger Moore), while reviewers from the American Right have praised it — again from a political perspective — for telling a story in which "heroes [stand] up for God and country" (Kahane). Adding to the debate, as well as contributing inadvertently to the film's ongoing free publicity, the Iranian government has publicly denounced the film for its depiction of Persian hordes as bloodthirsty, demonic zombies.

As happens so often when books are adapted into films, the authors of these reviews only rarely display any actual knowledge of the book. Especially in a case like this, where the original work is from the culturally disparaged comics medium, critics seem to have equated the film's politics with those of Miller's source text. But although the filmmakers went to great lengths to ensure visual fidelity to the graphic novel, a closer comparison between both works reveals that many of the issues that seem to have caused this controversy are ones that have been added to the original narrative by the film's screen-writers.

A Question of Authorship

The film's most obvious departure from the book is the addition of an extended subplot in which Leonidas's wife, Queen Gorgo, attempts to rally political support for her husband's efforts to counter the Persian invasion. As the battle of Thermopylae rages on, the audience is repeatedly returned to Sparta, where Gorgo wages her own battle against shiftless politician — and draft-dodger — Theron. This shifts the story's political balance quite strongly from where it lies in the book: in Miller's graphic novel, the blame for Sparta's decision not to go to war is placed firmly on the Ephors, the corrupt religious mystics who been bribed by the Persians, and who legitimize their decision by staging a predetermined rite in which they call upon an oracle. The portrayal of clerical figures of power as hypocritical, perverse and corrupt is a regular motif in Miller's work. It recurs prominently several times in his *Sin City* books, including two of the stories that appeared in their film adaptation, as well as in *Ronin* and *Batman: The Dark Knight Returns*. In the graphic novel *300*, they are explicitly described as "worthless, useless remnants of the old time — before Lykourgos the law-giver — before Sparta's ascent from darkness" (Miller 1999, 20).

But although the scene with the Ephrons is faithfully included in the film version, the introduction of Theron shortly thereafter deflects blame from the deformed mystics (who never reappear after their only scene in the first part of the film) to scheming, self-serving politicians who would rather seek diplomatic solutions than go to war. Even well-meaning political allies in the Spartan council ultimately prove ineffectual against Theron, who betrays Queen Gorgo after she has bribed him with sexual favors. Only when the queen herself resorts to violence on the Senate floor after being humiliated by Theron are the other senators' eyes finally opened, and only then are they ready to support the war that will ultimately bring about the total annihilation of the Persian forces. It is precisely this depiction of politicians as pliable, cowardly and reluctant characters that makes the film's main point so problematic. As in Miller's *Batman: The Dark Knight Returns*, the filmmakers here seem to be "attacking what, in practice, they support," namely the implied advantages of a military dictatorship over a free democratic process (Klock 49).

Turning Spartans into Palatable Heroes

This issue becomes even more problematic when one considers the second major area of departure from the book. As Frank Miller has conceded in interviews, his book deliberately leaves out aspects of Spartan culture that might alienate contemporary readers from the story's heroes, because he wanted readers to be able "to root for the Spartans" (Miller, 2006). The book's opening establishes the Spartans as proudly suicidal fighting machines with a strict code of honor, before almost immediately leaving behind every kind of societal context. Miller is then free to plunge his main characters into the heat of an extended battle that celebrates Spartan stoicism, militarism, and utter lack of emotion.

The film, on the other hand, introduces elements that unwittingly emphasize the basic contradictions at the heart of this narrative. King Leonidas, for instance, is humanized by the fleshing out of his relationship with his wife and son. The harsh, brutal treatment of small children as they grow up to become fearsome warriors or die, as the film's prologue establishes so vividly, is also conspicuously absent from Leonidas's household. In fact, the film version of Leonidas repeatedly shows physical affection for his son by patting him on the head and shoulder and hugging him, while an elaborate sex scene with Queen Gorgo not only illustrates his "softer side," but also contrasts with the explicitly perverse, kinky, and mainly non-heterosexual forms of sexual behavior featured later in the film at the Persian court.

Leonidas's sex scene, shot in slow motion in the style of high-gloss Hollywood glamour, is referenced in the book in entirely different terms. It does not appear visually in any of the panels, but is referred to briefly by Queen Gorgo when she learns that Leonidas plans to set out on his own against the Persian army. "This explains your enthusiasm last night," she quips, to which Leonidas's curt response is merely: "Yes. Sparta needs sons" (Miller 1999, 22). The emotionless quality of this exchange again underlines the vast difference between the characterization of both speakers in book and film. The film's other sequence that features sexual acts is set in Xerxes' court, where the deformed Spartan Ephialtes is persuaded to betray his people. In the book, a single panel shows Ephialtes between two seductive naked women (Miller 1999, 62). In the film, this is expanded into a montage of images showing various grotesque figures engaged in lesbian sex, the scene clearly functioning "to differentiate 'good' sex (matrimonial) from 'evil' sex (everything else)" (Chaw).

These changes to the book's narrative structure bring Miller's already controversial politics to the fore much more powerfully. The book, which was first published in five installments in 1998, was never the subject of much controversy, fitting as it does in its author's long-familiar theme of macho vigilante (super)heroes who take the law into their own hands and make a stand against forces of evil (e.g. *Daredevil*, *Batman: The Dark Knight Returns*, *Sin City: The Hard Goodbye*). But while there is little doubt in Miller's work as to where the reader's sympathies should lie, the author does tend to leave room for ironic readings of his texts. His most celebrated work *Batman: The Dark Knight Returns*, for instance, casts Batman as "an older and slightly mad right-wing moralist in a dystopian Gotham City gutted by corruption and vice" (B. Wright, 267). In his *300*, the main theme of the story is not so much the importance of defending freedom and democracy from the evils of military dictatorship — for what was Sparta if not a military dictatorship? — but the power of mythological narratives and storytelling in cementing one's own immortality. Persian king Xerxes claims to be divine and immortal, which in his own eyes legitimizes his claim to be absolute ruler over Greece. The Spartan king Leonidas, by contrast, glorifies death in battle, which is what ultimately grants him the very immortality that Xerxes would claim for himself. By framing their battle explicitly as an oral narrative oft repeated among soldiers, the power of myth bestows upon Leonidas that which Xerxes explicitly loses at the climactic moment when he is wounded and, therefore, revealed as mortal by Leonidas's spear.

But because the film shifts our attention away from this aspect of the story, the emphasis, and hence the controversy surrounding the film, is placed on the screenplay's political subplot. The major turning point in the film comes not when Leonidas faces Xerxes and is granted immortality through the power of legend, but when Queen Gorgo reveals Theron as a traitor and convinces the Spartan council to support the war unambiguously.[2] The final scene, which celebrates the impending annihilation of the Persian forces by a smaller but vastly superior Spartan army is, in the film, the result of a political process that has been interpreted by many as an allegory for contemporary American policies concerning the war in Iraq. "Theron wants to persuade the Spartan council not to send reinforcements to the desperately outnumbered

300 (what is he, a Democrat?)," writes Dana Stevens in *Slate*, and her reading of the film's political leanings is typical of many critics on both sides of the American political divide.

Film critic Walter Chaw described the film's problems in contrast to the graphic novel most succinctly when he expressed his disappointment that the film had not

> resisted the desire to turn its band of homicidal Conans into loving fathers, husbands, and defenders of the bedrock of life, liberty, and the pursuit of happiness — albeit in the form of child abuse, brutal coming-of-age rituals, and a rejection of ideas of social responsibility and stewardship of the weak.

His analysis points out exactly where the film fails as an adaptation: the contradictions inherent in a story about a group of gung-ho militaristic white men in red capes following a dictator of their own to certain death become problematic when this fight is couched in overtly ideological terms that are so similar to contemporary real-world conflicts.

Somewhat predictably, the one subversive voice in the chorus of critical readings of the film has been that of Slavoj Žižek, who has defended it by suggesting that the Spartans of *300* are in fact closer to the Taliban than they are to any representation of American or Western ideology. The invading Persians, according to Žižek's line of reasoning, are clearly metaphorical embodiments of the U.S. army and its high-tech military might:

> [W]hen the last surviving group of Spartans and their king Leonidas are killed by thousands of arrows, are they not in a way bombed to death by techno-soldiers operating sophisticated weapons from a safe distance, like today's U.S. soldiers [...]?

But as provocative as Žižek's close reading of the film as a possible "site of resistance" may be, his analysis fails to take into account the power of American hero narratives to cast themselves in the defensive role of the underdog. More often than not, the heroic protagonists of popular American narratives have been presented as the outnumbered but morally superior victims of an unprovoked attack. They may have to make great sacrifices, but are preordained to emerge victorious in the fight against this new "other." Recent popular films that have featured representations of the attacks of 9/11, both symbolic (e.g. *Superman Returns* (Bryan Singer, 2006)) and literal (e.g. *World Trade Center* (Oliver Stone, 2006)) have consistently adhered to the dominant notion that the attacks were an unprovoked act of political terrorism that called for violent retaliation. This oft-repeated narrative has de-historicized the attacks and cast their perpetrators as embodiments of pure evil seeking to subjugate the liberal democratic West by depriving us of "our freedoms."

A second element that Žižek fails to take into account in his essay is the sheer power of racial and ethnic identities in popular culture products targeted chiefly at western consumers. The visual force of the film's depiction of a group of male Caucasians fighting off hordes of invaders who are defined by their ethnic "otherness," guides viewers in their understanding of the narrative's allegorical meanings. Since both the film and the graphic novel use exactly the kinds of ethnic and racial stereotyping that Edward Said described as western orientalist fictions, Xerxes and his Persian hordes are thereby automatically reduced to a uniform, de-individualized "other," lacking the qualities that define the Spartans as heroic protagonists.

These allegorical readings of the film have been dismissed by its director Zack Snyder in the interviews he has granted:

> When I see someone use words like "neocon," "homophobic" "homoerotic" or "racist" in their review, I kind of just think they don't get the movie and don't understand. It's a graphic novel about a bunch of guys that are stomping the snot out of each other.[3]

His rather dubious argument seems to consist of no more than that the film should not be read for any subtext, that it exists purely as an event that offers viewers a kinesthetic experience. According to the statement released by distributor Warner Bros. in response to the Iranian government's complaints about the film, it is purely "a fictional work with the sole purpose of entertaining audiences; it is not meant to disparage an ethnicity or culture or make any sort of political statement" (qtd. in Jaafar, n.p.). Frank Miller has also proved to be notoriously reluctant to allow for political or ideological readings of his texts. When pressed to offer a political reading of Batman in *Dark Knight Returns,* Miller states merely that "anyone who really believes that a story about a guy who wears a cape and punches out criminals is a representation of a political viewpoint [...] is living in a dream world" (Sharrett, 43).

Given the established fact that responses to the film, both positive and negative, have focused so strongly on its ideological contents, the question now becomes who exactly is living in this dream world. A Gramscian view would maintain that *300,* as part of our popular culture, exists within "an area of negotiation" between dominant ideology and oppositional cultures where "dominant, subordinate and oppositional cultural and ideological values and elements are 'mixed' in different permutations" (Bennett, 96). The variety of ways in which the film's message has been "decoded" clearly strengthens Stuart Hall's notion that popular texts can and will be interpreted by audiences in ways that can neither be accurately predicted nor controlled. As strong as Žižek's argument for reading the Spartans in the film as the metaphorical embodiment of America's enemy in the "War on Terror," most viewers still seem to have based their reception on ethnic and cultural stereotypes.

Meanwhile, the controversy about the film — compared to the lack of any kind of upheaval surrounding the graphic novel's publication — cannot be attributed to differences in public appeal and popularity between the two media. It also shows how strongly our readings of such tales are defined by the historical context in which they are produced and released. Whether the filmmakers had any intention of creating a political allegory is, therefore, all but irrelevant. The fact that the screenwriters ended up adding a subplot to the original story that demonizes political debate and democratic process in a time of war, says enough about the ideology the film espouses.

But whether Miller, Snyder and supporters of the film who dismiss these readings are being naïve, obtuse, or simply unwilling to reveal their own political agenda, their position "smacks of either disingenuousness or complete obliviousness" (Stevens, n.p.). In an age dominated by conflicts, both real and imagined, between West and East, it may be tempting to re-embrace the simple, oppositional dichotomies that justify viewing entire cultures as inherently "other" from a western "us." It is exactly this kind of reductive thinking, which was most comprehensively analyzed by Edward Said in his book *Orientalism* that, for instance, cast the perpetrators of the 9/11 attacks as "an irrational 'Other' bent on destroying the West" (Norlund, 3). In times like these, popular films that celebrate those very precepts and lionize a Eurocentric perspective on culture and history may represent as much of a danger as any other imagined threat to our well-being.

Notes

1. The movie poster further solidifies this link by somewhat misleadingly describing the film as "from the creator of *Sin City*."

2. Unlike in the book, where a single panel shows assorted council members responding to Leonidas's determination to counter the Persian army, the film features a long, climactic scene in a Spartan senate, further cementing associations with the origins of Western democracy.

3. See http://www.comicbookresources.com/news/newsitem.cgi?id=9982

PART FOUR

Men in Tights:
The Superhero Paradigm

9

The Last Action Hero's Swan Song

Graphic Novelty or Never-Ending Story?

Andreas Rauscher

For several years, the concept of the graphic novel, as established by Will Eisner in his semi-autobiographical comic book *A Contract with God* (1978), seemed to present an opposing view of the continuing adventures of never-aging super heroes. Graphic novels featured self-contained stories comparable to literary works or feature films. They often reflected real incidents in an artistic way, in contrast to Superman, Batman and their cohorts, who inhabited fantastic parallel worlds like Metropolis or Gotham City.

Superheroes also reflected changing mentalities in popular culture through periodic reconfigurations of their basic formulas. The heroes and super-villains were adjusted to different political climates and changing social values. Crucial to this development was the arrival of several Marvel comic book franchises created by Stan Lee, Jack Kirby, Steve Ditko, and others. The adventures of Spider-Man, the Fantastic Four, the Avengers and the X-Men were no longer situated in imaginary cities, but in present-day New York. Besides including numerous references to contemporary popular culture, the social issues and cultural changes of the 1960s were reflected in the comics, transforming the distanced and all-too-perfect men in tights into contemporary urban heroes dealing with the troubles of everyday life. By the 1970s, even Batman incorporated social change in stories written by Denny O'Neill (*Green Lantern*) and others. But in the long run, the more differentiated plot structures were only a critical redecoration of the Bat-Cave. The hero's status remained untouched by more ambitious storytelling even if his darker side, systematically ignored by the camp approach of the 1960s TV show, was brought into focus again. The deconstruction of the superhero did not truly enter the genre until the mid–1980s, when it seemed to come in through the back door with the publication of two mini-series released as graphic novels by DC Comics.

Who Watches the Watchmen?

In 1986, Alan Moore and Dave Gibbons offered an ironic and disillusioned take on a group of criminalized, aging superheroes in a world on the brink of World War III in their graphic novel *Watchmen*. Moore created characters that featured their own critical subtext in a typically postmodernist way: Rorschach, a vigilante superhero hidden behind a mask bearing an amorphous blot, is exposed as a right-wing madman who never recovered from his childhood traumas. The Nite Owl, who combines Clark Kent's clumsiness and Bruce Wayne's wealth, can only overcome his feelings of sexual impotence through his fetish for bizarre costumes. Heroine Silk Spectre embodies gender issues and generational conflicts related to the genre, having been pushed into her role by her demanding superhero mother. The commercial merchandise surrounding many comic book series, especially once they make their way into film, is parodied by the business awareness of Ozymandias, a retired superhero who manages his own brand and line of products.

The most innovative aspect of *Watchmen* is its focus on the protagonists' inner life and the revelation that the prosecuted phantom nemesis is actually one of the heroes. The conflict's resolution indicates that the superheroes have become either useless or guilty through their knowledge of crimes against humanity, which they cannot reveal without affecting the state of world affairs for the worse. In this regard, *Watchmen* can be read as a darkly satirical swan song to the genre itself.

In addition to its re-reading of the mythology of the American superhero, Moore and Gibbons' graphic novel set standards in regard to their reflections on the history of the genre and the inclusion of additional metatexts, such as a pulp comic that mirrors the conflict of the superhero characters and excerpts from several fictional publications. By incorporating cinematic composition, *Watchmen* also eschews cartoonish sound effects and presents panel layouts that emulate camera movements.

Deconstructing Batman

Moore and Gibbons created new characters that obviously referred to famous predecessors from the Golden and the Silver Age of comics, but they did not use any explicit source material. This creative decision enabled them to demystify the concept of the superhero in a way that would not have been possible had they chosen established iconic protagonists, because their rewritten versions would have been perceived as being out of character.

Nevertheless, in the same year, Frank Miller adapted a deconstructionist approach towards the genre in *Batman: The Dark Knight Returns* (1986), a graphic novel featuring an unconventional variation of its main character. Miller dramatizes a situation that would not have been featured in a classical serial superhero adventure. In his re-imagination of this familiar narrative landscape, an aging Batman returns to the streets of Gotham City after ten years of retirement. Despite his remarkable physical condition, he has obviously aged beyond the conventions established by the preceding comic books. The text's emphasis on his obsession with fighting criminals now highlights the thin line between the supposed madness of his enemies and his own embittered mentality. Unlike *Watchmen*, *The Dark Knight Returns* deals with one of the established icons of the superhero genre and considers the problematic violent aspects of the Batman mythology, and by continually including sound bytes from the media controversy that surrounds the comeback of Gotham City's hero in the book, Miller also addresses the fascination with violence.

The Dark Knight Returns reflects the ambivalent status of the superhero as a problematic role model. After invading a street gang's headquarters with a tank-like version of the Batmobile, Batman accepts the challenge of their leader. He follows their violent code by leaving his high-tech equipment behind and getting into a brutal fistfight with their boss in the mud. After defeating his opponent in this post-apocalyptic arena, the former gang members choose Batman as their new idol. The images of urban decay presented in *Dark Knight* provide a combination of the future noir aesthetics associated with cyberpunk literature and films like *Blade Runner* (1982), and the wasteland of post-apocalyptic scenarios presented in films like the *Mad Max* trilogy (1979–1985). Well-known settings like the Batcave, hidden under the luxurious Wayne Manor, appear in the narrative albeit radically redesigned. In contrast to the classical version of the superhero hideout stuffed with camp memorabilia, Miller only hints at these collectibles from the distance of an extreme long shot. He focuses on the cathedral-like structure and the overarching darkness of the Batcave, hinting at the metaphorical potential of this scenario to reflect Bruce Wayne's state of mind.

The psychological subtext tells readers that Batman is not really so different from his adversaries. This thread is already developed by the first segment of the story, in which he is confronted by Two-Face, aka Harvey Dent. Following severe facial injuries caused by acid, the former district attorney is transformed into a schizophrenic psychopath. In *The Dark Knight Returns*, he is released from Arkham Asylum but although his appearance has been altered by plastic surgery, he fails to give up his old habits. Harvey Dent's struggle with his alter ego Two-Face mirrors Bruce Wayne's own return to the role of the Dark Knight, which he gave up ten years earlier. Apparently forced by the patterns of the genre as much as by their own neurotic attitude, both take up their former roles again. After he has been arrested, Dent asks Batman to take a look at his supposed true nature, which cannot be hidden behind make-up or plastic surgery. As in a Rorschach test, the disillusioned hero sees the original grotesque appearance of Two-Face accompanied by the image of a giant bat reflecting his own manic obsession.

During the climax of *The Dark Knight Returns*, Batman does not confront any of the usual suspects. His opponent turns out to be former friend Superman, who has been commissioned by the President — a Ronald Reagan look-alike — to stop the outlawed hero. With the help of Green Arrow, Batman stages his own death in order to go underground and continue his work with a new team, including a female Robin. The confrontation between Batman and Superman does not only offer a spectacular superhero face-off similar to such matches in earlier crossover projects; it also comments on the conflicting pop culture mythologies associated with the two franchises, both of which result in a disillusioned perspective. One either becomes the errand boy of a reactionary system, like the Man of Steel, or one maintains an individualistic independent attitude like Batman, with the risk of becoming a self-righteous vigilante.

The iconography of one particular splash panel in the story's final chapter summarizes Miller's approach in *The Dark Knight Returns*. Batman rides a horse on his way to the showdown, accompanied by his new team of torch-bearing former gang members. The picture is reminiscent of images associated with the classical Hollywood Western, while also inflected with apocalyptic undertones. Like Clint Eastwood's *Unforgiven* (1991), *The Dark Knight Returns* conjures up the essential topics of the genre's mythology, and questions them while leaving enough room for a reaffirmation in the narrative. What looks like a dark eulogy for an outdated genre can also provide a starting point for its neoclassical resurrection.

In the 1980s, graphic novels provided a platform for visual experiments that could not be found in mainstream comics, but that have become quite common by now. The formal invention on an aesthetic level is mirrored by a differentiated concept of storytelling that includes multiple points of view providing additional subtext. In *Watchmen*, an avid comic book reader and a newspaper salesman stress the relationship between popular fiction and social developments. Part of Miller and Moore's self-reflexive approach is the inclusion of discourse on superheroes as an important part of the story itself. The excerpts from autobiographies, interviews and other imaginary publications in *Watchmen* and the omnipresent Greek chorus provided by several TV channels in *The Dark Knight Returns*, take aspects that are well-known from real debates on comics and integrate them into the diegetic world of the graphic novel. In *The Dark Knight Returns*, the media buzz surrounding the return of Batman brings to mind the debates about the effect of violent comic books on society.[1]

Watchmen and *The Dark Knight Returns* successfully transferred artistic strategies associated with graphic novels to the superhero genre, along with self-contained story arcs; aesthetically innovative techniques associated with the cinema, such as parallel editing and slow motion; ambivalent characterizations and multilayered forms of storytelling entered the world of men in tights. The term "graphic novel" was extended to include several collections of limited superhero runs. DC continued its series of prestigious stand-alones in the tradition of *The Dark Knight Returns* by hiring innovative British comic book authors like Alan Moore and Grant Morrison to produce their artistically ambitious versions of Batman. In *The Killing Joke*, Moore focused on the tragic backstory of the Dark Knight's archenemy The Joker within an extended flashback sequence paralleling a confrontation between the two antagonists. This results in the fatal injury of Barbara Gordon, daughter of Commissioner James Gordon. The hardcover publication *Arkham Asylum* (1989), written by Grant Morrison and illustrated by Dave McKean, employed a vast variety of graphic techniques associated with high art, including photographs and collages. The book's plot and visual style correspond to their unconventional approach to the mental institution inhabited by Batman's long-time adversaries. Following the Joker's instructions, they overrun Arkham Asylum, taking its staff hostage and forcing their favorite nemesis to join their bizarre party. He enters a psychological maze filled with references to Lewis Carroll's *Alice in Wonderland*.

After his rescue by Two-Face, the Joker bids Batman farewell. The notorious psychopath reminds the hero, who appears throughout the story as a shadow, that they will always keep a place free for him in the asylum. Typical of the more mature approach taken by many graphic novels featuring superheroes is the suggestion that Batman actually belongs among Arkham Asylum's gallery of psychopaths. Alan Moore named one important aspect of the crossover between individual artistic visions and well-established superhero franchises in his introduction to *Batman: The Dark Knight Returns*:

> [Frank Miller] has taken a character whose every trivial and incidental detail is graven in stone on the hearts and minds of the comic fans that make up his audience and managed to dramatically redefine that character without contradicting one jot of the character's mythology [qtd. in Miller 2002, 3].

The graphic novels from the late 1980s that feature Batman add to the complexity of the concept by creating a situation that may be out of character within the ongoing serial publication, but which is perfectly in tune with the more ambivalent approach of the graphic novel genre. The success of *The Dark Knight Returns* and *The Killing Joke* resulted in the establishment of a template for future graphic novels within the realm of the superhero genre, whose colorful costumes had suddenly been redesigned to incorporate new shades of grey.

Marvelous Storytelling

At first glance the more serious cinematic treatment of superheroes, as evidenced in film adaptations by Tim Burton, Ang Lee, Bryan Singer, Sam Raimi and Jon Favreau, would seem to be the direct result of the aforementioned graphic novels from the 1980s. These postmodern swan songs to outdated action heroes ironically resulted in the resurrection of a stagnated genre. But upon careful consideration, this influence is primarily felt at the aesthetic level. In regard to storytelling, an important inspiration comes from the Marvel comics of the 1970s. Their tendency to include references to earlier publications could easily be extended towards a more complex, self-referential approach. More than the mere occurrence of known characters' names or the inclusion of cross-references to events from other publications, these links reflect various concepts of character. One example is the moment when the rather liberal Spider-Man is confronted by right-wing vigilante The Punisher, who suspects him of being connected to a local mafia syndicate. All events in the story are told from two contrasting points of view: Spider-Man's ironic take on the mannerisms of the brutal crime fighter, and the Punisher's martial diary entries, fittingly entitled "the war journal."

Along with a reflection of the superhero's ethical and political beliefs, Marvel comics from the 1970s offered an interesting point of origin for concepts that can be recognized in later graphic novels. In hindsight, dramatic events like the death of major characters (e.g. Jean Grey of the X-Men in *The Dark Phoenix Saga* or Spider-Man's first love Gwen Stacy) provide exceptional situations that could easily be reissued as graphic novels, which would concentrate the cycle in a stand-alone story.

Those narratives do not offer a deconstructionist endgame for the genre and its mythology, but they do mark definite periods of change within the diegetic world of a franchise. It is indicative of their potential to be re-read as a separate entity within the continuing flow of the regular series that many of those story arcs were used as the basic plot for recent film adaptations. Although they were not originally conceptualized as graphic novels, these collections nevertheless provide a nexus between ongoing serial publications and the coherent dramatic events that characterize the graphic novel. In the mid–1980s, both DC and Marvel had created new product lines reserved exclusively for graphic novels.

Crossover Strategies

Almost every collection of superhero reprints is now advertised as a graphic novel, although some only offer a selection of separate issues that are neither connected aesthetically nor diegetically. Nevertheless, since Marvel's introduction of extended story arcs in the 1970s, and DC's artist-driven Batman reconfigurations of the 1980s, several governing concepts have emerged, mixing approaches that are characteristic of the graphic novel with the serial storytelling of ongoing superhero franchises. In recent years, four major trends can be observed in the field of crossover enterprises between superheroes and comic book auteurs:

1. The canonization of the author.

The individual style and storytelling of comic book artists like Alan Moore, Grant Morrison, Frank Miller and others resulted in the canonization of the author. This aspect is important when considering both the visuals and the plot. There have always been American comic book artists like Will Eisner, Stan Lee, Jack Kirby or Carl Barks whose creative handwriting is given as much consideration as European graphic novels. But following the successful adaptations of the graphic novel concept to the superhero genre, the influence of the artist is no longer only discussed after a series has become popular, but is already taken into account when a famous writer is signed for a certain number of issues. The publishers now expect established artists like Grant Morrison or Neil Gaiman to apply their recognizable individual styles to the franchise. For after the initial publication, the collected limited series can be released as a stand-alone graphic novel.

Prominent examples in recent years include the re-launch of DC's *Green Arrow* (2000) series scripted by filmmaker Kevin Smith. The Green Arrow, a talented archer and socially conscious left-wing activist, had previously been killed in an explosion. His resurrection by the cosmic powers of the Green Lantern resulted in a remodeling of the series, similar in many ways to the "reboots" of popular film franchises like *Casino Royale* (2006) or *Batman Begins* (2005). For a new perspective on the character, DC hired Smith, well-known for his sophisticated pop cultural referencing in films like *Clerks* (1994) and *Chasing Amy* (1997), who had previously authored a *Daredevil* run for Marvel. The re-launch of *Green Arrow* not only featured his trademark dialogues and ironic approach that made fun of Batman's mannerisms as well as Oliver Green's simple costume, which fails to hide his face effectively. Smith's writing also emphasized the Green Arrow's experience of feeling slightly anachronistic after his return to the world of the living, provided a central topic for the story arc.

The synergetic effect of having writers and directors from film and television signed as comic book authors is defining for the current convergence between media. The publication of a run by a well-known screenwriter in the format of a graphic novel also appeals to fans from other media, who would otherwise be less likely to follow an ongoing comic series. The strongest intermedial connection can be found in the fields of comics and television series: J. Michael Straczynski, creator of the science-fiction series *Babylon 5* (1993–1998), has written and supervised the main line of *Spider-Man* comics for six years. Director, writer and producer Joss Whedon, responsible for influential TV series like *Buffy the Vampire Slayer* (1997–2003) and *Firefly* (2002–2003), created scripts for *X-Men* that applied elaborate cinematic visuals echoing wide-screen compositions as well as angles that are unconventional for comics, but well established in popular cinema. Other comic book authors best known for their television work include Damon Lindelof (*Lost*) and Jeph Loeb (*Smallville* and *Heroes*). The intersection of several parallel story arcs and the long-term development of characters provide especially interesting parallels between both media.

2. "What if..."-scenarios and "Else-Worlds"

The concept of alternate worlds in which historical events took a different turn has been popular with new wave science-fiction writers of the 1960s like Philip K. Dick, who showed more interest in social issues than hard scientific facts. It is also employed by Moore and Gibbons in *Watchmen*, where Richard

Nixon is still President in the 1980s and where Watergate has never happened, because everybody researching it has been murdered, while the nuclear arms race is escalating into World War III.

A story set in a parallel world featuring superheroes outside their usual continuity suits the demands of the graphic novel very well, since it is generally reduced to a single volume. The subgenre includes a variety that ranges from bizarre crossover meetings between Batman and Dracula (*Red Rain*, 1991) to "Else-World" stories, in which not only a single character but the whole scenario of the comic series is transferred into another century or universe. This has resulted in examples like Batman and his adversaries becoming contemporaries of Jack the Ripper in a steampunk variation of their hometown (*Gotham by Gaslight*, 1989).

These "Else-World" scenarios are easily combined with deconstructionist approaches, as in *Superman — Red Son* (2003), where Superman grows up in the Soviet Union and is depicted in the exuberant kitsch of socialist realism. Graphic novels like *Marvel 1602* (2003) on the other hand present auteur-driven "Else-World" fiction by picking up a specific motif associated with the author's style, in this case Neil Gaiman's interest in the anachronistic collision of different mythologies that can also be found in his novel *American Gods* (2001) and his graphic novel series *The Sandman* (1989–1996).

3. Alternate takes on a well-known situation from a franchise

A graphic novel revisits a crucial moment from the mythology of a superhero franchise, offering a re-imagination of events already known to most readers. The reader's knowledge of later developments provides a more elaborate sense of drama. Many prequels to popular films like the second *Star Wars* trilogy (1999–2005) or David Lynch's *Twin Peaks — Fire Walk With Me* (1992) are based on the premise that the audience's involvement is generated by their advance knowledge of the ending. Frank Miller's graphic novel *Batman: Year One* (1987), which deals with Bruce Wayne's first appearance as Batman, was also a strong influence on Christopher Nolan's film *Batman Begins* (2005).

In 2003, Jeph Loeb wrote a series of titles dealing with pivotal moments in the early biography of popular Marvel characters. In the graphic novel *Spider-Man: Blue*, a retelling of the doomed romance between Peter Parker and his high school sweetheart Gwen Stacy, the narrative focus shifts from the action set-pieces to the atmospheric and romantic scenes from early *Spider-Man* issues. It is told in an extended flashback with voice-over narration by Peter, bringing a sense of closure to the story. Although the narrative builds upon several different episodes from the first ten years of *Spider-Man*, they are connected and brought into a formal unity by Peter's knowledge of Gwen's tragic death. The predominant genre in *Spider-Man: Blue* is no longer the action-adventure of the original publications, but the melodramatic element brought to the foreground by the voice-over narration. Peter's reminiscences of his first love here create a coherent narrative structure that only made up a minor element of the issues when they were originally published.

An alternate perspective on previously established events can also result from an unconventional point of view. In the graphic novel *Marvels* (1994), the history of the Marvel heroes and their universe is told through the eyes of a New York photographer incidentally stumbling across various key Golden and Silver Age moments.

4. Exceptional dramatic situations within a franchise's continuity

This type of superhero graphic novel is the logical continuation of story arcs like *The Dark Phoenix Saga* that can be read as stand-alone stories besides being part of an ongoing series. Crucial events that have a lasting impact on the franchise as a whole are told from within the narrative frame of a graphic novel. Among the exceptional situations depicted in stand-alone titles are events like the X-Men and militant mutant leader Magneto joining forces against a right-wing minister embodying the regressive attitude of the Reagan era and the moral majority, or the reactions of various characters from the Marvel universe like Wolverine, Spider-Man and Iron Man to the assassination of Captain America in *Fallen Son*. The death of this trademark character from the Golden Age of the 1940s marked the closing chapter to a narrative patchwork that has been developed within a seven-issue mini-series and numerous subplots across all regular Marvel publications in 2006 and 2007. The event, conceived by graphic novel writer Mark Millar, demonstrates how ambivalent narrative topics, critical reflections on superhero mythology and references to current political topics, which were defining attributes of the deconstructionist work of Frank Miller and Alan Moore in the 1980s, have since entered the genre's mainstream.

The influence of the graphic novel on superhero comics is no longer restricted to trade paperback editions and stand-alone narratives. Its epic scope and multi-layered storytelling can occasionally be extended to a publisher's entire line. For example, the *Civil War* (2006–2007) storylines reconfigured the Marvel universe so as to align it with changes in pop culture after 9-11. But in contrast to former eras in comics history, the insecurity, helplessness and paranoia was not projected on an external conflict. Instead, it was the restrictions of Homeland Security policies that affected the recurring protagonists in the Marvel universe. The status of the X-Men, previously interpreted by authors like Chris Claremont in the 1970s and 1980s as a metaphor for racism and the insecure social status of marginalized groups, was extended to include all superheroes. In the series' main narrative, an accident during the shooting on a superhero reality TV show results in the death of six hundred civilians. After the tragic incident, an obligatory registration act for all superheroes and superheroines forces them to reveal their true identities, resulting in a strict division of the American heroes into two factions. Iron Man, the superhero persona of wealthy industrialist Tony Stark, supports the neo-conservative government and begins hunting down those of his former colleagues who are unwilling to reveal their secret identities. Similarly, Captain America coordinates the underground opposition against government-regulated, forced registration, and after a near-fatal clash between the former allies, he surrenders and is arrested by the police. Before he can be brought to trial, a hypnotized assassin shoots him in public, creating an iconic image for the end of one of the oldest comic book heroes.

Civil War, then, offers multiple perspectives. Yet while one might argue that earlier works such as *Watchmen* and *The Dark Knight Returns* also contained multiple perspectives in the form of media inserts and metatexts, *Civil War* constitutes a drastic change to the world of Marvel heroes. Interestingly enough, however, the narrative never addresses the ultimate consequences of these changes, hence the death of Captain America avoids the necessity of his taking sides in controversial real-world topics like the Iraq war. The marital conflict between Reed and Sue Richards of the Fantastic Four caused by differences in opinion concerning the registration act is resolved when the characters go on an extended vacation. The X-Men, whom one would expect to be alarmed by current developments, take a neutral position in the conflict, and even the problems caused by Spider-Man's revelation of his secret identity are solved in unsubtle ways. The transfer of graphic novel concepts to mainstream superhero events as in *Civil War* works very well within singular sequences, like the incrimination of the Marvel characters protesting the restrictive law. But in the long run, the novelty of self-reflexive approaches is integrated and adjusted to the demands of serial storytelling that simply installs a somewhat more diversified status quo.

The aftermath of the *Civil War* series can be regarded as a synopsis of the current state of the crossover between graphic novels and superhero franchises. The ambivalent situations established by Miller and Moore in the 1980s have been picked up by the mainstream, but only in part, and more than likely only temporarily. Events that affect the continuity of the fictional world are included for dramatic effect, but are played down later on. The death of Captain America will presumably last until the film version of his solo adventures and his accompanying film-team-up with *The Avengers* will be released. In the fall of 2007 moreover, the Spider-Man universe was reset to a state more typical of the mid–1970s than of the late 2000s, ignoring nearly every change that author Michael J. Straczynski brought to the series during his time at Marvel. The revelation that Peter Parker is Spider-Man, a key moment that could potentially have changed the entire Marvel continuity, proved to have no consequences whatsoever. More radical concepts in the portrayal of superheroes seem to be reserved for "Else-World" stories and graphic novels set outside of the series' regular continuity.

Nevertheless, the integration of stylistically ambitious elements and new storylines has added substance to the stagnating men-in-tights formula. The last action hero's swan song proved to be only the prelude to the superhero's more sophisticated resurrection, allowing for darker and more ambivalent elements within the stories and a higher degree of cultural and political self-awareness. Nevertheless, it is important to keep in mind that this initial deconstructive moment has been recuperated and incorporated into the franchise as yet another element in the ongoing reconfiguration of the genre.

Notes

1. One specific example is the notorious public debate initiated by psychologist Fredric Wertham in the early 1950s.

10

Extraordinary People
The Superhero Genre and Celebrity Culture in The League *of Extraordinary Gentlemen*

JONATHAN E. GOLDMAN

The Brief Wondrous Life of Dorian Gray, Superhero

Dorian Gray makes only the most peripheral appearance in Alan Moore and Kevin O'Neill's *League of Extraordinary Gentlemen*, turning up in the supplementary material included in the first bound volume of the series. This, however, does not stop the creators of the movie from granting Oscar Wilde's character a starring role in their version. They transform Dorian's supernatural perpetual youth, achieved while the painting of his likeness displays signs of age, into a kind of immortality as long as he does not come face to face with the portrait. The first of these attributes, Dorian's magical ability to stay forever young, is taken directly from Wilde's novel; the second is pure cinematic license. The movie Dorian possesses the extraordinary ability to absorb attacks that would be lethal to ordinary people. In his first scene, an assailant riddles Dorian with bullets and then watches in awe as the punctures in Dorian's skin re-seal themselves. "What are you?" he gasps, to which Dorian haughtily replies: "I'm complicated," before running his enemy through with a saber. Readers of superhero comics will quickly recognize Dorian's power and the attendant astonishment as akin to the "healing factor" possessed by many characters in the Marvel Comics universe. In other words, this is a power drawn from the mainstream superhero genre.

142

Injecting Dorian Gray into the *League* plot and casting him as kin to Wolverine of Marvel's *X-Men* may seem a spurious change in an already frivolous movie adaptation.[1] However, the gesture points to a serious aspect of Moore and O'Neill's work: its implicit argument is that the superhero genre is a logical outgrowth of 20th-century celebrity culture, which itself first took root in the late 19th century, the historical moment in which *League* is set, and from which it derives its source material. In this essay I will briefly examine the *League* series to show that it positions the superhero genre as a mechanism of celebrity, and that it thus addresses the attendant implications of what celebrity means to our modern conceptions of the individual's place within technologized, reproducible, mass society. I see the *League* as both recognizing and revealing that comic book culture and celebrity culture are products of the same late-19th-century societal impulse to distinguish the individual within the crowd, as is suggested by its very premise. Introduced in 1999, the series draws famous characters from the British literary canon and turns them, in less outlandish ways than in the case of the filmic Dorian Gray, into archetypal superheroes: a Justice League for an older age. I will argue that the *League* is best read as a work about celebrity as its role in our culture has evolved over the last one hundred years or so. Ultimately, I will consider how Moore's central positioning of the superhero genre within comics generally reflects the ongoing effort to legitimize comics as art, and how it thus reflects a century's worth of contending that elite art must distinguish itself from the mass-reproduced object, even when it is one.

The copious studies of celebrity published over the last fifteen years tend to identify the initial decades of the 20th century as the moment in which the notion of celebrity, as we now conceive of it, came into being. Richard Schickel, in his oft-cited *Intimate Strangers*, goes so far as to claim that "there was no such thing as celebrity prior to the beginning of the 20th century" (31). In previous eras, fame had been "the by-product of concrete, commonly agreed upon, perhaps even measurable achievement," but Schickel sees celebrity as a new phenomenon that tosses aside longstanding hierarchies of accomplishment (ibid.). The many critics who share this view generally consider early 20th-century celebrity the "democratizing" of that earlier, more traditional form of fame.[2] The Hollywood star system becomes both a paradigmatic site of these formulations and the main example for writers arguing that celebrity functioned then, and functions now, as the embodiment of a desired individuality. According to P. David Marshall, "the star is universally individualized, for the star is representative of the potential of the individual" (17). Crucial to this form of celebrity was the advent of the cinematic close-up, which Warren Susman calls "a stunning example of the individual against the mass" (282). Through the Hollywood star system, so this argument goes, the culture could retain concepts of individuality within an increasingly depersonalizing culture.

While these accounts date celebrity to the early years of Hollywood, we can, and should, go back further to see this culture taking shape in the Anglophone world. In the 1800s, English agrarian culture finally succumbed to industrial culture, which soon gave way to mass-industrial culture. By the 1890s, this led to a new form of visual culture, inundating society with mass-reproduced images. The photographic image essentially altered the way society viewed individuals of accomplishment, a change the cinema would exacerbate. As Leo Braudy writes, "[t]he photograph, with its exaltation of a momentary state of physical being, and the motion picture, which further emphasized its subject's immersion in a passing time, helped create the more uneasy relation we now share with those in the spotlight," in contrast with earlier, pre-photographic versions of fame (554). If, as Braudy claims, this new celebrity depended to some degree on photographic reproduction, then it did not arrive fully formed in the year 1900, but rather evolved over the second half of the 19th century. Indeed, writing of technological advances over the last decades of the 1800s, John F. Kasson notes that "[t]he passion for studio portraits, awakened with the rise of photography, not only seized people of all classes but helped to make possible a new celebrity culture" (18).

One need only look at the career of Wilde himself to see 19th-century stirrings of celebrity's new role, a new way of self-fashioning in the face of the mass-reproducible society of images. Long before his achievements as a novelist, essayist, poet and playwright were recognized — for that matter, long before these achievements were achieved — Wilde was, to pirate Daniel Boorstin's well-worn phrase, well known for his well-known-ness: famous for being famous. In other words, Wilde had fashioned himself into an icon. Lisa Hamilton writes that "one of the less discussed attributes of celebrity after Wilde is its component of immediate physical recognizability. His face, his body, and his clothing all became distinctive stylistic hallmarks that were instantly attributable to him" (4). In other words, it is Wilde's celebrity that gives rise to the idea that the celebrity image, quite independent from traditional spheres of achievement, functions as a universally recognizable representation of the person, distinct and separate from the faceless masses.

If Wilde signals a turning point for celebrity, then that transition is flagged by his only excursion into the popular genre of the novel, *The Picture of Dorian Gray* (1889), and by his most famous character (excluding his own persona). In Wilde's novel, Dorian circulates throughout late 19th-century British salons as an image only. A supernatural portrait of Dorian remains sequestered and hidden as its appearance changes to match Dorian's insidious actions. Dorian's corrupt lifestyle is meanwhile disguised by his fantastically youthful appearance. We might say that Dorian himself emerges as a super-hero, whose superpower is his supernatural beauty, which serves both to dis-tinguish him among upper-crust society and to mask his exploits when he delves among the masses. In other words, his power may be defined as the ability to look different and to have a secret identity. Through his character of Dorian, Wilde portrays the implications of the new version of celebrity that he was concurrently creating in his own life, while simultaneously estab-lishing some of the parameters of the superhero. Seen this way, the refash-ioning of Dorian into a superhero constitutes an act of inadvertent but uncanny insight on the part of the *League* filmmakers.[3] In fact, Dorian's death in the film seems to be caused not merely by his coming face to face with the portrait, but also by his realization of how eroded its visage has become — by his confrontation with its ugliness, or the final neutralizing of his superpower. Thus Wilde, in the syncretism of his life and work, models an earlier version of the celebrity, and suggests the twin births of both celebrity culture and the superhero genre.

The War in Heaven, 1898

The superhero genre itself constitutes a symptom of celebrity culture, representing paragons of individualism that are familiar from audiences' earlier encounters with them, thus echoing the machinations of texts that are more visibly celebrity-oriented. If theorists of celebrity have been somewhat myopic in their emphasis on pinpointing Hollywood culture as the start of modern celebrity, thereby ignoring its 19th-century origins, it may be because early movies made adroit use of the rapidly rising celebrity culture. Hollywood cinema of the 1920s invokes the recognizability of a star, whose identity "is constituted elsewhere, in the discourses 'outside' the [text]" (de Cordova, 19). We might think, as an example, of Chaplin's repeated appearances as the Little Tramp, an identifiable personage from the moment he appears on screen, and how Chaplin incorporated audience expectations regarding the character into sight gags and plots. In other words, as part of the cinematic experience, audiences were meant to think beyond the narrative they were watching and to consider the public persona of the actor as represented in public appear-ances, fan magazines, and previous movies — what Walter Benjamin calls the "build-up of the 'personality' outside the studio" (1997, 231). Celebrity seems inextricably linked to cinema, in other words, because the medium's most-watched productions learned to write the celebrity contexts right into their narratives.

We find a similar dynamic in Moore and O'Neill's *League*, which enlists fictional characters that have a distinct relationship to celebrity. The series makes use of the fame of its titular protagonists, all known from popular 19th-century novels. *League* treats Stevenson's Dr. Jekyll and Mr. Hyde, Verne's Captain Nemo, Hawley Griffin of Wells' *The Invisible Man*, Rider Haggard's Allan Quatermain, and Wilhemina Murray, bride of Bram Stoker's *Dracula*, along with numerous figures less prominent in the plot, as if they were living in a single same parallel world. They are brought together by the British government to discover and foil plots against it. Moore's personae team up not only to fight Britain's enemies, but also to usher in a century in which ordinary people identify themselves neither by clan allegiance nor by class allegiance, but by allegiance to the individuals who represent the ability to distinguish oneself from the rest. Within the narrative, Moore incorporates moments of recognition into the narrative, making the intertextual contexts of the characters essential to the plot. For example, the opening dialogue of *League* rests not on pure exposition, but rather on (fairly obvious) hints regarding the identities of Murray, Nemo, and M. Like a Chaplin film, or the Rudolph Valentino, Mary Pickford, and Greta Garbo vehicles of early cinema, the *League* relies on audience identification of the character's signification beyond the immediate text.

Of course, one could make a similar claim of many intertextual works. In fact, Moore has been playing this particular game in various ways for years. His most celebrated series *Watchmen*, illustrated by Dave Gibbons, enlists the defunct characters of the MLJ and Charlton Comics imprints. In so doing, though, it actually trades on the generic qualities of its superheroes and their obvious resemblance to established characters (the Comedian to Wolverine, Night Owl to Batman, Dr. Manhattan to Superman, etc.). As Thierry Groensteen writes, "we do not fully understand the masterpiece that is *Watchmen* if we do not have any preliminary familiarity with superheroes" (2008, 125). But what sets *League* apart from *Watchmen* and other intertextual narratives is that it specifically enlists the recognizability of characters from Wilde's historical moment as it turns them into comic book heroes, raising the stakes by painting the personae with the luminosity of early celebrity culture.

As Karin Kukkonen suggests elsewhere in the present volume, *League* is not the only text linking superhero genre with British pulp fiction; she writes of how Warren Ellis' *Planetary* "connects the superheroes to their 'roots' in Victorian entertainment literature." Moore and O'Neill, following *Planetary* (1998), make a similar move, but following Wilde, use that link to correlate the superhero genre to the advent of celebrity. This pairing ultimately relies on a cultural logic of the individual and the mass. If, in mass visual society, the only way to rise above the faceless urban crowds was to use one's unique abilities to create oneself as an icon, as Wilde did, then surely the superheroes, flying above the crowds, dressed in their colorful costumes, each with an insignia (or trademark), serve as a manifestation of that impulse. And the years surrounding the turn of the century, which gave birth to modern celebrity, also gave momentum to the nomenclature of the superhero via Shaw's *Man and Superman* and Nietzsche's *Übermensch*. This popularity of the prefix "super-" during the first decades of celebrity's rise surely illuminates that these are twin versions of the same idea: the individual that cannot be subsumed by the crowd.[4]

A crucial sequence of panels in issue 5 of *League* illustrates how Moore and O'Neill imagine superheroes in terms parallel to celebrity. It arrives at the apotheosis of the plot: the League has just learned, through Griffin's intelligence, that it has been duped into working for the crime lord Moriarty, remanding for him the precious cavorite (the fictional super-element from Wells' *The First Men on the Moon*). As they prepare for action, this sequence removes them momentarily from the scene. In the first panel, a crowd of awed pedestrians gazes upwards in shock. O'Neill colors the moment darkly, in subdued hues, against which the upturned eyes and jagged teeth of these working-class metropolitans contrast. He registers their amazement variously: women raise hands to faces in horror, a man steadies himself by clutching his neighbors' shoulders, while another, agape, lets his cigarette burn down. O'Neill crams a great deal of visual information into this silent panel whose only word (an unspoken one) is the "blind" sign carried by a beggar who is so astonished that he forgets his charade and stares with the rest — a great deal of information, and a great number of faces, suggesting a claustrophobic street scene. The crowd, in fact, is dense enough to trammel the progress of Murray and Quatermain, as the four following panels show.

The subsequent page depicts the cause of this effect in an image that highlights the spectacular aspect of the crowd's wonder: a full-page panel reveals the monstrous airship captained by Dr. Moriarty, powered aloft by the cavorite. The contrast between these two pages is considerable, and underlines how superpowers are aligned with individuality and spectacle. The panels set among the claustrophobic crowd build in a traditional comic book sequence toward the issue's final panel, dominated by the airship, set against the sky, flying above St. Paul's Cathedral, the luminescent beam of the cavorite extending below. Groensteen, in his theorizing of comics, would almost certainly qualify this page as "ostentatious" as it focuses attention on the static image rather than on the unfolding of narrative (2008, 99). This ostentatious quality is heightened by the fact that the panel concludes the issue, halting narrative time, creating (especially if one reads *League* serially) plot suspense. The message here is clear: the ordinary citizens in the street, whom Moriarty will soon look down on and call "those countless little lives" (Issue 6) are indistinct and not individuated, and thus positioned below, among the crowd. But an extraordinary character such as Moriarty, culled from the classic fiction of Conan Doyle, armed with cavorite, culled from the fiction of Wells, exists above them, as an object of the plebeian gaze. Indeed, Moriarty is so loath to descend to the level of the crowds that he grasps the cavorite and flies upwards and out of this installment of the story.

Quatermain and Harker, joined by Nemo, Hyde, and Griffin, will position themselves above the masses as well, also taking to the skies to literalize their rise above the mundane. Nemo articulates this gap that separates them from ordinary people: "Tonight, Gentlemen, London shall witness war in heaven." The phrase richly incorporates both the book's title and the New Testament to suggest that the League's declaration of *non serviam* is its assertion of independence not only from Moriarty's schemes, but also from the crowd. In *League*, to fly through the London skies, looking down at the gathered masses, serves as a metaphor for distinguishing oneself from the *populi*. Moore's enlisting of novelistic heroes, re-conceiving them as comic book superheroes, correlates with the desire to articulate oneself as an individual.

Indeed, *League* translates this desire into posthuman terms. Griffin, wending through the urban peoplescape, laments: "What a squalid thing humanity can be! Would that they all might be made to vanish and be made invisible instead of I." Murray incisively rejoins that his disdain for the human explains why he is "so eager to become entirely other" (Issue 3). Murray's retort can be partly understood here as that of someone who remains emphatically human. However, neither she, nor Quatermain, who emerge as the two true protagonists of the series, will remain so. By the time of *The League of Extraordinary Gentlemen, Volume 3: The Black Dossier*, which follows the second collected volume of the series, they have bathed in a Fountain of Youth, making them, in Eric Berlatsky's account, "young, blonde, and perpetually randy." Other non- or extra-human characters that populate the series include, Virginia Woolf's Orlando, and the animal/human vivisections of Dr. Moreau. Moriarty too, seems beyond normal, as O'Neill draws him with a head oversized enough for phrenological fantasy. (And Sherlock Holmes, in his momentary, analeptic, appearance, could be Moriarty's twin.) The process that Wilde was commencing in the 1880s and 1890s, and in which Superman creators Jerry Siegel and Joe Shuster participated in 40 years later, is recognized by Moore and O'Neill as a product of the *fin-de-siècle* that pre-dates ours.

Looking Upwards

The sequence of panels described above finds a parallel moment in what might be considered an unlikely place: Virginia Woolf's *Mrs. Dalloway*, a novel universally recognized as central to modernist literature, that early 20th-century literary moment that authorized itself as a chronicle of Western culture in transition. The comparison to *Mrs. Dalloway* gains import when one considers what both scenes imply about the relationship between the crowd, the individual, and 20th-century technological society, and how that relationship bears on the division between elite and popular forms of culture. Early in Woolf's novel, a Westminster crowd gathers around a stalled motorcar that bears the state insignia. The onlookers are fascinated by the mystery of exactly which official personage — the prime minister? the Prince of Wales? — rides within. Yet the crowd's attention soon shifts to an airplane overhead and its mysterious skywriting that advertises toffee, Glaxo, Kreemo, or something else, depending on which of the onlookers one believes. As in the moment in *League*, the ordinary Londoners are here united in their reverence for those figures above them — first figuratively, then literally.

This moment from *Mrs. Dalloway* reads easily enough as an allegory of societal change: the masses shift their fascination from a traditional signifier of political and class hierarchy to a modern sign of the times. Overlooked in such an account is that which unites the car and the airplane: first of all their inscrutability, and secondly their position, metaphorical in one case, literal in the second, above the heads of the people. This pair of shared traits suggests that these two objects of fascination are set in apposition rather than opposition; they are mutually constitutive rather than opposed. Most of all they are linked through this impenetrability, the way the signs seem readable, but emerge as hieroglyphs that do not yield their secrets. Unfathomability subsumes the car and the plane behind the most famously difficult-to-read object of all: the modernist text, in all of its experimental, elliptical, stream-of-consciousness glory. Woolf's novel positions the formal qualities of literary modernism above the plebeian, uniting tradition and technology in a shared elevation of modernist form. Literary style takes on the role of Wilde's sartorial style, articulating itself, and by extension its creator, as the object of the gaze.

Woolf's traffic-stopping crowd scene merges marketplace culture (the advertising airplane) and traditional insignias of class hierarchy. This pairing emerges as a symptom of modernist originality, or what Aaron Jaffe in his study of modernism and celebrity calls the "*imprimatur*" of the author.[5] By twinning the two phenomena through their illegibility — the difficulty an ordinary reader experiences while attempting to penetrate the stylistically complex modernist text — Woolf elevates the inscrutable author above the level of the plebeian. Woolf's novel thus signals its redressing of the so-called Great Divide: the idea, as theorized by Andreas Huyssen, that modernist art affirmed its high cultural status by casting popular culture as feminized and debased popular culture, and by asserting its independence from that culture's mechanically reproducible objects.[6] The text that points beyond its plot to its creator necessarily posits itself as an extraordinary object, on the elite side of the great divide by virtue of its creator's unique capabilities. In Foucault's explanation of the author function, the text itself constitutes the author as discourse, a special class of being to serve as the source of complex, polysemic language. He describes this discourse as a "series of specific and complex operations" that argue for the author as "a perpetual surging of invention" (Foucault 1998, 216, 221).

Viewed from this perspective, the echoes of Woolf in *League* take on clearer significance. *League* similarly elevates the form of the work, the "imprimatur" of the author, or in this case, authors. The extraordinary people of the title become understood as not only the superhuman characters within the text, but also the comic book creators outside it, able to appropriate specific material from other textual realms and densely weave it into their own. This is particularly apparent in *The Black Dossier*, the first entry in the series (as of this writing) to be published only as a single volume. The plot concerns the titular dossier, which, amplifying hints offered throughout the series, chronicles the activities of the league's various incarnations over the centuries. Murray and Quatermain, having found themselves on the wrong side of the British government, contrive to steal and then peruse the dossier, a compendium of stylistically diverse documents. To read what they read, along with them, in real time, so to speak, comprises much of the experience of *The Black Dossier*. This premise provides Moore and O'Neill with the opportunity to demonstrate their virtuoso mimicry and postmodern sensibility. The book careens from a "lost" Shakespeare play to a "sequel," to John Cleland's soft-porn classic *Fanny Hill*, and from a Bertie Wooster memoir via a Tijuana bible to a concluding 3-D section (cardboard 3-D glasses accompany the book) set in the "Blazing World" — a 1666 science-fiction invention of the Duchess of Newcastle, Margaret Cavendish. In this further exercise in canonization, Moore and O'Neill not only attempt to re-draw British history, but in so doing they suggest that the true league of extraordinary gentlemen is their own. The manipulation of pulp heroes from famous novels, finally, endorses this triangulation of superhero-as-celebrity, author-as-superhero. In each case, it is the recognizability and, as the cases of Wilde, Chaplin and Woolf remind us, the singularity of the figure that seems to reside outside of the text, that is both enlisted and reaffirmed. Once again, the *League* filmmakers intuited this. As their Invisible Man (here named Skinner) foils a plot to reproduce his invisibility formula, they give him the punch line: "Any more like me and I'll lose the franchise."[7]

The Canonization of Comics

Clearly, Skinner's quip points to the basic lesson that Wells has already lost the franchise: that it is the character's fame and not the author's which transcends the text, name change be damned. This points directly to the *League*'s central dynamic, which argues for the primacy of author over text specifically by enlisting characters who generally have come to represent a strain of British fiction identified with plot and suspense rather than with progressive (meant literally) literary techniques. Again, modernism's war on popular, transparent modes of representation looms. The indefatigably avant-garde styles and manifestos of a hundred writers grappling with the explosion of reproducible culture in the early 20th century helped create definitions of and divisions in culture that, a century later, have rendered Wells and company to, if not the backwaters of literary reputation, then at least the suburbs.

To this point I have been arguing that the backwards glance of the *League* series articulates the way the superhero genre constitutes an outgrowth of celebrity culture as it emerged at the turn from the 19th to the 20th century, and this can be seen as part of a cultural impulse to distinguish the individual among the crowd. To conclude this essay, I offer some of the implications this gesture has for comics in general and for the superhero genre's role within it. Part of what the *League* suggests is that to consider the superhero genre a merely popular, and thus lesser manifestation of the art form that is comic books, is to re-inscribe prejudices we have inherited from critical schools that have failed to take comics seriously to begin with — relegating them to the underside of the great divide.

In *Understanding Comics*, Scott McCloud writes of how comic books have been dismissed throughout their history "as the 'bastard child' of words and pictures" (47). What he means is that comics have rarely been accorded serious critical treatment because of the view that they are mere entertainment — a view predicated at least on the modernist idea that something produced for mass consumption cannot possibly be worth taking seriously. Yet it seems there is another "bastard child" here: superhero comics themselves. In another moment of McCloud's book, as the protagonist/narrator attempts to define comics to an invisible lecture hall audience, a voice interjects, "What about Batman?! Shouldn't it have Batman in it?" (9). The interrupter is thrown out of the room for pointing out this particular white elephant. The moment represents a scene of legitimization for comic books within a professional or academic setting. However, the solitariness of the pontificate combined with the audience's invisibility — not the Hawley Griffin kind of invisibility, rather the kind resulting from the fact that it goes visually unrepresented — undermines the attempt. The comic book readership is not quite participating in the event. One speaks up, reminding the lecturer that superheroes, characters that, like celebrities, are transcendent, that exist beyond the text, that provide a notion of the individual are, for many people, what comics do best. Tellingly, this unruly voice is excommunicated, removed from the premises.

McCloud's moment also represents, satirically it seems, the desire for content to take a part in the discussion, a resistance to the focus on style whose flames were fanned by modernist aesthetics. This is the moment where Moore and O'Neill intervene most forcibly. By recycling celebrity characters from British pulp fiction, they turn the formulation on its head. Their use of content and character, their deployment of already familiar semiotic material points beyond the boundaries of the text to establish their own inventiveness. In this work, it is not technique but the reliance on content that both argues for the mastery of the authors and the primacy of a mainstream, popular genre within the comics medium. This is in no way to suggest that *League* polemicizes against less mainstream exercises in the comics genre. It does not (and neither do I). But to downplay the significance of the superhero genre for 20th-century audiences is to re-inscribe categories of high and low within approaches to the comics genre and to fall prey to an outmoded ideological approach to culture. Such a critical treatment of culture would maintain the great divide, and therefore help to perpetuate the public relegation of comics to inferior status, mere entertainment, a ten-cent plague fit only, one might say, for the gutter.

Notes

1. The adaptation is certainly of the "loosely-based" variety. Moore was famously (and understandably) unhappy with the film, though he did not go as far as to pull his name from the credits as he would later do with *V for Vendetta*.

2. The term is from Leo Braudy, whose *The Frenzy of Renown* is often cited as the most comprehensive and magisterial history of fame in western society.

3. Todd Haynes makes a similar point in his film *Velvet Goldmine*, which posits Wilde as the origin of pop-star culture. The film commences with the origin story of Oscar. He descends from space to arrive on the Wilde doorstep with an emerald medallion that is the source of his power: a fairly direct correlation to Kal-El's arrival on Earth.

4. See Guralnik (105) for a summary of the super-prefix.

5. See Jaffe pp 1–5. Indeed, numerous scholars have recently remarked that modernism, following hot on the heels of the 19th century and contemporary to Hollywood cinema, parallels celebrity discourse in its construction of the author. I myself, in another context, have referred to modernism as "the literature of celebrity." For example, in my study of James Joyce, I explained that, "his aesthetic constitutes a new kind of author — as not only the art object par excellence but also the master choreographer of the culture that celebrates him" (86). Thus the *Mrs. Dalloway* moment's re-appearance in *League* seems an apt representation of the role modernism plays in the construction of celebrity.

6. Huyssens writes: "Modernism constituted itself through a conscious strategy of exclusion, an anxiety of contamination by its other: an increasingly consuming and engulfing mass culture" (vii).

7. There is a pertinent story behind this, and it is a good one: the H.G. Wells estate refused to allow the studio to reuse its trademarked character, forcing the filmmakers to both improvise a new civilian name and origin story (he stole the formula from Griffin) for he-who-cannot-be-seen.

11

Warren Ellis's *Planetary*
The Archaeology of Superheroes

KARIN KUKKONEN

... my problem with avowedly postmodern fiction is that that is usually reduced to an excuse for an ironic gag.

— Warren Ellis[1]

The direct gaze out of the panel, as characters address readers directly; the parody through subversion, as the hero is reduced to a dupe: these postmodern tricks that attempt to achieve a complicity with readers, to make them part of the sophisticated crowd that looks through the myths and constructions of traditional storytelling, often result in little more than an "ironic gag."

Warren Ellis' own series *Planetary* (1998), however, attempts a deeper engagement with postmodernism in contemporary superhero comics. *Planetary* tells the story of a team of superheroes exploring the secret history of the 20th century as chronicled by its popular fiction. They call themselves "archaeologists of the impossible," and their field trips lead them to abandoned monster islands in Japan, the rainy streets of Hong Kong and the dark alleys of Gotham City. They meet Victorian characters like Sherlock Holmes and Dracula, pulp heroes of the 1930s, like Doc Savage and The Shadow, superheroes of the Golden and the Silver Ages, popular icons like James Bond (re-named "John Stone"), characters of 1980s British comics writers like John Constantine (called "Jack Carter" in *Planetary*) and even one of Ellis' own characters, Spider Jerusalem (of his series *Transmetropolitan*). The cast and setting of *Planetary* amount to nothing less than the main story worlds and characters of the 20th century's popular fiction.

Within this extensive field, the *Planetary* team sets about its work. As "mystery archaeologists," their initial task is not to fight super-villains or to save the world, but to unearth information about what happened in the 20th century according to popular culture. "There's a hundred years of fantastic events that *Planetary* intends to excavate," explains Elijah Snow, one of the team members (1:6:25). The *Planetary* team models its self-understanding as "archaeologists" on the method of cultural analysis developed by philosopher Michel Foucault in *Madness and Civilisation* and *The Order of Things*: they pursue an "archaeology of knowledge."

And indeed, an "Archaeology of Superheroes" is necessary for unearthing the traditions of this genre, as characters like Superman, Batman or Wonder Woman are decades old and their stories have been written and rewritten by different authors in different times. The Batman of the 1940s is not the same character as the camp figure of the 1960s TV-show, and neither is Frank Miller's rendition in his 1987 graphic novel *Batman: The Dark Knight Returns*. However, in the public imagination, all these individual instances and their contexts are forgotten and superseded by "Batman" as a coherent figure, transforming the superhero figure into a "modern myth" as defined by Roland Barthes in *Mythologies*.

It takes an archaeologist's analytical skills to reinsert these abstracted "modern myths" into their cultural contexts and this is exactly the task of *Planetary's* investigative mission. On the basis of Foucault's theoretical digest *The Archaeology of Knowledge*, we will trace how Ellis' *Planetary* conceives of texts of popular culture as "statements" that can be located in certain "discourse formations." This strategy undoes the "natural" and obvious quality of the modern myth, thus representing an application of postmodernism in contemporary comics which goes well beyond the "ironic gag."

The "archaeology of knowledge" as a method of analysis is supposed to abstain from the narrative continuities of history. *Planetary's* main interest, however, lies in telling a good story. The series therefore transforms the archaeological dig into the basic plot device of its story. Through their various excavations, the team members of *Planetary* learn about the secret history of the 20th century and about their own past; they will need this knowledge in order to defeat the comic's villains. The archaeological method is not transparent in *Planetary*, but an integral part of its storytelling. Through it, the comic combines the exuberant details of 20th century popular culture into a "master narrative" of its own. In telling such a "master narrative" of 20th century popular fiction by using the concepts of postmodern theory as plot devices, *Planetary* not only goes beyond the "ironic gag," but also beyond postmodernity itself.

Superheroes as a "Modern Myth"

In his discussion of the modern myth in *Mythologies*, Roland Barthes tackles wrestling, plastic, Einstein's brain, and Garbo's face, but he has nothing to say about one of the most persistent modern western myths: the superhero. Nevertheless, the superhero phenomenon fits perfectly into the more theoretical description of the modern myth provided by Barthes in his essay accompanying *Mythologies*, "Myth Today."

Barthes characterizes myth as a "type of speech," basing his argument on a very general understanding of Saussurean semiology (Barthes 1991, 109). The signifier and signified in language create an "associative total": the sign. Similarly, myth combines a signifier and a signified, creating not a sign, but a "signification" (ibid., 113, 116). Myth functions as a secondary semiotic level, taking the result of the primary semiotic level, the sign, as its signifier. The myth's signifiers can be the signs of different language systems, words or images. But as the language sign becomes the mythic signifier, it is evacuated of its original meaning and this original meaning is replaced by signification, the meaning produced by myth.

As a modern myth, Superman is the defender of "truth, justice and the American way"—whatever that may signify in any particular contemporary context. "Truth, justice and the American way" are not defined in the "metalanguage" of the modern myth, but stand for the socially acceptable, the "right thing to do" for the superhero. In the first edition of *Superman*, published in 1938, when the U.S. was still following an isolationist policy and did not want to intervene in World War II, the superhero prevents a weapons manufacturer from drawing the U.S. into the war. After Pearl Harbor, Superman joins the U.S. forces in their fight against Japan and Germany, spanking Japanese generals and demonstrating American superiority to fanatic Nazis. Both stories present Superman as an exemplum of "truth, justice and the American way," but contemporary contexts filled this phrase with a very different understanding of what it actually means.

As a sign, "truth, justice and the American way" can have many distinct meanings. But once it passes through what Barthes calls the "turnstile of form and meaning" of the modern myth, these distinct meanings are lost and it becomes the form, the signifier of the modern myth of the American hero Superman (Barthes 1991, 124).

By now, superheroes have a long history. They went through various incarnations and parallel worlds, and many an author has told their tales. Yet all these different versions of any single superhero are still perceived to be the same character. Batman can be the vigilante detective of the 1940s, the colourful camp hero of the 1960s TV series, or the neurotic avenger of Frank Miller's *Batman: The Dark Knight Returns*.[2] As Umberto Eco points out in his essay on "The Myth of Superman," the superhero lives through the same story structure time and again in each instalment of the series. Superman is thus "aesthetically and commercially deprived of the possibility of narrative development" (15). The storytelling in superhero comics generally follows an iterative scheme, in which no single story can establish facts that change the basic set-up.[3]

However, as demonstrated in the Superman example above, the idea that the same story is told over and over again is actually an illusion of modern myth. The same story is told, because the form of the mythic signifier, the superhero, remains functionally the same. But the story is also continuously changed, if we consider its actual meaning. If we reverse direction through Barthes' turnstiles, from form to meaning, from the myth to its actual instance, the differences between isolationist Superman and war hero Superman come to the fore, even though Superman continues to defend "truth, justice and the American way" in both cases on the level of the myth.

Planetary dispels the modern myth of the superhero through addressing its mechanism in a special issue called "Night on Earth." In this issue, the team travels to Gotham City in order to investigate a series of killings. As it turns out, the killer has the ability to cause a "partial multiversal collapse," making different story worlds merge into one (Ellis, 2004b 3:7). As they hunt him down through the different story worlds, which constitute the various versions of Gotham City from comics history, the *Planetary* team also encounters the different versions of Gotham City's most famous denizen: the Batman. Jakita Wagner, the *Planetary* team's martial arts expert, enters into combat with him. First, she fights the Batman of Jeph Loeb's *Hush* storyline (ibid., 3:16–26). But as the killer changes story worlds again, she is suddenly faced with the 1960s camp version of the Batman, who tells her "I can't hit a girl" and douses her with pepper spray (ibid., 3:27). Time and again, the story worlds change and with them the drawing style, the setting and the Batman himself, his weaponry, behavior and discourse. The Batman of the 1960s gives Jakita "Bat-Apologies" in imitation of the speech style used in the TV series. The Batman depicted in the style of Frank Miller's rendition of the character tells her: "From this position, there are nine different ways to take you down.— Six of them kill you outright" (ibid. 3:30). This refers directly to one of Batman's monologues in *Batman: The Dark Knight Returns*: "There are seven working defenses from this position.— Three of them disarm with minimal contact.— Three of them kill..." (Miller 2002, 39).

In this issue, *Planetary* takes readers back and forth through the Barthesian turnstiles between the myth and its versions. Ellis thus exposes the constructed nature of the modern myth of the superhero in what could be described as a postmodernist fashion. And, indeed, the issue has some very funny moments through the "ironic gags" that postmodernism can also engender. But exposing the constructedness and situatedness of the various versions of the superheroes is only part of the larger project in *Planetary*, which deals more directly with an "archaeology of superheroes."

The Archaeology of Superheroes

"We are archaeologists," says Jakita. "We'll dig you up and work it all out in a couple of years. The end." (2:9:21). When *Planetary* began its run in 1998, the 20th century was rapidly nearing its end. The series' perspective is thus directed backward in time, as the heroes begin to unearth elements of that century's popular culture and try to make sense of them.

In the first issue, the Planetary team is investigating the underground lair of a secret society of pulp heroes. They find out that Doc Brass, *Planetary's* version of 1930s pulp hero Doc Savage, was in league with characters like Will Eisner's The Spirit, Burrough's Tarzan (here dubbed Lord Blackstone instead of Lord Greystoke), The Shadow, Asian mastermind Hark (a reference to Fu Manchu), and Thomas Alva Edison (1:1:14). The pulp fiction heroes of the 1930s and 1940s did not enter World War II, but attempted to end it "from our armchairs" by rewriting reality through a supercomputer (1:1:19).

Planetary relocates these heroes in their contemporary context. Doc Savage, The Shadow and Tarzan are no longer simply pulp heroes, but become what Foucault calls a "statement" in *Archaeology of Knowledge*: the elementary unit of a discourse (Foucault 1972, 80). For Foucault, the individual pulp novel would not be interesting as an *œuvre* to be interpreted, but as a statement, an event in the historical discursive formation it is part of. "Discursive formations" are the underlying units of Foucault's history of ideas. As a "system of dispersion" they extend beyond discipline and genre boundaries (ibid., 37). The science hero Doc Brass/Doc Savage and the real-life inventor Thomas Alva Edison, with the iconic quality his name was to attain, are on the same level as "statements" in the discursive formations of the belief in progress and the urge towards escapism in the popular culture of these years. A discursive formation is the "coexistence of these dispersed and heterogeneous statements," as Foucault explains (ibid., 33). Understanding a modern myth, which seems to have a "natural meaning," a timeless reality, as a statement in a discourse formation, brings it back to its contemporary context.

Planetary presents for example the Superman of the 1980s as a statement of the discourse formation of disillusionment of its era in issue 7. The team travels to London to attend the funeral of Jack Carter, who is the series' version of the occult detective John Constantine, hero of the *Hellblazer* series. The *Hellblazer* series, started by British author Jamie Delano in 1988, presents a bleak and cynical worldview. Like Alan Moore's *V for Vendetta*, it reflects the atmosphere in Britain at the end of the Thatcher era. "England was a scary place. No wonder it produced a scary culture," as Jakita explains (2:7:7). Attending Carter's funeral are also several iconic characters by British comics authors of the time: Morpheus from Neil Gaiman's *The Sandman* (2:7:5), Alan Moore's *Swamp Thing*, Grant Morrison's *Animal Man*, and members of his *Doom Patrol* (2:7:6), which can all be seen as statements in this discourse formation.

With this funeral scene, *Planetary* establishes the contemporary context and, as the team is investigating Carter's death, they encounter the Superman version of this particular discourse formation: He is ragged, ill tempered, crazy, and the "S" logo has been removed from his suit (2:7:17). The character complains about what has become of him in the 1980s, when the Second British Invasion brought a great number of British authors into U.S. comics: "I wasn't hip, I wasn't trendy, I wasn't edgy, and you know what?— That was ok!— I didn't need the split personalities, the nervous breakdown [...] my life being a lie..." (2:7:18). The context of the 1980s and its discourse formations created a version of Superman very different from its traditional modern myth. The main instances of this 1980s Superman can be found in the reset of the DC universe in *Crisis on Infinite Earths* (1985), followed by the importance of Superman's evil doppelganger Bizaro in John Byrne's *Man of Steel* (1986), his "split personalities," and the DC Elseworld series, which present alternative narratives like Alan Moore's *Whatever Happened to the Man of Tomorrow?* (1986), making Superman's life "a lie."

Planetary points out the historical situatedness of the Superman versions by referring to the cultural contexts through the comics characters of British authors of the 1980s, and highlighting the difference between this Superman and previous versions in the character's discourse. Both the characters of the British authors and the 1980s Superman are statements of the same discourse formation. *Planetary* not only reveals their historical situatedness, but also highlights developments in the Superman character, thereby offering an insight into the workings of the modern myth.

The Fantastic Four is a longstanding superhero team from the Silver Age, which became a signifier of the modern myth of science heroes.[4] Dubbing them simply "The Four," *Planetary* brings them back into the discourse formation that provided the context for their original versions. When retelling the fateful space accident that gave them their superpowers, *Planetary* does not start with the preparations for their flight as in Stan Lee's original comic, but with the influx of scientists from Nazi Germany at the end of World War II. Wernher von Braun and his team of rocket scientists were only the front operation, while behind the scenes, on "the real front line of the Cold War," a flight to the moon was scheduled for 1961 (1:6:5). In reality, 1961 is the year in which the first issue of the *Fantastic Four* was published by Marvel and these science heroes took their fictional space flight. The Apollo program would not put men on the moon until 1969. The space race, the Apollo program and the Silver Age superheroes are all statements of the same discourse formation.

As *Planetary* relates their story to their contemporary contexts so closely, the Silver Age superheroes seem to lose part of their fictional status. As statements in a discourse formation, the distinction between fiction and reality becomes almost irrelevant, because from the discourse perspective events in the real world and fictions both exist on the same ontological level as "statements." According to Foucault, they are coexistent rather than one being an expression of the other, and therefore he rejects the notions of interpretation and of structure (Foucault 1972, 137). Foucault's archaeology "does not seek another, better-hidden discourse" (ibid., 139). Fiction is simply the fact of a statement when it comes to discourse formations, and *Planetary* presents the first issue of the *Fantastic Four* as such.

For the archaeology of knowledge, the ontological distinction between fiction and fact is not salient in the traditional sense. All statements need to be "made," they are all "enunciations," and thus everything is both a fact, in that it exists and influences, and a fiction, in that it is made.

The Master Narrative

This coexistence of fact and fiction is at the heart of the postmodern epistemological project: what seems a fact because it exists and influences, like "the work," the modern myth or the master narrative, can be exposed as a mere fiction through analytical thinking.

The modern myth works not only as a simplification, taking statements out of their contexts, but it also "naturalises" the signification of the myth. By abstracting it from time and place, it makes the myth seem "real." If the contexts, the discourse's agents and intentions, are forgotten, the modern myth becomes natural, obvious and disinterested. It is the critic's task to relate it back to its discourses and contexts, to show its constructedness and situatedness. Both Barthes' and Foucault's theoretical works are clearly designed to show that what seems like fact might well be fiction.

The classical master narrative has been exposed in a similar vein by Jean-François Lyotard in *The Postmodern Condition*. The master narrative provides a narrative explanation for cultural phenomena and helps to circulate such knowledge in a society. One of the central master narratives of Western society for example is the "emancipation of the rational" (Lyotard, xxiii). This master narrative projects different levels of meaning onto each other: the move from the darkness of the cave to the light of ideas in Plato's "Allegory of the Cave;" civilization's development from the "dark" Middle Ages to the Enlightenment; the mental development of a human being as he or she grows up. These metaphors (dark/uncivilized/young vs. light/civilized/experienced) are then organized into a story structure. Again, the difference between fact and fiction is obliterated and the situatedness of the master narrative is deliberately hidden.

The master narrative provides a story structure (i.e. narrative causality and coherence) to events; something which an archaeology of knowledge tries to avoid. Foucault does not aim at "totality" in his explanations, and thus he turns from the perspective of history to the perspective of archaeology (Foucault 1972, 11f.). He envisions his archaeology as "a method purged of all anthropologism" (ibid., 16). While history *interprets* phenomena and arranges them into narrative patterns, archaeology *describes* discourse formations, their statements, and the relationships that are established between them by discursive practices.[5]

Here, *Planetary* parts company with Foucault's archaeology: the series clearly purports to tell a story and not to merely describe the discursive formations of 20th-century popular culture through excavating its statements. *Planetary* begins with seemingly unconnected visits to an abandoned Japanese island, home to Godzilla-like monsters and a crew of political fanatics reminiscent of the novelist Yukio Mishima or to the streets of Hong Kong, where a policeman seeks revenge from the triads, a well-known plot of Hong Kong cinema's Heroic Bloodshed genre. These trips function as "archaeological digs" uncovering such discourse formations. But at the end of issue 4, the team decides, "It's time Planetary stopped watching things and started doing things" (1:4:22). *Planetary* does not merely unearth discourse formations anymore, but starts connecting their statements into a narrative, developing a larger explanatory frame.

The history of popular fiction corresponds to the biography of Elijah Snow in *Planetary*. He is one of the team's members, born on 1 January 1900 and, after a serious case of memory loss, he has to rely on his teammates to help him uncover what happened during "his" century. As the team learns about Snow's past and the secret history of 20th-century fiction, the events begin to fall into place, and a narrative causality and coherence develops between what has been identified as statements and discourse formations.

Snow's life is projected onto the history of popular fiction in the 20th century. Early on, he raids a lair of Frankensteinian monsters and kills Dracula. Later, he explores Africa, where he meets Blackstock, the Tarzan character, and in the 1960s he befriends John Stone, a suave MI6 agent who represents James Bond. Through these projections and their combination into a story structure, *Planetary* employs a strategy similar to the classical master narrative in its retelling of the history of 20th century popular fiction.

The series however does not aim for a mythical naturalness and disinterestedness in the master narrative. On the contrary, the archaeological analysis, the detection of fictions and discursive constructions, are the explicit modus operandi of the *Planetary* team. Elijah Snow has been an apprentice to Sherlock Holmes because he wants "to know secrets" (3:13:21). "The Four" are the villains of the series, placing "memory blocks" in Snow's mind to prevent him from questioning, "to prevent [him] from being quite so useful" (2:12:17). In *Planetary*, Elijah's memory loss functions to prevent him from seeing beyond the obvious, from uncovering the myth, from exposing facts as fiction. As Elijah regains his epistemological powers, he can "perceive [...] scaffold" and "then it stopped being elegant and flawless" (2:11:20).

The project of postmodern theory, the exposure of apparent facts as mere fictions, whether they are modern myths or master narratives, becomes *Planetary's* central plot device. The series integrates Foucault's archaeological method into its storytelling. It turns what seemed transparent and "purged of all anthropologism" back into a subjective endeavor (Foucault 1972, 16). *Planetary* tells a master narrative of 20th century popular culture not simply by projecting layers of meaning onto each other and ordering its elements into a story structure, providing narrative causality and coherence, but also by including central critical reflections into its story. It may be characterized, paradoxically but convincingly, as a master narrative after postmodernism.

Conclusion

Planetary is a comic *about* the superhero genre. Begun in 1998 (and, as of this writing, still not concluded), the series can look back on a long line of superhero comics that capitalized on the critical achievements of postmodernism. "[T]here was a time when most superhero comics seemed to be about superheroes," Ellis says and, indeed, self-reflexivity has been a major trait of the genre since the late 1980s (qtd. in Butcher).

But *Planetary* is different from most of these comics because it does not simply expose the modern myth of the superhero as a mere construction, nor does it simply identify facts as fiction. Ellis sets out to "do something that actually went deeper into the sub-genre, exposed [its] roots and showed [its] branches" (qtd. in Butcher). With *Planetary*, he connects the superheroes to their "roots" in Victorian entertainment literature and 1930s pulp novels, revealing its "branches" with his excursions into the British comics scene of the 1980s and the popular cultures of Asia. These roots and branches are not only *shown* to be important contexts for the superheroes: they are in fact an integral part of the story.

Planetary combines them into the master narrative of 20th century popular fiction it tells. Yet the series does not double back behind the critical achievements of postmodern thinking by telling an old-fashioned master narrative, which presents fictions as fact. It also includes Foucault's archaeological method as its central metaphor and thematises the epistemological breakthrough of questioning the surface and perceiving the actual scaffold beneath through the experiences of Elijah Snow. Postmodernism's hostility towards coherent narrative structures, which it rejects as totalizing and simplifying the complexity of reality, is addressed, yet the series does not succumb to such hostility. *Planetary* tells a superhero tale that is both self-reflexive and captivating. Being a superhero comic *about* superhero comics, it therefore not only returns to the genre's roots and branches, but as Alan Moore puts it in his introduction to the series, *Planetary* positively paves "a way into whatever awaits in the comic field's future."

Notes

1. In an interview with Mindjack <http://www.mindjack.com/interviews/ellis.html>
2. See Brooker for an extensive cultural history of the character
3. Since 1972, when Eco wrote his essay, the superhero comics have developed more sophisticated techniques than simple circular narrative structures to deal with such problems of continuity, like the multiverse concept addressed in *Crisis on Infinite Earth*s or parallel worlds as in DC's *Elseworlds* series or Marvel's *What If....*
4. Most of the Silver Age characters are "science heroes": Bruce Danner from *The Hulk* is a researcher, Peter Parker from *Spider-Man* is a science prodigy, both Charles Xavier and Magneto from *X-Men* are described as scientific geniuses.
5. See Hayden White's *Metahistory* for a discussion of narrative patterns in history writing.

PART FIVE

Drawing History: Nonfiction in Comics

Reconsidering Comics Journalism

Information and Experience in Joe Sacco's Palestine

BENJAMIN WOO

> But his comics about Palestine furnish his readers with a long enough sojourn among a people whose suffering and unjust fate have been scanted for far too long and with too little humanitarian and political attention. Sacco's art has the power to detain us, to keep us from impatiently wandering off in order to follow a catch-phrase or a lamentably predictable narrative of triumph and fulfillment. And this is perhaps the greatest of his achievements.
>
> — Edward Said (vii)

Joe Sacco is something of an oddity among today's "graphic novelists." His colleague, the cartoonist Seth, puts it simply: "He's definitely an oddball cartoonist, because he has very excellent social skills" (qtd. in McGrath, 46). But Sacco has also distinguished himself through the remarkable comics he has produced. In a field of cultural production that is dominated, at one end, by science-fantasy escapism and, at the other, by self-indulgent navel-gazing, Sacco's comics stand out, not simply for their technical proficiency but also for their agenda of social advocacy. In books such as *Palestine*, *Safe Area Gorazde*, *The Fixer*, and *War's End*, Sacco uses comics to report on the experiences of the victims of conflict and war with a rare depth, sensitivity, and sense of context.

Sacco uses the term "comics journalism" to describe this particular kind of non-fiction comic book. However, to conceptualize comics journalism *qua* journalism is to subject it to a whole set of predetermined expectations and standards and, as I hope to demonstrate below, these preconceptions do not always sit comfortably with the work itself. In this essay I will explore some of the issues raised by the non-fiction graphic novel and interrogate the concept of comics journalism. In order to do this, I appeal to another model of non-fiction representation: the documentary film. By comparing and contrasting journalism and documentary, I aim to develop an ideal-typical distinction between the reporting of information and the communication of experience, which is ultimately rooted in the work of critical theorist Walter Benjamin. I will then use examples from *Palestine* to situate Sacco on the continuum between information and experience.

Portrait of the Artist as a Cartoon Genius

Sacco was born in Malta in 1960. According to Monica Marshall's biography and retrospective, stories of his parents' experiences during World War II — Malta, then part of the British empire, was regularly bombed by Axis forces — provoked his early and lasting interest in stories of war and occupation. Sacco holds a degree in journalism from the University of Oregon and had originally desired to pursue a career as a foreign correspondent, inspired and influenced by the narrative journalism of writers such as Michael Herr, George Orwell, and Hunter S. Thompson (Marshall, 22–23). Given this background, the serious content of his best-known comics should be no surprise. Yet his earliest published pieces belong squarely in the tradition of satirical and autobiographical cartooning that grew out of the American underground comix movement. The collection *Notes from a Defeatist* opens with a story called "Cartoon Genius," in which Sacco gives us a bitingly self-deprecating portrait of his life as an impoverished cartoonist. Over the course of the story, he vacillates between counter-cultural celebrations of artistic autonomy and an almost manic willingness to sell out for dental insurance and a steak dinner. Sacco also suggests that his education has prepared him poorly for life in the "real world." So how does he get from stories about subsisting on Campbell's tomato soup to the very real world of the Palestinian Occupied Territories and the fractured states of former Yugoslavia?

Sacco says his artistic practice "developed organically, based on the fact that [he] was a cartoonist and [...] studied journalism" (Sacco, personal interview). However, we can see the roots of his method in earlier stories like "In the Company of Long Hair," "More Women, More Children, More Quickly," and "How I Loved the War."[1] Despite representing a very different kind of non-fiction storytelling than his later work, these stories obviously belong to the same corpus of texts and are important points of inflection in Sacco's career. Taken together, Sacco's pre-comics-journalism stories demonstrate an artistic trajectory, over the course of which Sacco increasingly applied the techniques and approaches of autobiographical cartooning to the lives of others and to ever more serious subjects. When Sacco began to combine his cartooning hobby with his professional interest in stories of conflict, he conceptualized this simply as journalism being practiced within a different medium. However, specific characteristics of the comics medium and the graphic novel format and particular decisions Sacco made in the execution of *Palestine* suggest that this is, at the very least, not journalism as usual.

Understanding Non-fiction Comics

In a recent book on non-fiction or "factual" television, Annette Hill describes the contemporary media-scape as "a space where familiar factual genres such as news, or documentary, take on properties common to other genres. It's a place where reality TV runs wild, crossing over into fiction and non-fiction territories, taking genre experimentation to the limit" (Hill, 1). This is arguably also the case for the burgeoning field of graphic novels which, despite its name, has been dominated by works of non-fiction. In graphic novels, autobiography and memoir rub shoulders with the slice-of-life short story, biography, history, and travelogue. On television, this presents a problem to audiences and citizens who rely on the various kinds of non-fiction representations to co-ordinate social action and, perhaps more importantly, meaningfully understand their place in the social totality. According to Hill, "[w]atching factual television [...] can feel like being trapped between fact and fiction [...]. Surrounded by factual programmes, viewers have to deal with the various ways programmes represent reality" (ibid., 2). It is my contention that, *mutatis mutandis*, the same basic problem pertains to comics and graphic novels.

Genre and Non-fiction

While it would perhaps be simpler to talk about them solely on the terms defined by their practitioners, genres are largely a function of audiences' expectations of individual works and their relationships to larger groups of somehow similar works. This is particularly true once we remember that cultural producers are themselves part of the audience and that their understanding of the tastes and desires of consumers is always partially grounded in their own experience as consumers. Thus, a genre is more or less the codification of a certain competency — one which shapes the individual objects of its knowledge even as it is itself shaped by the cumulative encounters between audience and text. As Steve Neale writes:

> Genres do not only consist of films: they consist also, and equally, of specific systems of expectation and hypothesis that spectators bring with them to the cinema and that interact with films themselves during the course of the viewing process. These systems provide spectators with a means of recognition and understanding. They help render films, and the elements within them, intelligible and therefore explicable [Neale, 158].

Such expectations may include formal and textual conventions associated with the genre as well as the institutional contexts surrounding production, distribution, and consumption of the work in question. However, Neale's most salient point is that these expectations always invoke generic regimes of verisimilitude, "various systems of plausibility, motivation, justification, and belief," that help the audience make sense of the texts that make up a generic corpus (Neale, 158). For example, in the context of a classical Hollywood musical, it does not seem "unrealistic" for the characters to break into song, and in the context of a science–fiction novel, the laws of physics can be stretched in ways that do not necessarily break the audience's suspension of disbelief. At the same time, audience expectations will be frustrated if the protagonists of a romantic comedy do not end the film living happily ever after, though divorce rates suggest that this may not be particularly "realistic" either. A genre's regime of verisimilitude helps the viewer or reader to define realism for a given work or set of works; however, non-fiction works are less concerned with real*ism* than with the real itself.

My intention is not to endorse a naïve epistemology of direct access to the real. Whether posited in the form of a poststructuralist death of the subject, a postmodernist disappearance of the referent, or good, old-fashioned scepticism, potent critiques have made such a position untenable. Yet non-fiction works still present themselves as representing reality. No matter how we might conceive the actual relationship between a representation and "reality," an epistemological wager is part of the code that governs the reception of non–fiction genres: the viewer or reader expects that a work purporting to be non-fiction will be true. The challenge for the author of such a work is to encode it with recognizable signifiers of truthfulness in order that the audience might believe in it. To put it another way, non–fiction genres rely on regimes of *authenticity* rather than verisimilitude.

For most people, journalism is the paradigmatic form of non–fiction representation, and its regime of authenticity is the most familiar. But, as the saying goes, familiarity may breed contempt. In a contemporary journalism textbook, Bill Kovach and Tom Rosenstiel attempt to defend journalism from public cynicism with a fresh investigation of its principles. The authors develop a set of best practices that constitutes a journalistic response to the problem of authenticity. However, this must be understood as the product of an effort to legitimate journalism as an institution (and industry). Thus, they express a vision of what journalism ought to be rather than an assessment of what it is in practice. But this in itself provides insight into the conflict between journalism's official discourse and the public's expectations of the news media.

The meaning of objectivity is the most significant battleground in this conflict, for it remains the most powerful value shaping popular perceptions of journalism. Yet, according to Kovach and Rosenstiel, "[t]he concept of objectivity has been so mangled it now is usually used to describe the very problem it was conceived to correct" (Kovach and Rosenstiel, 13). The popular understanding of objectivity comprises concepts such as balance, neutrality, and impartiality. But the authors argue that, as originally formulated, journalistic objectivity resided not in the practitioner but rather in the "discipline of verification," which is the "essence" of the journalistic method (ibid., 71). A journalist need not fret over his or her personal biases so long as the method is followed correctly. Thus, journalism guarantees authenticity through the appeal to a quasi-scientific methodology for verifying evidence. This guarantee is encoded in various ways in journalistic texts, such as an "impartial" writing style, the inclusion of photographic evidence, and the use of authoritative expert sources.

However, the re-signification of journalistic objectivity as a question of method elides the ideological labor that is inherent in any representation, and particularly in those that claim transparently to reveal reality. The contradictions between the representations journalists construct and the lived experience of the audience is the source of the public cynicism that so unnerves Kovach and Rosenstiel. Thus, even constituencies that directly oppose one another can simultaneously perceive the news media as biased against themselves. One might suggest that this proves the effectiveness of the journalistic method — if none of the ideologues are satisfied, then the news media must be doing something right. But journalism's ideal is supposed to be a phronetic one.[2] It is supposed to provide a "practical or functional form of the truth [...] by which we can operate day to day" (ibid., 42). If journalism is not enabling diverse groups to understand one another and their (social) world, is there a kind of representation that can?

As I have suggested above, another prominent form of non-fiction representation is the documentary. What distinguishes documentary films is perhaps less clear to lay and professional critics alike. Documentary and journalism have had an intimate, but surprisingly under-theorized, relationship over the course of their respective histories. Indeed, a great deal of documentary production takes place under the auspices of television news and current affairs programming, and the American direct cinema movement, which held a dominant position in the field during the post-war period, drew heavily on a quasi-journalistic conception of objective representation. But, according to Stella Bruzzi, "virtually the entire post-*vérité* history of non-fiction film can be seen as a reaction against its ethos of transparency and unbiased observation" (Bruzzi, 6). In working through this reaction, documentary filmmakers and theorists have attempted to construct distinct regimes of authenticity for this genre of non-fiction.

While documentary, like journalism, is a form of evidentiary representation — i.e. a record of people and events — it has a different relationship to this evidentiary function. As Bill Nichols writes, "[t]o remind viewers of the construction of the reality we behold, of the creative element in John Grierson's famous definition of documentary as 'the creative treatment of actuality' undercuts the very claim to truth and authenticity on which the documentary depends" (Grierson, 24). The documentary tradition has attempted to forge new articulations of "complex documentary truth" and authenticity, "arising from an insurmountable compromise between subject and recording, suggesting in turn that it is this very juncture between reality and filmmaker that is the heart of any documentary" (Bruzzi, 6). On this view, the truth of a recording seems to become more authentic the more it acknowledges the fact of its own recording. The contemporary documentarian may make use of a wide range of representational modes in order to document — if not strictly to reproduce — the experiences of his or her subjects.[3] All the above suggests a markedly different approach to representing reality than the "scientific" reporting of mainstream journalism.

Information and Experience: Two Ideal Types

I would suggest that the divergent regimes of authenticity embodied in mainstream journalism and the documentary tradition are reflective of a more fundamental distinction. Comparing and contrasting the two allows us to abstract from them a pair of ideal types. Max Weber is the writer most closely associated with this methodology. It is imperative to understand that ideal types are not strictly empirical categories but analytical ones. Their purpose is not to describe reality but "to give unambiguous means of expression to such a description" (Weber, 90). Ideal types are constructed as means for the interpretation and judgment of actually existing cases. Thus, the ideal-typical distinction between the relaying of information and the communication of experience will allow us to analyze the works that actually fall at various points on the continuum between them more adequately.

I have drawn my constructs from the work of Walter Benjamin — in particular, his essay "The Storyteller: Reflections on the Work of Nikolai Leskov." In "The Storyteller," a companion to his more famous essay, "The Work of Art in the Age of Mechanical Reproduction," Benjamin describes the disappearance of traditional storytelling as the social conditions that made it possible are eroded by capitalism. In this way, oral communication and literature follow the same trajectory as visual art in the age of its "technical reproducibility," becoming ossified in the commodity form ("Work of Art," 223).[4] The story has been displaced by information, the storyteller by the press. However, as Pericles Lewis notes, "[t]he modern age of *The Storyteller* resembles that of the *Artwork* essays in its essential alienation, but Benjamin is [...] kinder to the novelist and the novel-reader than to the artist and the aesthete" (ibid. 225). To account for this discrepancy, Lewis argues that the collapse of artwork's autonomy involves a shift from a focus on the art object itself— particularly as an object of devotion or contemplation — to the capacity of such objects to act as media of communication.[5] The story is a key concept for Benjamin precisely because it was a pre-modern and pre-capitalist example of the communicative function of culture, which Benjamin hoped to recover through the *refunctioning* of cultural (re)production.[6]

The story is "an artisan form of communication" that had its source in experience that was "passed on from mouth to mouth," and "the storyteller is a man who has counsel for his readers" ("Storyteller," 91, 86). In contrast, information is a fetishized form of communication, interpreting value-laden knowledge produced by subjects as if it were objective fact. Benjamin holds the story separate from information because the former served to communicate experience [*Erfahrung*], whereas the latter reports only the immediate impressions of the lived moment [*Erlebnis*][7]: "Because of this, [information] proves incompatible with the spirit of storytelling. If the art of storytelling has become rare, the dissemination of information has had a decisive share in this state of affairs" (ibid. 89). Information, like journalism, is a form of representation that strives to transmit the real as objectively and transparently as possible, while the communication of experience is based on a model of inter-subjective understanding. The latter serves not only to inform but also to constitute new collectivities out of its audiences on the basis of the experience that they now share (albeit in a mediated form). The sociality and solidarity produced in this way is of the utmost political and cultural significance. It is this aspect of Sacco's work that so impressed Edward Said:

> Nowhere does Sacco come closer to the existential lived reality of the average Palestinian than in his depiction of life in Gaza, the national Inferno [...]. Joe the character is there sympathetically to understand and to try to experience not only why Gaza is so representative a place in its hopelessly overcrowded and yet rootless spaces of Palestinian dispossession, but also to affirm that it is there, and must somehow be accounted for in human terms, in the narrative sequences with which any reader can identify [Said, vii].

Having traveled and returned to share his experience, Sacco is a rare example of a storyteller in Benjamin's sense. In the next section, I will attempt to account for this quality through an analysis of Sacco's best-known graphic novel, *Palestine*.

Return to Palestine

I do not consider *Palestine* a work of journalism. For one thing, it was produced without the support of a news agency and released by a publisher of alternative and pornographic comic books. For another, Sacco has effectively abandoned the traditional indices of newsworthiness: comics are labor-intensive and slow to produce; chapters are organized thematically rather than chronologically; he meets no "notable" people; and there is, sadly, nothing novel about injustice and grinding deprivation. As Said writes, "[t]he unhurried pace and the absence of a goal in his wanderings emphasizes that he is neither a journalist in search of a story nor an expert trying to nail down the facts in order to produce a policy. Joe is there to be in Palestine, and only that" (Said, vi–vii). My intention is not to disparage Sacco's exceptional graphic novel, but to clarify the regime of authenticity that pertains to so-called comics journalism. In abandoning the constraints of "scientific reporting," Joe Sacco has gained the ability to share his own experiences and those of his subjects with clarity and force.

One of the most powerful sequences in *Palestine* is called "Moderate Pressure: Part 2" (Sacco, 102–113). While one of his daughters sleeps in his arms, a man named Ghassan tells Sacco the story of his detainment by Israeli authorities (it is unclear whether they are police or military) on suspicion of belonging to an illegal organization. Despite a lack of evidence, a succession of judges extends custody: he is ultimately held for nineteen days without charge. In this time, he is interrogated, beaten, and tightly bound in painful positions. Before long, Ghassan, hooded and tied to a chair, begins to hallucinate: "My daughter is dead.... My brother is sitting next to me.... My brother is dead.... My father is dead.... My uncle is dead.... My mother is sick. She is in the hospital.... My mother is arrested" (ibid., 109). These hallucinations are vividly illustrated by Sacco. In each case, Ghassan's loved ones appear next to him: his daughter lying face-down on the floor of his cell, his father and uncle wrapped in shrouds, his mother lying in a hospital bed, and so on. The quoted text is contained in a series of irregularly shaped bubbles. They are distinct from Ghassan's narration, which is restricted to rectilinear captions and set off with quotation marks. Though they superficially resemble thought balloons, they do not emanate from Ghassan or any other character in frame, and Sacco does not generally use this device in *Palestine*.[8] Presented in a straightforward, understated manner, these words, like the images they accompany, take on a kind of "phantom" reality. They are unreal, and yet they *are*.

The effect here is extraordinary, but this sequence is only one example of Sacco's use of this formal trick, whereby authentic but unrepresentable experiences are matter-of-factly inserted into the diegesis. Sacco does not attempt to corroborate Ghassan's case; he simply shows what he has been told, and, in doing so, gives a solidity to his respondent's story. In some cases, verification would be impossible. Many of the injustices Sacco relates go unrecorded or are generic enough to make appeals to official documents all but meaningless. For example, depictions of the prison, Ansar III, are based on descriptions and maps drawn by former inmates because Sacco was not permitted to go there and take reference photographs.[9] The prison appears on the page instead as it was experienced by those who knew it best, and those experiences are made real by the text — or, at least, as real as anything else we have been shown (Sacco 2007, 82–92). Elsewhere, Sacco performs the same semiotic manoeuvre on a morbid Palestinian joke that involves a Shin Bet agent attempting violently to coerce a donkey into admitting it is a rabbit (ibid. 96).[10] In this case, a joke, which has no empirical truth content whatsoever but gives insight into an aspect of life in the Occupied Territories, is transformed into an event through its presentation to the reader, who is made a witness by the text.

These examples could potentially break the pact of trust established between author and audience by exposing the epistemological underpinnings of the work. That is, they remind us that *Palestine* is not a document of events but a deliberate re-creation after the fact.[11] If non-fictional representation is truly evidentiary in nature, then much of *Palestine*'s evidence is inadmissible as hearsay. And yet, reading *Palestine*, one does not have the experience of imminent crisis. Rather, the above examples add layers of depth to Sacco's reportage. This dynamic is one of the opportunities created (but not necessarily determined) by specific properties of the medium.

While all autobiographical representation has a performative dimension, Charles Hatfield writes that "[s]uch tendencies become doubly obvious in the cartoon world of comics, in which the intimacy of an articulated first-person narrative may mix with the alienating graphic excess of caricature" (Hatfield, 114). I would, however, push this point beyond the "alienating" effect of a cartoon aesthetic to the basic semiology of the comic book. Because the images in a graphic novel are drawn rather than photographed, their iconic signification is not accompanied by an indexical relationship to the referent, as it is in live-action television and cinema. The subject of a photographic image must have existed in reality if it was present to be photographed. Thus, non-fiction comics are inescapably hyperreal, for, although they maintain a truth claim, they do not provide any access to the referent outside of the system of simulacra contained on the page. This is not to say that comics are entirely non-indexical, however, as Philippe Marion points out:

> Beyond the very distinction of narration and monstration, the reader-spectator of the comics is invited to achieve a coincidence of his gaze and the creative movement of the graphiateur [the cartoonist's subject position]; it is only by acknowledging and identifying the graphic trace or index of the artist that the reader can fully understand the message of the work. From this viewpoint, graphiation is eminently self-reflexive and autoreferential [qtd. in Baetens, 149].

Therefore, while comics do not have a necessary logical relationship to objective reality, they do have such a relationship to the subjectivity of the artist: a drawn image implies that someone drew it. And Sacco has drawn everything, so the entire diegesis is mediated through and indexed to his own subjectivity. He thus sutures the gap between subject and object, between knowledge of a thing and the thing in itself, not by the eradication of the subjective (or the imposition of an objective method, which amounts to the same thing) but by absorbing the objective into the subjective and making the process of mediation self-evident. To quote Benjamin once more: "Thus traces of the storyteller cling to the story the way the handprints of the potter cling to the clay vessel" ("Storyteller," 92). Sacco never promises or hides behind a false sense of immediacy, allowing the play of subjectivity to reach the audience on an experiential and affective level.

"Subjectivity" has become comics journalism's catch-phrase. Making the "case" for the genre in *Columbia Journalism Review*, Kristian Williams writes that "its inherent subjectivity contrasts sharply with the newsroom's dispassionate prose" (Williams, 52). Williams ascribes this effect to comics' blending of word and image and its narrative qualities. As my brief foray into semiology has demonstrated, these characteristics have something to do with the impression of subjectivity created by comics journalism. However, the more fundamental break is caused by what one *does* with this form rather than its "inherent" qualities. One can certainly imagine a piece of comics journalism that functions according to the ideal type of information. Furthermore, where the news media have experimented with comics journalism, they have largely restricted it to covering "soft" subjects — the ghetto of "cultural coverage and human-interest stories"—where a certain degree of subjectivity has always been permitted, so long as it does not threaten to contaminate "hard" news (ibid., 53). Responding to Williams's essay, Amy Kiste Nyberg points to the commonalities between comics journalism and forms of narrative journalism. However, Nyberg also notes that this style of reporting "has not taken root in daily journalism" (Nyberg, 108). Indeed, comics journalism and narrative journalism both face an uphill battle for acceptance for the same reason: they resist the pragmatics of the mainstream press. Put simply, journalism, in its institutional form, is rationalized for the relaying of information.

Given the dominance of the discourses of objectivity and verification in the journalistic field, I maintain that the label "comics journalism" is misleading. Moreover, it may inadvertently subject works that serve to communicate experience to the standards and expectations that more properly pertain to "informative" modes of representation. *Palestine* is not informative, in that it does not teach or relay information *per se*, but that does not mean that we do not learn from it. I have argued that we learn the most from Sacco precisely when he strays from objective and strictly verifiable facts to communicate the experience of his subjects to us. Most of *Palestine*'s readers will never see Israel or the Occupied Territories for themselves. We must make do with what the news media give us. But thanks to Sacco and other cultural producers who prioritize experience over information, we may have a better chance of making sense of the stream of events that fills our newspapers and television sets.

Notes

1. All three are collected in *Notes from a Defeatist*.
2. On the intellectual virtue of *phronesis* and its relation to social analysis, see Flyvbjerg.
3. Cf. Nichols, 99–138.
4. "Technical" or "technological" reproducibility is a more literal translation of Benjamin's original German phrase, *technischen Reproduzierbarkeit,* which is frequently translated as "mechanical reproduction."
5. Lewis's own distinction between objectifying and communicative action is based on the work of Seyla Benhabib and Jürgen Habermas.
6. Cf. Benjamin, "The Author as Producer."
7. On the concepts of *Erfahrung* and *Erlebnis* and Benjamin's theory of experience, see Jay.

8. Sacco does not impute thoughts or motivations to his subjects, only depicting what they do or say — presumably, this is a legacy of his journalistic training. His own commentary on events is presented in captions rather than thought balloons.

9. See Sacco, *Palestine* xxii.

10. Shin Bet is Israel's internal intelligence service.

11. Re-creation is a form of documentation that is anathema to journalistic norms, but common in documentary filmmaking.

13

Comics, Trauma and Cultural Memory(ies) of 9/11

CHRISTOPHE DONY *AND*
CAROLINE VAN LINTHOUT

Historical (re)construction inevitably poses the problem of representation. In this essay, the authors inquire how, and to what extent, the comics medium represents the historical/cultural memory(ies) of the traumatic events of 9/11, asking how and why comics may be considered a source of memory.

In postmodern society, commemorative art, such as literature, poetry, cinema, sculpture and architecture, has made up for the gradual loss of historicity. The awareness of this loss has brought about a growing interest in historical memory, which has inevitably raised concerns about the appropriate language or medium to communicate memory. The accuracy and faithfulness of artistic representations of historical memory has been theorized by historians, sociologists and philosophers alike, within the dialectic "event/code" (Wagner Pacifici, 304). This dialectic, central to the memory debate, raises the issue of which cultural encodings (memorials, fictional narratives, movies, sculptures) best represent and commemorate traumatic cultural events, considering "the moral, political and aesthetic imperative[s]"entailed in the representation of trauma (ibid.).

From within this code/event framework, we would like to reflect on two questions concerning the appropriateness of the comics medium to convey the traumatic historical/cultural memory(ies) of 9/11. First, is comics an adequate medium for bearing witness to the past? In other words, in applying Pierre Nora's idea of *lieu de mémoire* [site of memory] to selected comics texts, we ask whether or not comics are appropriate cultural encodings that may be considered memorials or, to use Nora's concept, as "objects of memory"? The second question we want to raise is whether or not the comics medium, in terms of form and structure, can appropriately and adequately convey the memory of a traumatic experience. Or else, do the specific structural and aesthetic features of the medium give comics a privileged status when it comes to render the memory(ies) of 9/11?

Comics as "Objects of Memory"

According to Nora in his book *Realms of Memory*, a site of memory is anything that contains the memory of a community: an individual, an object, a place (15). Nora goes on to add that these sites of memory, or objects of memory, have no real referent. Rather, they are their own referent (Nora, 42– 43). In that sense, Nora's definition suggests that, unlike the object of history that belongs to a particular historical moment, both in content and form, the object of memory escapes history itself and embodies the past. In other words, Nora argues that the form of the site of memory is "areferential": it cannot be reclaimed by history, whereas its contents refer to history. Within Nora's framework, we would like to argue that our corpus of research, namely a wide array of mainstream 9/11–related comics, makes up a site of memory and therefore merits close attention.

According to Nora's claim, comics belong in the category of objects of history because they are rooted in current events and thus pertain to history. Indeed, this major characteristic of comics enables them to provide an overview of the mentality of a society at a specific moment in history, and to be first-hand signs of the historical and cultural reality in which they were created. However, some comic books, like the ones under scrutiny in this essay, are also, and above all, objects or sites of memory. Nora explains that memory appears in more and more various institutional shapes, so that mainstream comic books, despite their populist nature, can rightly be considered to be memorials of a past event and to bear witness to a traumatic historical/cultural reality. They are created to incarnate history and shape a collective memory in the same way as any other film, museum, novel or monument does.

The comics under study, including Art Spiegelman's *In the Shadow of No Towers* and narratives from the comics compendia *Emergency Relief* and *9/11: Artists Respond*, can all be regarded as memorials to the tragic events of September 11, 2001. Created shortly after 9/11, they all contain fictional and personal accounts, and interpretations of the events, and they all tell the (hi)story of a past that now only exists in memory and in artistic or other mediated forms. In fact, because of their populist and commercial nature, comics act as objects of mass culture and play an important role in the production of collective memory due to their mass appeal.

Time, Space and Memory: The Comics Medium and Traumatic Memory

Comics are therefore capable of bearing witness to the past and of being "objects of memory." But can a comic book be considered an appropriate form to convey the memory(ies) of a traumatic experience? Because of their mass appeal, common-sense logic would dictate that comics cannot, aesthetically speaking, represent the "unrepresentable." However, we want to show that it is possible to draw interesting parallels between the breakdown and layout of comics and the structures of traumatic memory. Indeed, both comics and memory and, more specifically, traumatic memory, can be understood in terms of fragments and totality because they construct a whole (a narrative or story) by assembling multiple parts (such as panels, testimonies, or memories). Moreover, both the comics medium and traumatic events shatter notions of time and space as they are perceived under "normal" conditions.

Scholars do not agree on a definition of the term "comics," which we use as a generic term. However, they generally agree on Will Eisner's famous term, "sequential art." This particular appellation suggests that one of the intrinsic characteristics of the medium is its multi-episodic format, which uses static panels arranged in a specific order to convey a narrative. This method is tremendously interesting in the sense that it allows the reader to experience time spatially and, therefore, to consider movement and duration visually, while in "reality" time is more illusory because perceived through "the memory of experience" as Will Eisner has argued (Eisner, 38).

Along with the fragmentation of time and space, the comics medium can also associate parts or fragments (panels) in order to construct a whole narrative or page. French theoretician, analyst, and comics writer Benoit Peeters insists on the fragmentary nature of the panel as it inscribes itself within a whole, i.e. the plate, or even the book (Peeters 1998, 29–31).[1] The different narrative units of the comic book can actually be considered to be both independent as well as parts of a larger unit. Scott McCloud puts it simply as follows:

All of us perceive the world as a whole through the experience of our sense. Yet, our senses can only reveal a world that is fragmented and incomplete. Even the most wildly travelled mind can only see so much of the world in the course of a life. Our perception of "reality" is an act of *faith*, based on mere fragments. [...] This phenomenon of observing the parts but perceiving the whole has a name. It's called closure [McCloud 1994, 62–63].

This logic of seeing the part(s) as standing for the whole applies as much to the breakdown/layout of comics as to the structures of traumatic memory. Both are indeed built up from fragments, and both shatter the notions of time and space. In discussing the traumatic events of 9/11, many commentators claimed that "time was broken" and that *nothing would ever be the same again*, which resulted in the now widely-spread notions surrounding pre– and post– 9/11 eras (Campbell, 1–9). According to Campbell, the struggle for the ordering of things "into a sequence that allows understanding [...] is emblematic of trauma" (1). In addition, space(s) previously void of any particular significance become "sites of memory," to use Nora's terms, which can constantly engender new meanings. This is the case with the location where the WTC formerly stood, now known as Ground Zero — a site of pilgrimage for New Yorkers and tourists alike (Lentricchia and McAuliffe, 359). Within this collapse of the notions of time and space, the memory of the traumatic event can only be fragmentary, given that the act of remembering itself implies fragmentation. As Lock contends, "to *re-member* something is to perform the act of re-assembling its members, thus stressing the importance to the memory process of creative reconstruction" (Lock, 112). In other words: the process of remembrance is partial and incomplete as well as creative because it consists in the juxtaposition of parts in order to (re)construct a coherent whole.

Spiegelman's In the Shadow of No Towers *and Traumatic Memory(ies)*

In this brief theoretical overview, we have shown that the relationship between fragmentation in comics and memory lends the comics medium an advantage over other media in the representation of the unrepresentable. This is because the structural features of comics, such as sequentiality and fragmentation, lend themselves particularly well to the fragmented structures of memory and, more specifically, to the structures of traumatic memory.

In order to illustrate this claim, let us introduce Art Spiegelman and his book *In the Shadow of No Towers* (2004) as our first example of how comics narrate memory. Spiegelman is a Jewish-American cartoonist and comic book author, best known for his graphic novels *Maus I* (1984) and *Maus II* (1991). In both volumes, Spiegelman tackles the difficult and traumatic subject matter of the Holocaust in the form of graphic memoirs that tell the history of his parents during World War II, especially during their internment at Auschwitz. In typically postmodern fashion, Spiegelman uses the meta-fictional device of self-reflexively appearing in his own narrative. This technique highlights the fictionality or artificiality of the work, as a means of undermining any illusion of authenticity which he, as someone who did not experience these events, may not claim. Hence, Spiegelman himself is presented as a character who expresses his struggle while writing and drawing his father's memories of the Holocaust. And in both volumes, sections about his complex relationship with his father, set in the present day, regularly interrupt the telling of his father's memories, thus demonstrating the tension between history and memory as well as the tension between personal and official historical accounts.

In the Shadow of No Towers, a *comix* testimony of Spiegelman's own experience of 9/11 in Lower Manhattan, incorporates meta-fictional devices to mirror his hesitations and difficulties in representing his traumatic experience of 9/11[2]. In addition, he renders the plurality of feelings and perspectives he went through by means of his original use of the inherently fragmentary comics medium. In this work, Spiegelman parts company with the traditional pattern of comic books, which involves a conventional reading from left to right and from top to bottom. Instead he uses the technique of *collage*, juxtaposing fragmentary thoughts and memories in different styles. As Benjamin Noys puts it, "one formal strategy that Spiegelman uses is a radical break with the traditional comic book arrangement of its images into a series of 'boxes' in a grid" (Noys, 367). While the grid format is still omnipresent in *Maus*, *In The Shadow of No Towers*, puts it "into play with other arrangements of images that cut across and disrupt this structure" (ibid.). While this technique communicates the chaos that followed the events of 9/11, it also demonstrates Spiegelman's ability to reflect on mnemonic structures and to adequately adapt them into comics.

Each plate in the text is made up of various strips and panels, resulting in the coexistence of several narrative/memories/fragments on the same page, all of which vary in size and style. The eclectic style and layout of the book makes any reading difficult, any general understanding of a page at first glance seemingly impossible without affecting its meaning. Likewise, it is virtually impossible to develop full understanding of a traumatic experience — which by definition exceeds experience — within a single memory, thought or testimony.

An excerpt from the middle of page two of *In the Shadow of No Towers* exemplifies this stylistic heterogeneity, which gives rise to the difficulty in finding a direction for reading, as well as the fragmentary structure of pages throughout the book. In this excerpt, one can distinguish three overlapping narratives or fragments, each in a different style. On the left, Spiegelman illustrates his anxiety about the political conflict between the U.S. and Al Qaeda as symptomatic for individuals suffering from Post-Traumatic-Stress Disorder. In the center panel, Spiegelman addresses the issue of self-representation and his difficulty in defining his identity in the aftermath of 9/11. In both these narratives, Spiegelman's self-representation is an intertextual reference to his character in *Maus*. This metafictional device establishes continuity between the traumatic events of 9/11 and the Holocaust and problematizes the issue of representability. On the right, Spiegelman depicts his personal experience of 9/11 in Lower Manhattan, by showing himself and his wife on the street when the planes hit the Twin Towers. As he and his wife realize that their daughter Nadja "had just started high school at the foot of the towers three days before," Spiegelman and his wife are transformed into the twins from Rudolph Dirk's *Katzenjammer Kids*.

In combining various strips that account for differing thoughts, fragments of memory, mixed feelings, and interrogations of his personal traumatic experience of 9/11, Spiegelman uses the sequential and fragmented format of the comics medium in a challenging fashion so as to reflect the chaotic and partial process of remembering that is characteristic of traumatic memory. In fact, the chaotic structures of the page, and that of the whole book, shatter conventional conceptions of time and space, and are themselves representative of "the moment of collapse and disintegration" of the Twin Towers (Noys, 369). In his closing essay of *In The shadow of No Towers*, Spiegelman contends that "comics pages are architectural structures — the narrative row panels are like the stories of a building" (Spiegelman, 11). Therefore, as Noys argues, the "attack on the physical structure of these symbolic buildings ... is mirrored in [Spiegelman's] attack on the architecture of the traditional comic book page" (Noys, 367).

Pushing the Envelope: Other 9/11–Related Comics Narratives Sequencing Trauma

Other comics narratives commemorating the events of 9/11 use the fragmentary format of the medium particularly well in order to convey the author's fragmentary, partial, and incomplete recollection of the traumatic events, mixed feelings, and the plurality of perspectives that may be encountered after a traumatic psychological shock. In his narrative *Four Memories of Two*

Towers, Alex Robinson shatters the conventional grid format of the comics medium, dividing the page into four symmetrical stories, fragments, memories, perspectives, or feelings (Mason, 137). Because of the stories' symmetrical format (in terms of size and shape), readers do not know where to begin reading, or what part to interpret as the opening of the narrative. The panels containing different memories, fragments, or feelings seem to be of equal importance, and do not correlate in any sense, except perhaps in subject matter, given that they all reveal a particular story or memory of the Twin Towers.

Interestingly enough, though, these narratives seem to be articulated within a dichotomy of being versus destruction. The top and bottom panels present memories concerning the iconic shape of the Twin Towers. The top panel features one of the first appearances of the Twin Towers in film, from the movie *King Kong* (1974). The bottom panel mirrors the importance the towers had to the New York skyline, while both panels emphasize the destruction of the towers. In contrast, the left and right panels present more trivial and anecdotal memories about the Twin Towers. For example, the panel on the left depicts the memory of a joke about the WTC shared by the author and one of his ex-roommates who were incited to quip "I betcha someone's having sex in the World Trade Center right now" whenever they saw the towers (Mason, 137). The panel on the right is the memory of the author's only visit to the World Trade Center on the occasion of a dinner with his girlfriend and her father in the "fancy restaurant at the top of tower one" (ibid.). In both these panels, the Towers' existence is emphasized.

Despite this articulation of memories of the Twin Towers within the binary opposition of existence and destruction, the narrative nevertheless lacks both continuity and closure. In a traditional narrative, continuity and closure are two features that allow the reader to make sense of the story events. In this comic, however, this strategy of placing similar panels of equal importance in an unconventional order challenges the conventional grid format of the comics medium, as well as the medium's traditional notions concerning the representation of time and space. Indeed, this narrative does not convey time spatially, and in that sense, Alex Robinson uses the fragmentary format of the comics medium in a challenging fashion, so as to convey his fragmentary memories of the events of 9/11, as well as his plurality of perspectives and mixed feelings that resulted from the severe psychological shock he experienced. In addition, this comic lacks continuity and closure, and reveals the artist's incapacity to develop a coherent story out of the events of 9/11, and mirrors how the concepts of time and space collapsed after 9/11, as well as the fragmentary nature of the process of memory following a traumatic experience.

Jessica Abel's 9/11–related narrative (Mason, 13–14) also illustrates how the comics medium transmits the fragmentary process of memory of a traumatic event. While this narrative adheres to the traditional grid format of the comics medium, Jessica Abel manages to blur the distinction between the parts (the panels) and the whole (the narrative) to reflect the fragmentary memory of her traumatic experience of 9/11. The first page of the narrative portrays friends speaking with each other as they gradually disappear from the narrative in the dust that gathered after the collapsing of the Twin Towers. On the second page, dust penetrates entire panels, making the surrounding frames disappear. This effectively blurs the distinction between the parts (panels) and the whole (story) and challenges the ways in which duration and temporality are traditionally rendered in comics, i.e. through the use of panels and gutter spaces. As a result of the disappearance of the frames that typically shape and enclose panels, this comic conveys an impression of timelessness. In addition, the disintegration of the sequential structure in this comic creates a void of meaning similar to the memory of the traumatic event, which cannot be understood in any straightforward chronological fashion because of its overwhelming intensity. In essence, Abel's deliberate use of comics' structures problematizes the issues of representability that surround traumatic events.

Spiegelman's work and these other two narratives reveal that the comics medium can make use of its specific sequential format in challenging new ways, thereby mirroring the fragmentary remembering process of a traumatic event, or representing the diversity of feelings and perspectives that those who experience troubling psychological shocks often report. One last example of this kind of innovation is Frank Miller's response to 9/11 in *9/11: Artists Respond* (Levitz, 64–65). Although Miller does not use the fragmented format of the medium to reflect the fragmentary structure of traumatic memory or the multiple perspectives and feelings one can experience after trauma, he nevertheless uses panels and colors in subtle and innovative ways to suggest how trauma affects individuals repetitively, and how those who suffer from Post-Traumatic Stress Disorder constantly relive their experiences of the horror as they attempt to make sense of it.

Miller's short narrative features a clear visual and rhythmic pattern. The first two panels of the first page depict a black symbol on a white background. They also each contain a sentence containing four syllables; hence, a strong sense of repetition is induced through the visual and musical similarities on the first page of the narrative. The full-page splash panel of the second page, in contrast, clashes with this sense of repetition, given that the size of the panel is doubled and there is a striking inversion of colours, which contrasts sharply with the pattern established on the first page, namely a white symbol over a black background. In addition, the sentence on the second page contains eight syllables, doubling the rhythmic pattern of the text in the two previous panels.

These sharp visual and rhythmic contrasts between the first and second pages reveal both an echo and a crescendo effect that culminates in the last panel. The sentence "I've seen the power of faith" resonates visually through the emptiness suggested in the black background. In addition, because the rhythmic pattern is broken, this last sentence operates as the closure of the rhythmic pattern. The narrative's musicality, therefore, gains importance in volume through the growing size of the panel and the prevalence of blackness. In the last panel, the echo effect is also enhanced by the shift from a two-dimensional perspective on the first page to a three-dimensional perspective on the second page. In the two first panels, the artist has drawn flat symbols on a background, so no visual perspective is indicated. On the second page, however, the appearance of the shattered structures of the Towers seems to fall away in the black background, suggesting a three-dimensional perspective.

As a result of these visual and musical echo and crescendo effects, the reader is plunged into a nihilistic "repetitive emptiness," or a response that might encourage the reader to question patriotism ("I'm sick of flags") and religion ("I'm sick of God"). The shattered structure of the towers falling forward in the background seems to attract the reader, plunging her into the black empty space of the panel, while the last sentence, because of its musicality and rhythm, seems to echo and grow in volume in the reader's head. These visual and musical techniques reproduce the re-experiencing and reliving of the events in ways that suggest the PTSD and post-traumatic compulsion that victims experience through nightmares and flashbacks. Frank Miller's short work, although it does not rely on fragmentation to convey trauma in the comic form, is nevertheless rich and complex in terms of the structural and formal aesthetics that traditionally inform it, illustrating how the comics medium can represent an ongoing dialogue between words and images. As such, it suggests that the comics medium can mobilize its formal characteristics to adequately or appropriately relate the trauma of 9/11.

Conclusion

In this essay, we have argued that these comics confirm the notion that the medium is perhaps the most appropriate form for capturing the essence of traumatic experiences. Though trauma, by definition, imposes a barrier between the imaginable and the expressible, comics can overcome and emphasize the "unrepresentability" of the traumatic events via its fractured sequential format. However, few comics artists commemorating the events of 9/11 have used the medium's fragmentary format to convey their difficulties in remembering the traumatic events of 9/11. In fact, many artists have used plain images, single panel images, or "splash pages" to represent the events of that day.

We have shown that the examples discussed here represent trauma in new ways that carry on a tradition of remembering traumatic events through single images. The collective memory of American national traumas such as the Civil War, the Maine, or the Alamo has often been expressed in single images in a range of various media, such as popular prints, newspapers, illustrations and paintings. These images, printed in 19th-century magazines like *Harper's Weekly*, *London Illustrated News*, or Frank Leslie's *Illustrated Newspapers*, often used conventional modes representations of traumatic events that emphasized notions of heroism or relied on allegories and icons in order to support meta-narratives of American unity. We have argued that the medium has since developed the ability to represent traumatic memory in new and compelling ways that comics research is only now beginning to grasp.

Notes

1. Peeters, 29–31. Benoit Peeters has written a number of books on the comics medium. His historical work *Tintin and the World of Hergé* (1988), his extensive analysis on Hergé's album *Les Bijoux de la Castafiore*, and his theoretical work on the medium *Lire la Bande Dessinée* (1998), rank among his most famous works.

2. Spiegelman prefers the term *comix* to *comics* to describe his mixing of images and words. However, neither Spiegelman's neologism, nor the term "graphic novel" can clearly define *In the Shadow of No Towers*. The book, with its outsized format and its eclectic style and structure, challenges the boundaries of the comics genre so that no single term can adequately describe it.

14

"Be vewy, vewy quiet. We're hunting wippers"

A Barthesian Analysis of the Construction of Fact and Fiction in Alan Moore and Eddie Campbell's From Hell

JULIA ROUND

This article examines the construction of the non-fictional tale presented by Alan Moore and Eddie Campbell in *From Hell*, a philosophical meditation on the Jack the Ripper murders. The events depicted in *From Hell* are based on Stephen Knight's *The Final Solution*, a publication that has been marketed and received as both a serious exposé and elaborate hoax.[1] Knight's theory alleges that the Ripper's victims knew of Prince Albert Victor's secret marriage and child with shop girl Annie Crook, and had attempted to blackmail the Royal Family, who responded by having them removed. He therefore identifies the Ripper as a group of men led by Sir William Gull, Queen Victoria's royal Surgeon-in-Ordinary and member of the Freemasons.

Using the narrative models of word and image proposed by Roland Barthes, this article considers the comics medium as it successfully fictionalizes the Whitechapel murders as well as the ways in which the content of *From Hell* foregrounds these processes. My observations will be related to Barthesian narrative models, considering notions such as narrative atemporality, image/imitari, the non-mimetic nature of narrative, and the active/passive reader. I will conclude that the qualities of the comics medium support Barthes' observations on the nature of narrative, making this medium ideally suited to conveying historical faction such as the Ripper myth.

The Comics Medium

The three main elements underlying a semiotics of comics are the depiction of time as space; the construction of an open narrative that relies upon the reader's contribution; and the creation of the hyperreal. This is, of course, only an overview: multiple visual and textual strategies are also used to limit and structure the text into its chapters, installments, and so forth. These, however, are additive techniques rather than integral to the medium's narrative structure. Of these strategies, the depiction of time as space is most obvious and is essential in constructing the comic book panel, which the reader must read from left to right in order to allow events to proceed in sequence.

The medium's reliance on interpretation operates on two levels, as the reader works alongside the creators as a contributory author, not only deciphering the panel contents, but also filling in the gutters. In this manner, the medium's narrative structure informs the treatment of symbolism, where meaning is open to interpretation. This form also allows for the creation of a linear story from the panel layout of fragmented and isolated events.

Comics' non-realistic aesthetic and use of panels-as-signifiers offer fictional seeing rather than literal representation. The juxtaposition of various perspectives also helps construct the hyperreal by offering the reader multiple (and often contradictory) points of view. As such, the world of comics may best be described as the world of the fictional signifier (Verano, 326). This approach accords with Rosemary Jackson's model of the Fantastic, by which definition the comic book world is an alterity that, no matter how much it may resemble our own, is not the same: it is "this world re-placed and dislocated" (Jackson, 19).

I turn now to a discussion of how these elements inform the construction of faction in *From Hell*. As Lisa Coppin notes, "[i]n *From Hell*, the border between fiction and reality is continuously played with: almost every detail is supported with possible evidence, and yet, the conclusions drawn by Moore remain conjectures." Stephen Knight's theory, the main source for this story, attracted a lot of interest when it was first published in 1976, but has since been derided by many Ripperologists. Knight's theory is based on the story of the painter Walter Sickert, as recalled by his son Joseph. This article does not seek to address the merits of Knight's hypothesis but rather, to analyze the contribution of the comics medium in reconstructing such a tale. *From Hell*'s dramatization of events that are themselves largely speculative means that its content will not be assessed in terms of fact versus fiction. Instead, this article seeks to consider the ways in which the comics medium fictionalizes the tale by smoothing the joints between fact and fiction, and in so doing illustrates Barthes' theories regarding the construction of narrative, word and image.

Alan Moore comments, "*From Hell* is the post-mortem of a historical occurrence, using fiction as a scalpel. [...] it isn't history. It's fiction" (1994: 337–38). He continues, "perhaps it's worth remembering that *all* history is to some degree a fiction; that truth can no longer properly be spoken of once the bodies have grown cold" (ibid.). Viewed in this way, the dramatization of Knight's theory is in itself a fictionalizing process, as specific words, relationships and incidents are necessarily created out of thin air. There can be no recourse to evidence regarding the specifics of conversation, or the emotions felt by the story's characters.

The dramatization of Moore's research in Appendix 2, "Dance of the Gull Catchers," offers a similar perspective. Positioned as an appendix and taking as its subject the emergence of "Ripperology," this again is a tale based on fact. However, its pictures operate on a metaphorical level, as for example when Moore and Campbell are shown among a crowd of Ripperologists carrying nets in an attempt to catch their elusive quarry. This article's title is drawn from this sequence, and its cartoon vernacular (familiar to most from Warner Brothers' *Looney Tunes* cartoons) invokes the comedic, and acknowledges the fictionalized nature of its content. This panel is also captioned "The rest is dodgy pseudo-history" and together the two statements seem to imply that, simply by being translated into a narrative, the events leading up to the book's conception have become, in some sense, false (2000, II.16.3).[2] As Moore explains:

> In studded football boots they [Ripperologists] endlessly cross-track and over-print the field of their enquiry. They reduce its turf to mud. Only their choreography remains readable [II.1.6].

The implication is that there is no fact left in the Ripper mythos, only conjecture upon conjecture and, as Moore concludes, "[i]t isn't getting drawn into Masonic Death Conspiracy that troubles me, you understand. It's getting drawn into the vortex of a fiction" (II.19.3). He uses the example of Koch's snowflake to illustrate his point. This is a mathematical formula which shows that, although the edge of this shape can, in theory, be infinite, its area is always limited by the circle around it. Within Ripperology an infinite number of details and new theories continue to emerge, but the area they delineate remains limited to that of the "initial circle": autumn, 1888, Whitechapel (II.23.3–6).

From Hell takes pains to establish its content as fiction by pointing out the inherently fictional status of all history; emphasizing the conjectural nature of the Whitechapel events; and using self-conscious metaphor in its pictorial elements, thereby drawing attention to the fictionalizing process of comic book visuality. "As if there could ever be a solution," Moore exclaims (II.22.1). "Murder isn't like books. [...] Jack's not Gull, or Druitt. Jack is a Super-Position" (II.16.7). *From Hell* is not concerned with simply recreating a grisly tale, or promoting Knight's "final solution," or even with exploring its validity. Instead it is a treatise on the nature of fiction and human psychology; on the function that the Ripper myth holds in modern life. "It's about us. About our minds and how they dance" (II.22.7). As such, this article will discuss the ways in which both the form and content of this text address these processes.

Chronological Illusion

Alan Moore explains:

> When books are closed, they represent a model of post–Stephen Hawking space-time, the events within the book depicting past, present and future all contained within a simultaneous whole. When books are opened, two modes of time come into play; time as it seems to pass for the characters within the book and time as it appears to pass inside the reader's mind [Moore 1994, 13].

Alongside the dual construction of narrative versus perceived time, *From Hell* also seems to recall the type of co-present chronology Moore assigns to the notion of a book-as-a-whole, because events are multiplied and revisited without recourse to a single, linear chronology. Gull's murder of Mary Kelly contains scenes drawn from a previous operation and his later Masonic trial, and his final imprisonment in an asylum (p)revisits earlier conversations, childhood memories, and even future events. In this way, Moore constructs an "architecture of history" that relies on a notion of co-present time and cyclical patterns. Based on a pamphlet published by C. Howard Hinton, it suggests that "[t]ime is a human illusion [...], that all times co-exist in the stupendous whole of eternity" (2.14.2–3). Patterns within this "fourth dimension" merely seem to be random events from a human perspective.

Moore goes on to identify such a pattern as "[a]n invisible curve, rising through the centuries," a notion he deems "most glorious and most horrible" (2.15.3–4 and 14.14.5–6). Beginning in 1788, he notes slashing attacks on women by Renwick Williams, nicknamed The Monster. A century later, in 1888, the Ripper stalks the streets of London. Fifty years on, in 1938, an investigation into the Halifax Slasher takes place. In 1963, Ian Brady and

Myra Hindley begin their murders on the Moors, and twelve years later, Peter Sutcliffe, the Yorkshire Ripper, claims to have received murderous instructions from a supernatural voice while working as a gravedigger. In this way, the Ripper legacy continues.

This heritage is likewise expressed in terms of fiction within *From Hell* when we are shown Robert Louis Stevenson awakening from a nightmare of "a doctor with the soul of a terrible beast inside him," the inspiration for *Dr Jekyll and Mr Hyde* (14.15.6) (1886).[3] A few pages earlier, we are given a glimpse of William Blake and, at panel 14.16, an apparition of Gull is revealed to be the source for Blake's *Ghost of a Flea*. The historical circumstances of the sketch are again reproduced truthfully and are conceptually accurate, as Blake apparently explained the name of his strange vision by saying that "all fleas were inhabited by the souls of such men as were by nature bloodthirsty to excess" (Miles). Both events take place before the Ripper murders and, therefore, a philosophy of co-present time is essential.

As noted, events such as these are repeated throughout *From Hell*. In chronological terms, Gull's flight of fancy over the city takes place in 1896, while he is locked up in an asylum under the name of Tom Mason after committing the Ripper murders. However, this vision includes events that occurred earlier in his lifetime, such as a childhood conversation with his father or the "architecture of history" discussion with Mr. Hinton. It even includes events far beyond it, such as his visitation of Ian Brady and a vision of what appears to be an open-plan, twentieth-century office. The mixing of temporalities is also emphasized textually at other junctures in the book, as, for example, when Gull seems to have a prescient knowledge of his murder of Liz Stride, saying "This is the one that I didn't finish, isn't it?" (8.33.5).

Earlier in the text, his murder of Mary Kelly is also interrupted by a flashback to a previous operation, and flash-forwards to his Masonic trial and subsequent confinement in the asylum. His speech in all of these scenarios includes the same words he utters during their appearance in his "hallucination." As the text explains, "movement, and yet there is no movement. There is not space. There is not time, and therefore nothing moves, but only is" (14.14.7). The time-as-space narrative structure of comics informs this statement at various levels. For example, the depiction of co-present time obviously relies on a comics aesthetic, where all moments are co-present on the page in the spatial layout of panels. Although the events must be read in sequence, in a linear fashion, they are positioned spatially in relation to each other. The locations Gull visits in his out-of-body experience are, therefore, able to be juxtaposed despite their differences in time and place. From this point of view, the role of the reader in constructing a sequential narrative from fragmented panels recalls the statement from within the text that "time is a human illusion" (2.14.2).

It also recalls Roland Barthes' work in his "Introduction to the Structural Analysis of Narratives." In this text, Barthes proposes a common model for narrative across media and is at pains to include all narratives, whether "myth, legend, fable, tale [...] stained glass windows, cinema, comics, news items, conversation" (Barthes 1977, 79). Barthes argues that narrative contains within itself relations that exist at both a horizontal level (that of the words themselves) and a vertical level (regarding levels of meaning) (ibid., 87). This relates, very loosely, to the Russian Formalist distinction between "*story* (the argument), comprising a logic of actions and a 'syntax' of characters, and *discourse*, comprising the tenses, aspects and modes of the narrative" (ibid., 87). Barthes then divides narrative elements into functions and indices, noting that functions operate on the horizontal level (story), whereas indices (although still functional at this level) also refer to the relations between levels of meaning. The resultant model contains three levels of description in the narrative work, namely functions, actions, and narration.

Importantly, Barthes argues that all elements of narrative are functional, so that even if a sentence appears to be meaningless, its absurdity is still a meaning assigned by the narrative. He goes on to identify various types of functions, initially dividing them into cardinal functions (which are necessary to advance the plot, for example in terms of consequence) and catalysers (other functions, such as the discursive function, which affect pace) (ibid. 95). In deconstructing these elements, Barthes identifies a strange temporality within narrative as when two cardinal functions (such as the ringing of a telephone and someone answering it) are separated by a variety of catalysers, or simple events that fill time between the two events. As he explains:

> [...] the tie between two cardinal functions is invested with a double functionality, at once chronological and logical. Catalysers are only consecutive units, cardinal functions are both consecutive and consequential. Everything suggests, indeed, that the mainspring of narrative is precisely the confusion of consecution and consequence, what comes *after* being read in a narrative as what is *caused* by [...]. It is the structural framework of cardinal functions which accomplishes this "telescoping" of logic and temporality [Barthes 1977, 94].

This model contrasts with theories of narrative such as that proposed by Vladimir Propp, which privilege the notion of time as reality and therefore argue that chronological order is irreducible. However, Barthes' model concurs with Claude Lévi-Strauss's proposition that "the order of chronological succession is absorbed in an atemporal matrix structure" (qtd. in Barthes 1977, 98). Lévi-Strauss's work focuses on identifying the elements of this underlying structure, which are often arranged in opposition. By way of brief example, the type of matrix one might perceive underlying *From Hell* could arrange notions and symbols such as rich, poor, blood, grapes, ceremony and conspiracy in order to examine the tensions and oppositions that are used to create the tale.

As Barthes asks, then, "is there an atemporal logic lying behind the temporality of narrative?" (ibid. 98). He elaborates further that "time belongs not to discourse strictly speaking but to the referent; both narrative and language know only a semiotic time, 'true' time being a 'realist,' referential illusion" (ibid. 99). This statement certainly seems to be illustrated by *From Hell*, most obviously in its story content ("What is the fourth dimension?") and structure (Gull's visitations in Chapter 14). But the comics medium, whose panel-based aesthetic requires that the reader consciously create the illusion of linear time, also forces us to acknowledge the processes by which we create narrative temporality.

Image and Imitari

As might be expected, *From Hell* makes use of some striking imagery that pertains to its content, the most remarkable of which is the pentagram motif that links Gull and Netley's tour of Masonic landmarks within the geography of London. However, visual elements are also used to blur fact and fiction as, for example, in the scenes discussed above, which are revisited in different contexts. The climactic murder of Mary Kelly is simultaneously represented as an autopsy in a sequence that is clearly William Gull's fantasy (10.14) as the audience observing his scientific demonstration includes Ian Brady and Myra Hindley, recognizable from their arrest photographs. Within the terms of the narrative, though, this sequence can be deemed no less real than Gull's other contact with the couple — whom he observes watching a Jack the Ripper movie at the cinema (14.13.8) — or his appearance to a younger Ian Brady (14.18).[4]

As noted, the visuality of comics has been defined as the world of the fictional signifier. Traditionally, both contents and aesthetics are aligned in order to depict fictional events in a non-realistic manner, offering fictional seeing rather than literal representation. The incredible events of superhero narratives take place in a world whose primary colors and heavily stylized art seem to draw attention to their impossibility. By contrast, historical events in *From Hell* are rendered entirely in black-and-white line drawings, a conscious choice to unite style with content in a similar manner.

The comics medium is essential in conveying this fiction, because photographic or other realistic depiction would alter the status of this narrative significantly, thereby fictionalizing it in an entirely different manner. In "The Rhetoric of the Image," Barthes analyzes a photograph, identifying three messages carried within it: the linguistic (any written content), the coded iconic (the symbolism of the elements themselves and their composition), and the non-coded iconic (the literal message of the photograph's content) (Barthes 1977, 36). By contrast, Barthes notes that the drawing, which incorporates a process of transformation ("there is no drawing without style"), is always coded (ibid. 43). The photograph only appears to constitute a message without a code, although the truth of this is dependent on its context.

Barthes again returns to the question of temporality arguing that, rather than immediacy, the photograph establishes an awareness of *having-been-there*. This represents a new space-time category: "spatial immediacy and temporal anteriority" (Barthes 1977, 44). This, however, does not hold true for the drawn image, which, by being highly coded, is effectively dislocated from both space and time. The coded message obviously requires interpretation, and Barthes goes on to discuss the importance of this process and the factors affecting it. Multiple elements are selected and interpreted by the reader, and it is important to note that this number will vary from person to person, according to the different kinds of knowledge they possess. "This is the case for the different readings of the image: each sign corresponds to a body of 'attitudes'— tourism, housekeeping, knowledge of art — certain of which may obviously be lacking in this or that individual" (ibid., 47). This process is clearly observable in comics, where the reader must interpret the panel contents. As comics creator Will Eisner notes,

> [i]t is inherent to narrative art that the requirement on the viewer is not so much analysis as recognition. The task is then to arrange the sequence of events (or pictures) so as to bridge the gaps in action. Given these, the reader may fill in the intervening events from experience [Eisner 1990, 38].

The content of *From Hell* further emphasizes this message, as in the duality of meaning attached to the pentagram symbol. The pentagram is itself a minor Masonic symbol, but is more generally associated with religious iconography. Although it is popularly understood as Satanic, this is a relatively recent association, and originally the pentagram was a Christian symbol. Broadly speaking, its modern interpretation may depend on whether the point is up or down, but historically this distinction was rarely made.[5] As such, the pentagram is a divided symbol that stands for both good and evil, and is therefore entirely dependent on interpretation. In this sense, the content of *From Hell* again echoes the tenets of comics narrative form as regards a reliance on codification and interpretation. Furthermore, the treatment of these processes conforms to a Barthesian analysis of the rhetoric of the image.

Textual Mimesis

In depicting fictional events at a visual as well as a textual level, the comics medium may be described as hyperreal: creating a comic is not a way of telling a story with illustrations that replicate the world it is set in, but a creation of that world from scratch. This might seem a strange statement to make about *From Hell*, as the accuracy with which the various locations of London are rendered, the use of historical characters, and the historical importance of the murders themselves all link the events in the text strongly to our world. However, Moore's comments on the fictional status of his tale, together with the treatment of its meta*factional* background in "Dance of the Gull Catchers," firmly denote the world of the text as a fictional one. As he notes, "[t]his reality [the murders] is dwarfed by the vast theme-park we've built around it" (II.22.6).

His character Mr Lees offers an opposing point of view, saying "[b]ut that's just the thing, it isn't just stories. Those women really died" (Epilogue 5.2). But as Moore points out, the events themselves are no longer the focus of the tale, which has instead shifted towards the cohesion between theories. Furthermore, these theories — Masonic conspiracy, royal sanction, and a secret marriage — are certainly fantastical in the extreme.

In the broadest possible terms, the genre of the fantastic is based around a notion of hesitation between reality and the marvelous, achieved through the co-presence of natural and supernatural elements (Todorov 1975, 25).[6] It takes place in an "alterity" that may be defined in terms of its relationship with reality, a term introduced and further defined in the later work of Rosemary Jackson. She comments that "[f]antasy re-combines and inverts the real, but it does not escape it: it exists in a parasitical or symbiotic relation to the real" (20). Fantastic worlds are therefore alterities: "this world re-placed and dis-located" (ibid. 19). Although the terminology has not been widely adopted, other critics such as Amaryll Chanady concur with this perspective, noting that fantastic literature is set in a world "very similar (though not identical) to our own," in contrast to fairy tales, which take place in the world of the outright marvelous (5). A narrative with a fantastic element is thus set, by definition, in a world distinct from the consensus reality. The importance of the comics medium to this conclusion is apparent, as its visuality immediately creates this new world. But is this medium relevant to the fictionalizing process more generally?

The Barthesian model seems to accord with this perspective. Barthes notes a "mythical appearance of 'life'" in narrative that he also defines as creativity (Barthes 1977, 123). He notes, however, that this narrative creativity is heavily restricted, as it must always operate under two codes: the linguistic and the translinguistic. It is situated between the code of language and the code of narrative (as identified previously in terms of functions, indices and so forth). He continues:

> Claims concerning the "realism" of narrative are therefore to be discounted. [...] The function of narrative is not to "represent," it is to constitute a spectacle still very enigmatic for us but in any case not of a mimetic order. The "reality" of a sequence lies not in the "natural" succession of the actions composing it but in the logic there exposed, risked and satisfied [ibid. 123].

Narrative is therefore exposed as the result of these two operations, and a deconstruction of the same will reveal only an adherence to its own specific rules, created by the interaction between linguistic and translinguistic codes, rather than to external reality.

Barthes also attacks the notion of realist narrative in a different manner, by pointing out that "[n]arrator and characters [...] are essentially 'paper beings'; the (material) author of a narrative is in no way to be confused with the narrator of that narrative" (ibid. 111). If true of the author/narrator relationship, this statement may also inform the relationship between historical figures and literary characters, again supporting a conception of comics narrative as an alterity, peopled not by the "real" but by fictional characters. The comics medium again has the capability to emphasize this point, because narrative, when included, is typically typeset in a similar manner to the story's (fictional) dialogue and demarcated within a box (rather than dialogic speech bubble).

The typography used by comics also emphasizes this distinction. Although traditionally hand-lettered, the mass-production of comics means that the handwritten appearance of their lettering is essentially a fiction. Many modern publications go still further by featuring computerized lettering that nonetheless mimics the appearance of handwriting. This "fiction of fonts" may be read as another signpost indicating that the narrator is, like his characters, also fictional.

Moore uses no omniscient narration, with the exception of informing us of places and dates, in the main body of *From Hell*. Wherever explicit narration does occur, it is variously drawn from police reports, or attributed to William Gull during his out-of-body experiences. By clearly attributing instances of narration such as these to exact sources or characters, *From Hell's* content also highlights the falsity of narrative voice. That both the aesthetic and typography of the comics medium emphasize this distinction is, again, an example of the form and content aligning in support of a Barthesian tenet: the fiction of the narrative voice.

The ending of *From Hell* also provides us with what seems to be a further alterity, as Gull's vision takes him to Ireland in 1904, where he encounters a woman who strongly resembles Mary Kelly and her four young girls. It is tempting to interpret this scene as an afterlife, but Moore has suggested another possibility, pointing out that "obviously, the simple truth of it is, how could anybody have identified what was in 13 Miller's Court? [...] I've seen the photographs, it's difficult to actually tell which way up she is for a while, let alone who she is. There is no positive evidence" (qtd. in Kavanagh). Moore thereby offers the possibility that Kelly might have escaped — a notion that finds some support in other elements of the case, such as her boyfriend Joe Barnett's testimony that he and Mary had been arguing due to her inviting other prostitutes to stay in their room. Two independent witnesses also stated that they saw Kelly alive the following morning, which is also a matter of recorded testimony and represented in Chapter 11 of *From Hell*.

Moore explains that he "just wanted to give the poor woman a happy ending [...] without actually going against what was possible, I wanted to sort of give her a way out" (ibid.). Perhaps it is only wish fulfillment, but a scenario in which Mary Kelly escapes to Ireland seems no less likely than any other element of the text. Although it obviously goes directly against traditional *interpretations* of the events, this conclusion still adheres to the facts as known, and could actually be considered more plausible than most theories, as it manages to make the known facts cohere with the troublesome testimonies of Mrs. Maxwell and Mr. Lewis. However, in the final event, the onus is on the readers to interpret this scene.

The Active Reader

In *The Pleasure of the Text*, Barthes offers a series of vignettes addressing the ways in which relations between the reader and the text operate.

> On the stage of the text, no footlights: there is not, behind the text, someone active (the writer) and out front someone passive (the reader); there is not a subject and an object. The text supersedes grammatical attitudes: it is the undifferentiated

eye which an excessive author (Angelus Silesius) describes: "The eye by which I see God is the same eye by which He sees me" [1975, 16].

The role of the reader in interpreting panel content has been previously noted, but this statement seems to go beyond a simple notion of decoding or deduction of meaning. Although noting that Silesius's analogy is somewhat excessive, Barthes nonetheless concurs with his principle: that the relationship between the writer and reader is reciprocal in nature.

Although sounding somewhat unlikely within our understanding of reality (for if the text has been finished by the writer before it has been passed to the reader, how can there be any kind of two-way effect?), this identification of the writer/reader connection was also pointed out by theorists such as Maurice Blanchot, in *The Space of Literature*, which offers an inverted approach to literature as a silent empty space. Blanchot argues against common literary perceptions in proposing that art is not the real made unreal, proposing instead that we do not ascend from the real world to art, but that we emerge from art towards what appears to be a mutualized version of our world (Blanchot 1982a: 47). Literature dwells in a silent, empty space and is inward-looking: concerned only for its own essence.

Although space does not permit a detailed discussion, it is worth noting that Blanchot's denial of an external reality as the text's referent supports my previous analysis of Barthesian theory regarding the non-mimetic nature of narrative and its lack of an objective referent.[7] Blanchot also notes the performative nature of narration, a notion that aligns strongly with comics' presentation of the hyperreal (1982b: 63). His theories also incorporate an analysis of the disjointed temporality that is produced by the writing and reading experience, where literature arises from the death of the subject while simultaneously sustaining this subject (1982a: 198, 247).

Therefore, although it is located in a dubious temporality and within a purely fictional state, the writer/reader relationship is deemed by both critics to be more than simply that of an active writer and passive reader. In *Understanding Comics*, Scott McCloud identifies the active role of the reader in interpreting comics, using two sequential illustrations. The first of these depicts a man being threatened by an axe-wielding maniac, while the second only shows a scream echoing out over a silhouetted cityscape. McCloud comments:

> Every act committed to paper by the comics artist is aided and abetted by a silent accomplice. An equal partner in crime known as the reader. I may have drawn an axe being raised in this example, but I'm not the one who let it drop or decided how hard the blow, or who screamed, or why. That, dear reader, was your special crime, each of you committing it in your own style. [...] To kill a man between panels is to condemn him to a thousand deaths [McCloud 1994, 68–9].

As this example shows, the gutter is often the site of major events with the result that readers are implicitly involved, investing the story with their own identities and experiences. This creates the illusion of linearity, as writer and reader constantly exchange positions throughout the narrative, depending on whether the story is being told within a panel (by the creator) or between panels (by the reader). This encourages a view of narrative sequential art in line with Jean-François Lyotard's notion of language games, in which speaker and addressee interchange positions constantly.

The content of *From Hell* emphasizes this process, using it to great effect to create its most graphic scenes. The murder and mutilation of Mary Kelly lasts over thirty pages, and is a horrific sequence by any standards. Gull's cuts progress slowly, with one panel showing his knife entering her body, while the next shows the resulting wound and the new position of the knife. As such, our deduction of the knife's motion necessarily takes place between the panels. As Mary Kelly's body becomes more and more unrecognizable we are left with the ghastly realization that, thanks to the nature of the medium, these cuts are ours.

Conclusion

This article has demonstrated some of the ways in which the content of *From Hell* emphasizes the role of the comics medium in constructing fiction, and explored the ways in which these processes may be linked to the Barthesian models of narrative, word and image. *From Hell*'s theory of co-present time emphasizes the medium's use of a time-as-space narrative structure, and so form and content together demonstrate the atemporality that characterizes narrative. The codification of the image identified by Barthes necessarily informs the medium's stylized aesthetic, and this is particularly apparent in *From Hell*'s use of symbols such as the pentagram. This aesthetic is also essential to the creation of the hyperreal and enables the comic-book world to be viewed as an alterity, a notion that informs Barthes' observations on the non-mimetic nature of narrative. The possibilities for interpretation of certain alterities and symbols also emphasize the active role of the reader, another key Barthesian concept. Finally, the importance of the reader's role is again emphasized by the content of *From Hell*, which quite literally makes the reader Gull's accomplice.

Not only does *From Hell* expertly manipulate the possibilities of the medium to create this fiction, but it also draws attention to these processes. It displays the ways in which fiction is created, and emphasizes the notion that every story, whether ostensibly non-fictional or not, exists in this state. In demonstrating the applicability of Barthesian models and theories, it seems clear that the comics medium has much to teach us, not just about the construction of fiction, but also about the processes by which we derive meaning.

Notes

1. Moore notes Knight's use of the Shakespearean quotation "Here comes my noble gull-catcher," and points out that gull-catcher means trickster (II.15.5).

2. References taken from *From Hell* will be cited in this format, which correspond to Appendix II, page 16, panel 3. Please note that references drawn from Chapter 2 (rather than Appendix II) will be delineated 2.16.13.

3. Interestingly enough, the circumstances depicted are factual; Stevenson got the idea for his story from a nightmare his wife awakened him from.

4. With reference to my comments on temporality, it is worth noting that this vision takes place some pages after the cinema scene, although it is obviously earlier in Brady's lifetime.

5. This popular belief appears to have originated in the work of Éliphas Lévi, who claimed that the direction of the rays of the pentagram determine whether it represents the good or evil principle: one point up representing order and light, two points up representing disorder and darkness (Lévi 1970, 55). Lévi gives no justification or citation for this distinction, and no research associating the pentagram with evil appears prior to this, yet this commonly held belief is now ingrained in the dogma of heavy metal music, occult circles, the American Satanist Association and so forth (Yukon A.F. and A.M, 2007).

6. This conception of the fantastic owes much to the Freudian notion of the uncanny, which is discussed by Lisa Coppin in her 2003 article "Looking Inside Out: The Vision as Particular Gaze in *From Hell*."

7. See Blanchot 1982a: 47; 1982b: 118.

15

Graphic Black Nationalism

Visualizing Political Narratives in the Graphic Novel

JAMES BRAXTON PETERSON

Classical Black Nationalism is defined in a global sense as "an ideology whose goal was the creation of an autonomous black nation-state, with definite geographical boundaries — usually in Africa" or in a national sense "as the effort of African Americans to create a sovereign nation-state and formulate an ideological basis for a concept of a national culture" (Moses, 1). In this chapter I employ theories of comics and narrative in order to excavate an historicized re-engagement with Black Nationalist themes in Frank Miller's *Give Me Liberty*, featuring Martha Washington; Aaron McGruder, Reginald Hudlin and Kyle Baker's *Birth of a Nation*; Kyle Baker's *Nat Turner*; and Reginald Hudlin's *Black Panther*. Martha Washington, Fred Fredericks (protagonist of *Birth of a Nation*), Nat Turner and T'Challa/Black Panther are all Black Nationalist figures with peculiar and at times historically interstitial valences with African Diasporic realities.

Thus in Miller's *Give Me Liberty*, Martha Washington is named after America's first president's wife, but she emerges as a Black heroine who almost literally pulls herself out of an impoverished inner city hell by the figurative bootstraps of sheer gumption. Fred Fredericks, whose name doubles and signifies Frederick Douglas, one of America's first fugitive Black heroes, is an indefatigable civil servant in the recently seceded Blackland, a fictional renamed East St. Louis in *Birth of a Nation* — a title which itself signifies the White supremacist Nationalism depicted in D.W. Griffith's film. Nat Turner as historical symbol and Baker's haunting historical graphic novel both project the violent imagery of a Black Nation enraged by the brutality of oppression. Baker's *Nat Turner* graphically puts into bold relief the vision of a Black Nationalist revolution. *The Black Panther*, through Reginald Hudlin's writing, challenges some of the overly structured templates of the character's super-heroic narratives as a genius ruler over an eternally sovereign Black nation named Wakanda.

Each of these texts constructs and projects Graphic Black Nationalistic (GBN) narratives through overlapping but largely distinct literary genres. Frank Miller's Martha Washington narratives contain satire and irony, but they all largely truck in the dystopian themes of a consumerist American society of the not-so-distant future. *The Black Panther*, on the other hand, is largely based on the utopian notion of Wakanda, a Black African nation untouched by colonialism that paces the world in technological advancement and largely stable socio-political structures. Likewise, Baker's *Nat Turner* is meticulously historic and historicized, whereas *Birth of a Nation* is satirical and boasts comedic timing unrivalled in sequential art.

Nationalistic and historic protagonists inform various aspects of my analysis, but each of these graphic narratives produces various manifestations of what Owen Whooley refers to as "political work." According to Whooley, "narratives are saturated with political relevance" and do political work on individual and collective levels (Whooley, 295). "To achieve a comprehensive understanding of the political work performed by a given narrative, both the historical context and local context must be analyzed" (ibid.). My exegesis of the political work in the *local contexts* of the GBN narratives wrestles with the relationship between the author(s) and the narratives or the nationalistic heroes and, in some ways, the relationship between the graphic narratives and the audiences that receive them. The *collective level* of analysis, and/or the historical contexts out of which these GBN narratives emerge, produces a radical re-imagination of Black Nationalistic thought.

Moreover, my analysis of these four distinct Black graphic narratives renders a dialogic deconstruction of classical Black Nationalism through the visual and linguistic artistry of Miller, Baker, McGruder, and Hudlin. This is, at least partially, the rationale for employing narratology to investigate the medium of comics. Douglas Wolk in *Reading Comics* suggests that "since comics simultaneously feed the parts of the brain that make sense of written language and pictures, narrative seems natural or at least formally appropriate to them" (Wolk, 23). The intertextual discourse in and around nuanced notions of Black Nationalistic thought in the GBN narratives warrants subtle narratalogical analyses that allow readers, scholars, and critics to fully engage the complex history of Black Nationalism as well as its brilliant re-depictions in 20th- and 21st-century graphic texts, narratives, and/or novels.

Graphic Black Nationalism (GBN) is a sort of "catch all" term that I employ to reference the various ways in which Black Nationalism is depicted in graphic narratives.[1] The historical development of Black Nationalistic thought is as complex, powerful and reflects as much about African American and African political thought as it does American history. Reducing nationalistic ideology to its essence, William L. Van Deburg writes that "[a] common denominator of these robust nationalistic expressions is the high value placed on self-definition and self-determination" (Van Deburg, 2). For the purposes of this essay, Black Nationalism is subdivided into its classical and modern manifestations. For the most part, classical Black Nationalism is a chronological designator reflecting Black Nationalistic thought in America during the 19th century. Its proponents and ideologues included various historical figures: Frederick Douglass, David Walker, Edward W. Blyden, Alexander Crummell, and Martin R. Delany.

Several of theses figures were privately and publicly at odds with each other over the socio-political semantics of the terms Black and Nation. Some felt that Black included the entire African Diaspora, while others were more focused on African Americans. Even more contested was the notion of nation, or more specifically whether or not Black Nationalism required emigration and repatriation to Liberia, Canada, South America, or some annexed portion of the United States (Moses, 6–30). These "Nation" debates were unsettled through the 19th century, finding some resolution in Marcus Garvey's extraordinary Universal Negro Improvement Association (UNIA) movement. Garvey's movement, a peak transitional moment between 19th- and 20th-Century Black Nationalism, raised money and recruited tens of thousands of African Americans to the cause of emigration.[2]

Despite the nuances of Black Nationalistic ideology in the 19th century, there were at least two interlocking narratives that provided some cohesion amongst the various discursive positions. According to Wilson J. Moses: "[t]he major proponents of classical Black Nationalism in the 19th century invariably believed that the hand of God directed their movement" (Moses, 2). The near-ubiquitous belief in Christianity's innate capacity to civilize African Americans as well as black folk throughout the African Diaspora provided slaves with a religious optimism that insulated them from the social, psychological, economic, and spiritual detriment of white supremacy. This same Christian optimism also supported various utopian narratives of a promised land and ideal Black Nation States (in Liberia, Canada or the U.S.), while serving to re-inscribe flawed narratives of the civilizing properties of Christianity.

Garvey's UNIA movement of the 1920s and the Black Power Movement of the 1960s and 70s were two peak periods of activity for 20th-century African American Nationalism (Van Deburg, 10). The mission statement of UNIA underscores its pivotal role in the transition between classical and modern Black Nationalism:

> To establish a Universal Confraternity among the race; to promote the spirit of pride and love; to reclaim the fallen [...] to assist in civilizing the backward tribes of Africa; to assist in the development of Independent Negro nations and communities; to establish a central nation for the race [...] to promote a conscientious Spiritual worship among the native tribes of Africa [...] to improve the general conditions of Negroes everywhere [Van Deburg, 11].

Note the 19th-century desire to "civilize" a "backward" Africa and the abiding belief in a utopian "central nation for the race." This dogma was mitigated by the more modern narratives of reclaiming the fallen; an emphasis on spirituality over the Christian imperative; and a Pan-African sensibility that promoted cultural solidarity throughout the Diaspora.

The other "peak" of 20th-century Black Nationalism, the Black Power movement, produced public discourse through speeches, poetry, political treatises and the mediated presence of the Black Panthers, Malcolm X, Angela Davis, and others. Aggregated upon the history of Black Nationalistic ideology, "the sheer volume of discourse coupled with the repetition of key themes legitimized the idea of black people as a kind of nation" (Robinson, 71). In *Black Nationalism in American Politics and Thought*, Dean Robinson suggests that even amongst the intellectually wide-ranging scholars and activists who subscribe to Black Nationalism in the 20th and 21st centuries, all tend to focus on four core principles or ideas:

> (1) [T]hat Black Nationalism reject[s] integration-as-assimilation; (2) that Black Nationalism [has] a tradition with "roots" in earlier times; (3) that the black population [has] a colony (or something like one); and (4) that, like other national communities, Afro-Americans [have] distinct cultural characteristics [Robinson, 71].

This 4th principle distinguishes classical 19th-century Black Nationalism, featuring Christian ideology and a misdirected impulse toward civilization, from its modern version. By the mid–20th century the anxiety surrounding African origins was displaced by an "ethnic paradigm" that focused on a set of cultural attributes like dialect, dress, music, and, most importantly, an Afro-centric historical narrative. Not surprisingly, ideologically dense slogans like "black is beautiful" were important discursive components of this newer form of Black Nationalism.

The Black Martha Washington

Martha Washington, the sole female character of the GBN narratives selected for this essay, was created by white men. This presents several problems, both from a Black Nationalist perspective and from a feminist perspective. Consider the history of the Student Nonviolent Coordinating Committee (SNCC) and its abrupt transition to Black Nationalist ideology. By the mid–1960s "black-white tensions within the organization and the growing attraction of nationalism as an ideology and organizational tool caused SNCC leaders [...] to conclude that their work would be made easier if non-blacks were excluded from participation" (Van DeBurg, 119). Thus a 1980s African American female character created by two white men was and is an anomaly both in this essay and as an iconic image of Black Nationalism in the comics medium.

Nonetheless, Frank Miller's *Martha Washington* is an intriguing and complex example of the graphic Black Nationalist narrative. According to Owen Whooley's notion of "political work," the collective level of the Martha Washington narrative initiates its political work in the asymmetrical juxtaposition of the historic Martha Washington, and Miller's Martha Washington, who is African American. Aside from sharing the same name and an assumed abiding sense of American nationalism, the two women have nothing in common. Miller's African American Martha Washington hails from the future while the original Martha Washington is white and hails from the ur-narrative of American presidential history. History's Martha Washington was a wealthy land and slave owner, while Miller's Martha Washington — most likely descended from enslaved Africans in America — was born into poverty in the notorious Cabrini-Green Projects of Chicago, Illinois.

But Miller's Martha Washington engages in an uncanny form of Black Nationalism by becoming an American nationalist who also happens to be black. According to late historian Hans Kohn:

[n]ationalism is a state of mind in which the supreme loyalty of the individual is felt to be due the nation-state. A deep attachment to one's native soil, to local traditions and to established territorial authority has existed in varying strength throughout history [Kohn, 9].

Native soil, local traditions, and established territorial authority engender various pragmatic meanings for physically and/or mentally colonized people of African descent throughout the Diaspora, represented brilliantly in the nominative connections between Miller's Martha and history's Martha. Professor Kohn also asserts that nationalities maintain objective elements that

define them against other nationalities. Some of the distinguishing characteristics are: "common descent, language, territory, political entity, customs,
traditions and religion" (Kohn 1965: 9). He also maintains that these characteristics are not essential to nationalism: "the most essential element is a living
and active corporate will. [A will that] asserts the nation state [as] the ideal
and the only legitimate form of political organization and [*sic*] the nationality
[as] the source of all cultural creative energy and economic well-being" (Kohn,
10). Each of Kohn's keen insights into the ideology of nationalism is mani-
fested in Miller's dystopian portrait of 21st-century America.

Miller's Martha Washington is born into a decrepit housing project under
an ascending fascist American president. The historical counterpart of the
fictional housing project is the notorious Cabrini-Green "projects" located
on Chicago's north side, ironically located in close proximity to wealthy neigh-
borhoods and high-end shopping districts. Constructed between 1942 and
1962, and mostly demolished by 2008, the Cabrini-Green housing project
was a notorious signifier of all that was wrong with inner city public housing
across America: rampant violence fueled by various underground economies
run by drug lords, pimps, and gangs.

Miller's Martha Washington narratives were released on an intermittent
monthly basis from the 1990s until 2008, when *Martha Washington Dies* was
released. The collected first installment, entitled *Give Me Liberty: An American
Dream*, begins in Miller's version of the Cabrini-Green projects. In the opening pages, Martha reflects on the death of her father as she recounts her humble
beginnings: "Dad died in a protest against The Green. Dad said The Green's
a prison for people who haven't done anything wrong" (Miller and Gibbons,
3). Martha's father's politics reflect those of the 20th-century Black Nationalism, concerned with confronting the socio-economic conditions of the poor-
est black folk. Her father's death in "The Green" is a result of his political
work and underscores Martha's destiny as a Black Nationalist.

When Martha is a young girl, the infamous President Rexall comes to
power. His administration's transition to a regime is signaled by Martha's
reflection on the fact that Rexall repealed the 22nd Amendment to the Con-
stitution, and each time he takes office his rule is accentuated by parade-like
visuals and a strong military presence. Rexall's nominative narrative is an
unsubtle suggestion of his autocratic political power (hence his name Rex).
The extent of his power is evidenced in the acceleration of ruin of America's
political, social, and economic infrastructure that takes place under his rule.

As Martha wrestles with the insurmountable challenges of her youth,
many of which are a result of Rexall's governance, she is mysteriously followed
by a black cat. This subtle visual suggestion is more fully realized later in the

narrative, when Martha discovers that she is able to master technology. This "power" enables her to bond with a volunteer teacher whose kind-heartedness is clearly out of place in The Green. So when he is abruptly murdered by one of the most notorious thugs in the projects, Martha, after witnessing his death, murders the thug. Thus begins her narrative of emergence from The Green. Her murderous act renders her silent, and this silence is reason enough for her to be committed, so that Miller and Gibbons now depict the erosion of yet another social institution.

As Rexall's reign continues to dismantle the social fabric of America, the walls of the institution literally come crumbling down. Through her fighting skills and her extraordinary technical prowess, Martha is able to escape the fascist drug police who track down and drug the roaming "out"-mates of the Insane Asylum. She decides that her only option is to join the military, also known as PAX, another not-so-subtle Latinate dig at the American military's claims to police the world in the interest of peace. Martha enlists, her record is cleared, and she exchanges "The Green" of America's concrete jungle for the green of the Amazonian jungle.

Just as Martha joins PAX, a terrorist assassination attempt kills nearly everyone in President Rexall's regime and puts him into a coma. The acting Secretary of Agriculture, Howard Johnson Nissen, is thrust into the presidency. His presidency initially shows promise, and Martha develops a strong nationalist ideology under Nissen's short and troubled presidency. Nissen does not rule with the autocratic force of Rexall, and is too easily controlled by sinister political forces led by Martha's arch-nemesis, Moretti, a rogue officer in the military who spearheads the group that controls President Nissen. Nonetheless, Martha emerges as a war hero and nationalist poster girl for PAX. As Moretti explains,

> Nissen was priming [her] to become a media event. "She's perfect," he said [...] "she's black. She grew up poor. Would've ended up a junkie or a hooker if it weren't for PAX" [Miller and Gibbons, 98].

Surviving the Green and mastering the Amazon as a PAX soldier, Martha's story is a strangely symmetrical narrative that works politically by reflecting a particular American national history, and present-day "reality," as it gestures toward a Black Nationalist political narrative. Although the fictional and historical Washingtons are binary opposites in virtually all other respects, both are nationalists and patriots of the first order. The graphical Martha sacrifices her life time and time again for the United States as the country becomes increasingly fragmented and nationalism is fragmented into various warring factions. Through it all, Martha holds firm to her conviction that the U.S. is worth defending; that her mother will be proud of her; and that liberty is attainable, even if "by any means necessary."

Miller and Gibbons reflect the fragmented nature of a dystopian America via a full two-page map of the United States. This map expresses the divisive America against which Martha Washington must struggle. Each shaded area represents an ideological secession from the federalized United States: God's Country (the Pacific Northwest), Wonderland (Southern California), Real America (Arizona and Coloroado), The Lone Star Republic, Florida, The First Sex Confederacy (Viriginia, West Virginia, Maryland, Georgia, and others), The East Coast Capitalist Dictatorship (New York City), and The New England Federation of States. The two-page "Nation Divided" image and text are imbued with a potent *pictorial narrativity*, requiring readers of graphic novels, "who [are] much more active in (re-)constructing a narrative than would be necessary in verbal texts" (Wolf, 435). Thus in order to fully grasp the narrativity of The Lone Star Republic, comic book readers need to be able to recall the history of Texas, just as they need to be able to re-construct the history of Hollywood and southern California to understand the text's Wonderland; and in order to fully appreciate the irony of The First Sex Confederacy, where women enjoy supremacy, readers need only recall the gender-conservative region out which this new confederacy arises. Although Miller provides a brief description of each nation within the nation, the pictorial narrative resides in the redefined cartography of "A Nation Divided." This is a version of America where nationalist ideology is unchecked, out of control, and where even a hero is unequal to the task of rescuing it from the brink of destruction.

In the Amazonian jungle, a black alley cat that followed Martha and witnessed the murder that she committed in "The Green" becomes a wild black panther whose presence is unmistakable. The black panther is both Martha Washington's avatar and the visual articulation of her Black Nationalist persona. Although I would argue that Martha Washington is more a nationalist who happens to be black than a black nationalist per se, Miller and Gibbons still inform their GBN with the central iconic image of the modern Black Nationalist movement, namely the black panther. The black panther appears sometimes in "pin-up" style, without any direct relationship to the narrative itself, or it interacts with Martha Washington in the jungle. But the black panther's most significant appearances in the narrative include Martha being depicted as resembling a panther as she faces off with Wasserstein, her future love interest and leader of the Apache Nation. Wasserstein is a native American/American Indian represented by the bald eagle, "White" America's central patriotic icon. The connection between Wasserstein and the eagle is one of reclamation and it informs ways of reading and seeing the connection between Martha Washington and the black panther, thereby producing "political work." Moreover, although Wasserstein's reconstituted Apache Nation is subject to a second genocide at the hands of America, he still represents the aboriginal American, while his icon, the eagle, underscores the notion that the connection between the construction of the American national identity was predicated on the genocide of Native Americans.

Martha's depiction as a black panther is similarly dense. The image reflects her defiant spirit, but it also renders her American nationalist sensibilities inseparable from the Black Nationalist narrative. As a soldier and a patriot, Martha is a nationalist in the most traditional sense, but as a result of her upbringing, her time in both the concrete and natural "Green," as well as Miller and Gibbons' choice of iconography, Martha Washington is never separate from the history of Black Nationalism, or in this case the GBN of *Give Me Liberty*.

Black Panther Perspectives

The other black panther in this essay has a much more explicit connection to the iconography of the Black Power movement so central to modern Black Nationalism. Stan Lee and Jack Kirby created the Marvel Comics superhero known as the Black Panther in the mid–1960s. They initially named him the Coal Tiger, but in July of 1966, the Black Panther debuted in the 52nd issue of the Fantastic Four. His moral status was initially unclear, but he was shortly revealed as a hero — the first African hero in Marvel Comics. The Black Panther would not receive his own comic book title until 1977, but his first appearance preceded the establishment of The Black Panther Party for Self-Defense by only a few months.

Without question, the ideas and iconography for the Black Panther Party (BPP) were either in place or germinating prior to the July 1966 appearance of the Black Panther in *Fantastic Four* #52. Several organizations emerging out of the Civil Rights movement, such as the SNCC, were exploring more progressive and aggressive Black Nationalist agendas. The Revolutionary Action Movement (RAM) was one such organization that slightly predates the formation of the BPP for Self-Defense but harnesses the same nationalistic energies that were prevalent in the American public sphere during the 1960s. RAM, SNCC, and the emergent BPP reflected the Black Nationalistic *Zeitgeist* of the 1960s, and the founding members of the BPP were looked upon as political folk heroes. Their black leather blazers, black berets, and dark shades contributed to the overall heroic imagery of the party, but the insistence on armed self-defense cemented their near-superheroic status. Figure 1, first published in an issue of the BPP's widely circulated political newspaper, *The Black Panther*, will illustrate this (Black Community News Service). This comic image captures the full force of the BPP presence in the public sphere, especially as it relates to the graphical Black Nationalism (GBN) narratives outlined in this essay, while demonstrating the important political work of comic book narratives as articulate indicators of real-world experiences. Hence these images, like so much political cartooning, became a means by which Black Nationalist ideology was circulated throughout the community.

In 1977 Lee and Kirby delivered Marvel's *Black Panther* into this ideological milieu. When Kirby took on full writing and drawing duties of the first volume of the *Black Panther* comic book narratives, the BPP had

Fig. 1. *The Black Panther News*

been infiltrated by COIN-TELPRO, and the party's image in the media was associated with thuggish behavior and terrorist ideology. Thus Kirby's *Black Panther* was in many ways over-determined by the BPP's dominance in the public sphere, and much of this is apparent in the early issues.

The opening story arc involves a conflict over the "Brass Frog," a time machine removed from King Solomon's tomb for which the Black Panther embarks upon a perilous journey. The Black Panther, also known as T'Challa, is a Wakandan Prince and heir to the throne of the most powerful and wealthy African nation in the world. In the series' opening narrative he sets out on a journey to assist Mr. Little, a diminutive Caucasian, because of his supposed connection to the Prince's grandfather. Little details T'Challa's grandfather's responsible handling of the Brass Frog and the totem's peculiar historical narrative as a portal for every unexplained "grotesque being," from Ali Baba's genie to the Loch Ness monster. T'Challa's alliance with Mr. Little is strange, but necessary for comic book audiences to connect with their first African hero. But the fact that Mr. Little must relate important portions of T'Challa's familial history to him undermines the Black Panther based on the fundamental Black Nationalist principles of self-knowledge and autonomous education. T'Challa should know all about his grandfather, and indeed, in the next issue he proclaims: "I am a King's son — raised in a noble tradition! My people are builders and scholars!" (Kirby, 30).

Another challenging issue in this volume of the *Black Panther* narratives surrounds Princess Zanda, T'Challa's first adversary. She is a member of a mysterious illuminati group called The Collectors. The Collectors serve as an important critique of colonial exploitation of culture, and illustrate the ways in which folk art and ethnic artifacts are transformed into exotic products by imperialistic forces. The Collectors want to possess the most precious material items of the world's cultural history, and they are prepared to kill, bribe, lie, and destroy entire civilizations in order to get what they want. Princess Zanda is the only female and the only person of color amongst this nefarious group, and the narrative decision to make her the face of The Collectors seems odd at first glance.

One way of interpreting the face-off between Princess Zanda and Black Panther is that Kirby centralizes the narratives of the protagonist and the first antagonist around Afro-centric themes. They are both Black rulers (future King and Queen), powerful, well educated, "articulate," and beautiful. However, careful consideration of the gender distress of the Black Power movement, particularly reflected in the narratives of Assata Shakur, Afeni Shakur, and Elaine Brown — all former Black Panther Party members — suggests that the confrontation between Princess Zanda and Black Panther can also be interpreted as a narratological capitulation to the prevailing fissure of Black Power politics: the irreparable rift between black men and women.

These ideological and political "glitches" may have been the prerequisites for Marvel, Kirby, et al. to publish this comic book at all. There would have been no way for a 1977 comic book to pass the censorship standards of the Comics Code Authority and closely align itself with Black Nationalism or the BPP, which explains why Kirby's *Black Panther* has an expressed aversion to guns. In a revealing confrontation with Princess Zanda, T'Challa exclaims: "Bloodthirsty female. Is the gun the only answer to your problems? [...]. No! We've got to face this as *civilized* human beings" (Kirby, 28, emphasis added).

Here, Black Panther directly opposes one of the organizing principles of the BPP, the civil right to bear arms, particularly to defend oneself from the oppressive forces of a white supremacist police force. An excerpt from a 1967 essay entitled "Armed Black Brothers in Richmond Community," originally published in the inaugural issue of the *Black Panther*, April 25, 1967, is instructive:

> 15 Black Brothers, most of them armed; with Magnum 12 gauge shot guns, M-I rifles, and side arms, held a street rally at the corner of Third and Chelsey in North Richmond last Saturday afternoon about 5pm. The nice thing about these Bloods is that they had their arms to defend themselves and their Black Brothers and Sisters while they exercised their Constitutional Rights: Freedom of Speech, and the right to Peacefully Assemble. And while they exercised another Constitutional right: the right to bear arms to defend themselves [Van Deburg, 242].

T'Challa/Black Panther then distinguishes himself markedly from the political party that shares his iconography. Black Nationalist rhetoric suggests that this is what happens to a black hero in the hands of a white artist, but based upon Jack Kirby's life experiences as an artist for the Communist Party and his own personal travails as a mid–20th-century Jewish American, he may well have had some insight into the challenges he assumed in writing and drawing the *Black Panther* comics through the late 1970s.

After Kirby's run on *Black Panther*, Christopher Priest began writing the comic in the late 1990s, and continued through the early part of the millennium. Although Chris Priest was the first African American to write the *Black Panther* comic, his run remains somewhat less remarkable than Kirby's in terms of its artistic and/or political impact and timing. In Scott McCloud's discussion of the fight for minority representation in comics, or the "Eighth Revolution," he suggests that "Black Superheroes began appearing occasionally but their white creative teams often seemed unsure how to present positive role models without draining their subjects of their humanity" (McCloud 1994, 107). Here he pictures the Black Panther in a classic crouch with the following caption: "Marvel Comics' better-than-average *Black Panther*" (ibid.). McCloud does not elaborate visually or verbally what exactly made *Black Panther* "better-than-average," but I would suggest that at least part of what "humanizes" the Black Panther is the GBN narrative that drives each incarnation of the character. T'Challa's adherence to Black Nationalist ideology of the classical and modern varieties positions him as an authentic original, even in the anxious hands of his white — or black and white — creative teams. The Priest version of *Black Panther*, and the McGregor and Turner mini-series, use a black writer-white artist team, and a white writer-black artist, but neither of these *Black Panther* narratives transcend McCloud's "better-than-average" criticism.[3]

More recently, a third volume of Marvel's *Black Panther* series debuted, featuring the writing of Reginald Hudlin and the art of John Romita, Jr., which lacks the racial and ideological anxiety so apparent in the work of previous writers and artists. Nearly all superhero comics contain an abstract, and here the abstract helps to explain some of this artistic and nationalistic confidence of the various volumes. By way of introducing the character to new readers, Kirby's original abstract tells readers that "[w]ith the sleekness of a jungle beast, the Prince of Wakanda stalks both the concrete of the city and the undergrowth of the veldt, for when danger lurks he dons the garb of the savage cat from which he gains his name!" (Kirby 5). Christopher Priest's 1998–2001 version adds: "So it has been for countless generations of warrior kings, so it is today — and so it shall be for as long as the law of the jungle dictates that only the swift, the smart, and the strong survive! Noble champion. Vigilant protector" (Priest 3). Note how the narrative in each of these abstracts accentuates Black Panther's animalistic qualities. He is sleek and "savage" as he "stalks," thus creating an implicit equation between the urban jungle and the African "veldt."

Connecting the veldt to the streets of American cities reveals a racial ideology that views residents of the inner city as dehumanized animals. For example, throughout the 1980s "[t]he Zoo became a metaphor for the whole borough" of the Bronx" (Kevin Powell, *Beyond Beats and Rhymes* — documentary). Kirby ends his abstract amidst animal allusions, but Priest attempts to extend beyond them and a surface of the nationalism that informs the character, setting, and plot of *Black Panther*. His reference to "generations of warrior kings," and the Darwinian conclusion (the strong survive) to the abstract seem paltry attempts to balance some of Kirby's language, which could well have been interpreted as racist in the 1990s, when Priest began writing the series. In this light, Priest's addition to the text could be understood as being in narratological dialogue with Kirby's words. Yet the result is unimpressive, since neither Priest nor Kirby's version of the *Black Panther* abstract touches on the core nationalistic principle of T-Challa's character.

This omission is, however, amended in Hudlin's abstract for the *Black Panther*:

There are some places you just don't mess with. Wakanda is one of them. Since the dawn of time, that African warrior nation has been sending would-be conquerors home in body bags. While the rest of Africa got carved up like a Christmas turkey by the rest of the world, Wakanda's cultural revolution has gone unchecked for centuries, unfettered by the yoke of colonization. The result: A hi-tech, resource-rich, ecologically-sound paradise that makes the rest of the world seem primitive by comparison [Hudlin, 1].

In Hudlin's *Black Panther*, abstract animalistic allusions are replaced by allusions to carved turkeys — a powerful geo-political distinction between Black Nationalist Wakanda and the rest of Africa. Moreover, the threat of "places you just don't mess with" suggests the African American vernacular that informs this most recent version of the *Black Panther*. The signal shift from non-nationalistic referencing in Kirby's abstract to Priest's "generations of warrior kings," to Hudlin's "African warrior nation," suggest the chronological emergence of the GBN narrative in the *Black Panther* comics. Recalling Whooley, "[n]arratives do political work on both the individual and collective levels" (295). The linguistic shifts in the *Black Panther* abstracts reflect both individual and collective levels of political work that the GBN narratives produce. Both Kirby and Priest write or rewrite abstracts that concede specific mainstream stereotypes about Africa, the inner city and people of African descent in America. Hudlin, as an African American in the 21st century, creates a powerful discursive distance from his artistic predecessors through an individual artistic decision that has the collective effect of rendering the Black Panther as a Modern Black Nationalist figure. Modern Black Nationalism's expressed emphasis on distinct cultural attributes is clearly articulated as Wakanda's "unchecked cultural revolution," resulting in a utopian Black Nationalist state, resource rich and equipped with a powerful enough military to resist any and all attempts at colonization.

One of the clearest examples of this militant strength and colonial invulnerability occurs in a story recounted by a U.S. official in the first issue of Hudlin's *Black Panther*. "Captain America entered Wakanda during World War II on a search and destroy mission [...]. He had an extended hand-to-hand battle with the Black Panther [...]. He lost" (Hudlin, No. 1, 28–29). According to the comic, Captain America's 1944 mission in Wakanda was to contend with the Nazis there, who wanted to steal Wakanda's most precious resource, a mysterious and potent substance known as vibranium. Unbeknownst to Captain America, the Wakandans had already captured and decapitated the Nazis, yet he was spared by T-Challa's father, then ruler. The narrative of America's best being defeated by Wakanda's best is one of the more powerful examples of GBN narratives and their attendant political messaging through visual and verbal texts.

Visions of Nat Turner

There may be no other narrative in American history as infamous as the 1831 Nat Turner Slave Revolt. Cryptically and meticulously detailed in

Thomas R. Gray's *The Confessions of Nat Turner*, the Turner-led slave revolt of 1831 has the dubious distinction of being the only "successful" slave rebellion on United States soil. Success here is measured by the revolting slaves' brutal murder of nearly sixty white men, women, and children before the rebellion was put down and those responsible along with hundreds of other innocent slaves were brutally murdered as a show of white supremacist law and order. Turner was reported as being reclusive and singular as he came of age; he was also extremely intelligent: "Turner's grandmother, his master, and many others repeatedly remarked that his extraordinary intelligence made him unfit to be a slave" (Greenberg, 1). He was a devout Christian, and by some accounts he was a healer and prophet. Ironically, Nat Turner was considered a "semiotic rebel — a man moved to action by reading and interpreting the signs of heaven and earth" (ibid., 2). In a visually powerful panel from Baker's graphic novel, an eclipse signals the time to act for Nat Turner, who then quickly prepares a "last meal," including a roasted pig for him and his cohort. In spite of recurring references to Turner's semiotic narrative, history provides little or no evidence of the man himself, and few (if any) historically accurate portraits or paintings of Nat Turner exist. Moreover, the only access we have to his words is through the questionable filter of Thomas R. Gray who, although a lawyer, was not Turner's lawyer, and would not have been an objective witness.

Kyle Baker inserts himself into this complex historical narrative through his award-winning graphic novel, *Nat Turner*. Unlike Miller's Martha Washington narratives or any of the versions of *Black Panther*, Kyle Baker's Nat Turner was originally self-published. As he explains:

> I originally chose to publish *Nat Turner* myself, rather than through the comic book publishers I usually work for (the two largest). I liked that one of my first books as an independent publisher would be about a self-freed slave. I knew nothing about publishing, having only worked as an artist before. In the tradition of my hero Nat Turner, I went out and found books about being a publisher [Baker, 7].

Baker's *Nat Turner* sold through its initial printings and was collected and republished as a single volume. His individual professional decision to self-publish exemplifies the ethos of Black Nationalism, and the fact that his artistic production chronicles the history of one of Black Nationalism's greatest heroes cannot be overemphasized. Kyle Baker's *Nat Turner* is the archetypal GBN narrative, gesturing as it does toward the ideological roots of classical and modern Black Nationalist thought, and visually realizing the "semiotic" rebel who for the most part has been invisible in the narratives of American history. In Whooley's terms, Baker's *Nat Turner* conducts political work through the

(GBN) narrative on both individual and collective levels. Baker's own narrative about his decision to self-publish *Nat Turner* underscores the individual level of this argument, while the work's success and his multiple Glyph and Eisner Awards reflect the narrative's potential to connect with audiences on the collective level regarding an important historical figure.

In a complex discussion on distinguishing "art comics" from "auteur comics," Douglas Wolk writes:

> Kyle Baker was the auteur of his 2004–2006 run on Plastic Man. With the exception of a couple of fill-ins, he wrote and drew the whole series himself. [...] But they're not quite art comics because he's playing with someone else's toys: Plastic Man [...] is the property of DC Comics [Wolk, 35].

According to Wolk, auteur comics and art comics have the strongest potential for autonomous style in the work of the artist, and they also tend to value substance over style in both the visual and verbal arts of the graphic narratives. But he makes a further distinction between art and auteur comics by suggesting that when an auteur writes and draws someone else's property, s/he will be somehow limited, while when drawing his or her own property the inherent creative freedom produces the most potential in art comics. Thus the creative oversight, direction, and control of an auteur are prerequisites for the "art comics" designation. Although he is reluctant to admit it, Wolk ultimately concludes that "art comics" are at the top rung of comics in general.

The art and auteur comics discourse cannot, however, account for Kyle Baker's *Nat Turner*. Clearly Wolk considers Baker to be an auteur, yet referring to Nat Turner as a "property" is problematic at best; at worst, it ignores historical narratives of slavery. As an artistic property, *Nat Turner* is also troublesome because he does not fit neatly into the dichotomized ownership categories of either creator-owned or company-owned, and Baker had the freedom to depict Nat Turner in his own visual vocabulary. Given this, the auteur/art distinction does not hold and Baker's *Nat Turner* becomes both, since the artist had artistic freedom on the visual side of the project. In other words, while Baker has created a visual representation of Nat Turner from his own artistic imagination, his art is the only visual depiction of Nat Turner in history. The verbal side of this equation poses an altogether different set of issues. One of Kyle Baker's signature artistic choices is the complete absence of thought bubbles, boxes, or in-panel dialogue. All dialogue is positioned outside of the box, usually beneath the corresponding panels. Baker used a similar style in *Nat Turner*, but did not write the dialogue. Instead, he appropriated the dialogue between Thomas R. Gray and Nat Turner as the text, which he reconstructed from historical documents, including Nat Turner's

Confessions. Baker's reconstructed historical narrative lends the text a palpably authentic aura, making this a powerful and engaging graphic novel.

The historical narrative of Nat Turner is fragmented, incomplete and filtered through Thomas R. Gray, who may have feared and hated Turner for his crimes. Nonetheless, as a successful revolutionary, Turner is a paragon of Black Nationalist ideology. Kyle Baker has likewise distinguished himself as an auteur of a classic GBN narrative, and the self-publication of *Nat Turner* and its success suggests that there is indeed a creative space in the marketplace for graphic Black Nationalism.

Just a few years before Kyle Baker began work on *Nat Turner*, he was asked to illustrate *Birth of a Nation: A Comic Novel*, written by Reginald Hudlin and Aaron McGruder. Hudlin (writer, *Black Panther*) and McGruder (creator, *The Boondocks*) were working on a script that would satirize contemporary politics through a story about "East St. Louis seceding and forming its own country" (McGruder et al, v). They worked on the idea for over a year and realized the likelihood of a major film studio financing a film informed, even through comedy, by Black Nationalism.

> Rather than have it sit on a shelf, waiting for Jay-Z to buy Paramount, we decided to publish it as a graphic novel. Aaron and I quickly agreed that Kyle Baker would be the perfect artist to bring the story to life [...]. I knew his storytelling skills and versatile art style would be invaluable in translating our script into a illustrated style that would appeal to both comic snobs and first-time readers of the format [McGruder, et al, v].

Again, the artists' business decisions take into account the limitations of producing and distributing GBN narratives in the mainstream market place. At the same time, they have to radically re-imagine society's power structure in order to assess its limitations and discover a more self-oriented, nationalistic outlet. Hence, "Jay-Z would have to buy Paramount" in order for McGruder, Hudlin, and Baker's version of *Birth of a Nation* to be made into a movie.[4] Baker would eventually go through this same process before he decided to self-publish *Nat Turner*, but McGruder and Hudlin were able to publish *Birth of a Nation: A Comic Novel* in 2004.

The single most nationalistic figure of McGruder, Hudlin, and Baker's "comic novel" is the mayor-turned-president of Blackland, Fred Fredericks, the civic-minded mayor of East St. Louis, a section of St. Louis proper. This area has secured its sovereignty from the United States after their blatant disenfranchisement and the subsequent election of President Caldwell, who bears a caricatured resemblance to George W. Bush. While Fredericks bears no resemblance to any particular historical figure, his name suggests Frederick Douglass, and brings to mind his powerful autobiography, *Narrative of the Life of Slave.*

The doubling of Douglass' first name is an important mimetic invocation of the historical figure, and although Fred is not a slave, he is as relentless as Douglass in his commitment to challenging America's relationship to its own constitutional ideals. He is equally committed to the emergence of Blackland as a sovereign state, and when Fredericks delivers his secession speech, he posits himself as a "defender of freedom," echoing the words of his historical counterpart. Moreover, Fred Fredericks' indefatigable work ethic for freedom (Fred-Fredericks-Freedom) refigures his character as an embodiment or personification of freedom itself.

Birth of a Nation is a fantastical, graphic narrative of Black Nationalism depicted through the emergence of Blackland, the renamed region formerly known as East St. Louis. The red, black, and green national flag of Blackland, with a white Jesus superimposed over the traditional Black Nationalist colors, is an important signifier of freedom, democratically selected by Blackland's citizens. The panels that narrate the citizens' discussion around the design of their flag are constructed as an interesting satirical narrative of cultural and generational ideology in the African American community. The first flag of Blackland, an afro-centric simulacrum of the American flag, garners "gas-face" looks from a predominantly older black audience. At the appearance of the second flag, which features an image of the continent of Africa superimposed over the traditional Black Nationalist colors, McGruder et al repeat the same response-panel from the previous flag, indicating that the audience disapproves. The final flag, a Kinte cloth on which a Nike symbol is superimposed over the traditional Black Nationalist colors, elicits smiles and approval. This response is possibly due to the design (a kinte cloth Nike symbol), suggestive of the consumerist ethic of Black Nationalism in the 21st century, or it may also be attributable to the fact that this flag "comes with a generous donation from Nike" (McGruder et al, 58).

Although the ultimate decision to use the Jesus flag occurs off-panel, the selection is nonetheless iconographically complex. The Black Nationalist narrative of the black "Jesus" has been wrestled with throughout the history of African American artistic production and popular culture.[5] Hence, the idea that Blackland would select a white Jesus for the flag typifies the kind of narrative irony that McGruder, Hudlin, and Baker inject into their rereading of Black Nationalism. The discourse surrounding the flag of Blackland crystallizes a comedic theme within the narrative of *Birth of a Nation*. Black Nationalism and Graphic Black Nationalist narratives are replete with iconic and ironic contradictions and the white Jesus, superimposed upon the red, black and green of Blackland's flag, suggests ironic and iconic inconsistencies. The historical development of Black Nationalist thought decodes this particular

GBN image since classical Black Nationalism embraces Christianity, especially its ability to "civilize" Africans and African Americans. Modern Black Nationalism rejects Christianity as a "white man's religion" and embraces the cultural colors of red, black, and green as signs of the ethnic paradigm through which the Black Power and Black Arts movements have emerged and thrived.

These inconsistencies strengthen the ideology of Black Nationalism rather than weaken it, by giving it a sense of history, and opening the door to emergent, multi-faceted readings of Black Nationalism in the 21st century. Blackland ultimately survives and maintains sovereignty and its all-important independent revenue streams. The community's initial response to the Kinte-cloth Nike symbol flag underscores the central importance of economic (not civil, religious, or cultural) sovereignty in the discourse on Black Nationalism. And, at the same time, the white Jesus Blackland flag captures the history of Black Nationalism in the broadest sense, even as it points to both the religious and economic underpinnings of Christianity.

Conclusion

The GBN narratives briefly discussed in this essay proffer specific nationalistic spaces: imagined, real, utopian, and dystopian, from which readers can engage with the past, present, and future of Black Nationalism. Miller's rendition of the Cabrini-Green projects is a reflection of the state of public housing in inner-city America, lived in and ruled by African Americans who find this is no consolation in the U.S.A. that Miller imagines. On the opposite end of this spectrum is the fictional African nation of Wakanda, a free Black Nationalist state that is wealthy, powerful, and utopian in every way. Nat Turner's Virginia was a site of horror for white slave owners in 1831, but through those few days of rebellious mob rule, Turner projected his own brand of Black Nationalistic heroism through the narratives of American history. And creatively, somewhere amidst these fictional and historical locales resides Blackland, an impossibly sovereign urban 'hood right here in America. Each locale of the GBN narratives unveils the incisive vision of its respective creator/writer/auteur, but it is ultimately the extraordinary potential of these places, real and imagined, to interact with history that signals the political valance of nationalist ideology with the graphic novel genre.

Notes

1. Note here that there are relatively few characters, narratives, or graphic novels that engage, depict, or wrestle with Black Nationalism, but the few that do proffer a complex range of interpretations of the ideologies of Black Nationalism.

2. Garvey's UNIA fell apart when he was indicted for mail order fraud, allegedly based upon his fundraising tactics for the Black Star shipping line intended to bring folks "back to Africa."

3. Keep in mind that, although McCloud is considered a brilliant and groundbreaking critic of comics, he is also white and by the standards of Black Nationalism is necessarily ill-equipped to render judgment on the presentation of Afro-centric characters.

4. It is worth noting that Hudlin is the writer and director of the popular 90s film series *House Party*. McGruder has achieved similar popularity with *The Boondocks* comic strip and animated series. They are proven commodities in the marketplace. Hence one may conclude that it is largely the political and Black Nationalistic content of *Birth of a Nation* that stymied Hollywood interest in their projects.

5. A 1974 episode of the television sitcom *Good Times* is entitled "Black Jesus," and it features a painting of a black Jesus rendered by Jimmie Walker's character, "J.J." Other noteworthy examples include lyrical allusions to Black Jesus by Kanye West and Tupac Shakur.

About the Contributors

Christophe Dony obtained his MA in Germanic languages at the Université Catholique de Louvain in 2007. His dissertation *May 9/11 Bless America: Trauma, Identity and Memory: The Representations of 9/11 in American Comics and the Ideologies Behind Commemoration* combines interdisciplinary awareness with insightful comments on comics. He continues to carry out research on comics and their use in the ESL classroom. Parts of his research have been published in *The International Journal of Comic Art*, (vol. 9:2). He is currently editing a collection of essays on the mediations of 9/11 in comics, films, and fiction.

Kurt Feyaerts is a full professor in the Linguistics department of the Katholieke Universiteit Leuven. He teaches courses on German grammar and proficiency, structural features of spoken German, constructions in interaction, and, since 2007, humor and creativity in language. After an MA in Germanic linguistics (1990), he studied at the Westfälische Wilhelmsuniversität in Münster (1991), and worked as a research and teaching assistant at the University of Antwerp. In 2003 he founded the CHIL–research unit in which cognitive linguistic perspectives are adopted to study creativity in interaction.

Charles Forceville studied English at Vrije Universiteit Amsterdam and lectured in the departments of English, comparative literature, and word and image. Since 1999 he has worked in the Media Studies department of the Universiteit van Amsterdam, where he directs the department's Research Master program. He has published *Pictorial Metaphor in Advertising* (1996), and the co-edited volume *Multimodal Metaphor* (2009). His research and teaching are inspired by cognitivist-oriented models in linguistics and film, and focus on the structure and rhetoric of multimodal discourse in advertising, documentary, animation, comics, and cartoons.

Joyce Goggin is an associate professor of literature, film and new media at the University of Amsterdam, and head of Studies for the Humanities at Amsterdam University College. She has published numerous articles on the novel, Hollywood film, television and computer games, as well as the history of money, gambling, finance, art history, and economics.

Jonathan E. Goldman is assistant professor of English at the New York Institute of Technology. A teacher and scholar of twentieth-century literatures and popular cultures of the United States and Europe, Goldman is the author of *The Modernist Author* *in the Age of Celebrity*, forthcoming from the University of Texas Press. He is co-editor of a collection of essays entitled *Modernist Star Maps: Celebrity, Modernity, Culture*, forthcoming from Ashgate Press. He has published articles in *Novel: A Forum on Fiction*, *Narrative*, and *M/C*, and written review-essays for *Modernism/modernity*, *The James Joyce Quarterly*, and *American Studies Journal.*

Dan Hassler-Forest holds MA degrees in English literature and film and television studies, and has taught extensively in the Media Studies department and the English literature department of the University of Amsterdam. He combines his teaching activities with ongoing work on his PhD project, which deals with the politics and rhetoric of superhero figures in (graphic) literature and film from a post–9/11 perspective. He regularly presents papers based on his ongoing research at international conferences, and serves on the advisory board of the journal *Studies in Comics.*

Karin Kukkonen works on comics, cognitive narrative studies, and postmodernism. She is currently in the final stages of her PhD project "Storytelling Beyond Postmodernism: Fables and the Fairy Tale" (Mainz/Tampere), which investigates how the comics series *Fables* engages with postmodern modes of storytelling. She has published a book on superhero comics (*Neue Perspektiven auf die Superhelden.* Marburg, 2008). In her article publications and conference presentations, she discusses the impact of postmodernism on superhero comics.

Kai Mikkonen is an associate professor of comparative literature at the University of Helsinki, Finland. He obtained his MA at the University of Iowa in 1991, and PhD at the University of Tampere in 1997. He is the author of *Kuva ja sana [Image and Word]* (Gaudeamus, 2005); *The Plot Machine: The French Novel and the Bachelor Machines in the Electric Years 1880–1914* (Rodopi, 2001) and *The Writer's Metamorphosis: Tropes of Literary Reflection and Revision* (Tampere University Press, 1997) as well as various journal articles.

James Braxton Peterson is an assistant professor of English at Bucknell University. Peterson's academic work focuses on Africana studies, narrative, graphic novels and Hip Hop culture. He is the founder of Hip Hop Scholars, LLC, an association of Hip Hop generational scholars dedicated to researching and developing the cultural and educational potential of Hip Hop, urban, and youth cultures. Peterson is a regular contributor to theroot.com and has appeared on CNN, Fox News, CBS, MSNBC, ABC News, ESPN, and various local television networks as an expert on Hip Hop culture, popular culture, urban youth, race and politics.

Andreas Rauscher works as a research assistant at the department of Film and Media Studies at Johannes-Gutenberg-University Mainz. He has published several articles on film history, cultural studies, genre concepts, and game studies, and has edited books on *The Simpsons*, superhero movies, and the James Bond series. His dissertation, which deals with the cultural and cinematic implications of the Star Trek phenomenon, was published in 2003. He is currently finishing his post-doctoral lecturing qualification on genre concepts in video games.

Julia Round lectures in the Media School at Bournemouth University, UK, and edits the academic journal *Studies in Comics*. She has published and presented work internationally on cross-media adaptation, television and discourse analysis, the application of literary terminology to comics, the "graphic novel" redefinition, and the presence of gothic and fantastic motifs and themes in this medium. She holds a PhD in English literature from Bristol University, England, and an MA in creative writing from Cardiff University, Wales.

Angela Szczepaniak is a PhD candidate at the University at Buffalo. She has published and presented papers on innovative fiction, poetry, and comic books. Among other honors, her scholarship has been awarded the McKeen Prize and the Wynn Francis Award. More of her work can be found in her books *Unisex Love Poems* and *The QWERTY Institute of Cosmetic Typographical Enhancement* (forthcoming).

Dirk Vanderbeke teaches English literature at the University of Jena and at the University of Zielona Góra. His doctoral thesis, "Worüber man nicht sprechen kann" (Whereof One Cannot Speak), deals with aspects of the unrepresentable in philosophy, science and literature. He has published on a variety of topics, including Joyce, Pynchon, science fiction, self-similarity and vampires. In addition he has co-edited an annotated edition of the German translation of James Joyce's *Ulysses*, published in celebration of the Bloomsday centenary.

Caroline van Linthout obtained a degree in modern languages and literatures from the Université de Liège (Belgium) in 2006, and an MA in contemporary American literature and Native American studies at the University of Illinois at Urbana-Champaign (U.S.A.) in 2008. Her dissertation, "Art Spiegelman: Between Memory and History: An Analysis of the Appropriateness of the Comics Medium to Convey Traumatic Historical Memory in *MAUS* and *In the Shadow of No Towers*," offers insights on the tension between history and memory via Spiegelman's works. She currently teaches English at the Université de Liège.

Tony Veale is a lecturer in the School of Computer Science in University College Dublin and the School of Software Engineering at Fudan University, Shanghai. More recently, he was a visiting fellow at VLAC, the Flemish Academy for Arts and Sciences in Brussels. He obtained his PhD in computer science at Trinity College Dublin in 1996, on the topic of computational models of metaphor processing. At UCD he continues to research the computational treatment of metaphor, analogy, blending, irony and humor.

Benjamin Woo is a PhD candidate in the School of Communication at Simon Fraser University in Burnaby, BC, Canada. His master's thesis examined nationalist themes in Canadian superhero comic books, and he is currently conducting media-ethnographic research on "nerds" for his doctoral dissertation. Versions of his chapter were presented at Visible Evidence XII in Montreal, QC, and the 2008 Western Graduate Communication Conference in Nelson, BC.

Daniel Wüllner is currently enrolled as a doctoral candidate at the LMU–Munich, where he has taught a course on American comics. After finishing his master's thesis on reader-response theory in correspondence to the sequential structure of Dave Sim's comics epic *Cerebus*, he will illuminate the concept of seriality further with regard to the novels of William Gaddis in his doctoral thesis. Other research topics include neo-baroque aesthetics and 20th century American literature.

Daniel Yezbick is an assistant professor of English at Forest Park College, where he teaches literature, mass media, writing, and humanities courses. He has lectured and published on diverse interdisciplinary topics, including Victorian stereoscopic views, American radio drama, blaxploitation cinema, and New Deal Shakespeare. He also pioneered the first undergraduate surveys of American comics art at the University of Illinois, Peninsula College in Washington, and Forest Park College.

Works Cited

Abbott, Lawrence A. "Comic Art: Characteristics and Potentialities of a Narrative Medium." *Journal of Popular Culture* 19.4 (1986): 155–76.

Andrew, Dudley. "Adaptation." *Film Adaptation*. Ed. James Naremore. New Brunswick and New Jersey: Rutgers University Press, 2000: 28–37.

Auster, Paul. *City of Glass*. Adaptation by Paul Karasik and David Mazzucchelli. New York: Picador, 2004.

Baetens, Jan. "Revealing Traces: A New Theory of Graphic Enunciation." *The Language of Comics: Word and Image*. Ed. Robin Varnum and Christina T. Gibbons. Jackson, MS: University Press of Mississippi, 2001:145–55.

Baker, Kyle. *Nat Turner*. New York: Harry N. Abrams, Inc., 2008.

Barros-Lémez, A. "Beyond the Prismatic Mirror: *One Hundred Years of Solitude* and Serial Fiction." *Studies in Latin American Popular Culture*. Vol. 3 (1984): 105–114.

Barthes, Roland. *Image, Music, Text*. Trans. Stephen Heath. London: Fontana Press, 1977.

_____. *Mythologies*. Trans. Editions du Seuil. New York: The Noonday Press, 1991 (1957).

_____. *The Pleasure of the Text*. Trans. Richard Miller. New York: Hill and Wang, 1975.

_____. *A Roland Barthes Reader*. Ed. Susan Sontag. London: Vintage 2000, 1983.

_____. *S/Z*. Trans. Richard Miller. London: Blackwell, 1996.

Bartual, R. "William Hogarth's A Harlot's Progress: The Beginnings of a Purely Pictographic Sequential Language." *Studies in Comics* Vol. 1:83–105.

Baudrillard, Jean. *Simulacra and Simulation*. Trans. Sheila Faria Glaser. Ann Arbor: University of Michigan Press, 1994.

Bazin, André. "Adaptation, or the Cinema as Digest." Trans. Alain Piette and Bert Cardullo. *Film Adaptation*. Ed. James Naremore. New Jersey: Rutgers University Press, 2000: 19–27.

Bell, David F. *Circumstances: Chance in the Literary Text*. Lincoln and London: University of Nebraska Press, 1999.

Benjamin, Walter. "The Author as Producer." Trans. Edmund Jephcott. *Reflections: Essays, Aphorisms, Autobiographical Writings*. Ed. Peter Demetz. New York: Schocken, 1986: 220–38.

_____. *Charles Baudelaire: A Lyric Poet in the Era of High Capitalism*. Trans. Harry Zohn. London and New York: Verso, 1997.

_____. "The Storyteller: Reflections on the Work of Nikolai Leskov." Trans. Harry Zohn. *Illuminations*. Ed. Hannah Arendt. New York: Schocken, 1969: 83–109.

_____. "The Work of Art in the Age of Mechanical Reproduction." Trans. Harry Zohn. *Illuminations*. Ed. Hannah Arendt. New York: Schocken, 1969: 217–51.

Bennett, Tony. "Popular Culture and the Turn to Gramsci." *Cultural Theory and Popular Culture: A Reader*. Ed. John Storey. London: Pearson Education, 2006.

Beresiner, W. Bro. Yasha. "William Hogarth: The Man, the Artist and His Masonic Circle," *Masonic Papers*, <http://www.free

masons-freemasonry.com/beresiner11. html> (22/03/09).

Berlatsky, Eric. "Lone Woolf and Cubs: Alan Moore, Postmodern Fiction, and Third Wave Feminist Utopianism." *The Gay Utopia*. <http://gayutopia.blogspot. com/2007/12/eric-berlatskylone-woolf-and-cubsalan.html> (12.04.09).

Black Community News Service. *The Black Panther*, Volume II No. 9. Oakland: BPP, 19 October 1968.

Blanchot, Maurice. *The Sirens' Song*. Ed. Gabriel Josipovici. Trans. Sacha Rabinovitch. Brighton, Sussex: The Harvester Press, 1982b.

_____. *The Space of Literature*. Trans. Ann Smock. London: University of Nebraska Press, 1982a.

Bolter, Jay David, and Richard Grusin. *Remediation: Understanding New Media*. Cambridge: MIT Press, 2001.

Boorstin, Daniel. *The Image: A Guide to Pseudo-Events in America*. New York: Atheneum, 1975.

Braudy, Leo. *The Frenzy of Renown*. New York: Vintage, 1986.

Brooker, Will. *Batman Unmasked: Analyzing a Cultural Icon*. London: Continuum, 2000.

Brown, Joshua. *Beyond the Lines: Pictorial Reporting, Everyday Life, and the Crisis of Gilded Age America*. Berkeley: University of California Press, 2002.

Bruzzi, Stella. *The New Documentary: A Critical Introduction*. New York: Routledge, 2007.

Burney, Frances. *Evelina*. London: Penguin Books, 1990.

Busiek, Kurt, and Alex Ross. *Marvels*. New York: Marvel Comics, 2004.

Butcher, Christopher. "Profile: Warren Ellis Interview" <http://www.popimage.com/ industrial/103100ellisprofileinterview1. html> (06/06/2008).

Calhoun, Craig, Paul Price and Ashley Timmer, eds. *Understanding September 11*. New York: New Press, 2002.

Calhoun, Pat. "In Praise of Pretzelburg." *Comic Book Marketplace*, Dec. 2003: 32–49.

Campbell, David. "Time Is Broken: The Return of the Past In the Response to September 11," *Theory & Event*, vol. 5:4: 1–9.

Chanady, Amaryll Beatrice. *Magical Realism and the Fantastic*. London: Garland, 1985.

Chatman, Seymour. *Story and Discourse. Narrative Structure in Fiction and Film*. Ithaca: Cornell University Press, 1978.

Chaw, Walter. Review of *300*. *Film Freak Central*. 2 April 2007. <http://www.film freakcentral.net/screenreviews/300.htm> (22/03/09).

Chute, Hillary, and Marianne DeKoven. "Introduction: Graphic Narrative." *Modern Fiction Studies* 52:4 (Winter 2006): 767–782.

Claremont, Chris. *X-Men: God Loves, Man Kills*. New York: Marvel Comics, 1982.

Coppin, Lisa. "Looking Inside Out. The Vision as Particular Gaze in From Hell." *Image [&] Narrative*, 5 (2003). <http:// www.imageandnarrative.be/uncanny/lisac oppin.htm> (28/03/08).

Couch, C. "The Publication and Format of Comics, Graphic Novel, and Tankobon." <http://www.imageandnarrative.be/ narratology/chriscouch.htm> (10/12/08).

_____. "The Yellow Kid and the Comic Page." *The Language of Comics*. Jackson: Mississippi University Press, 1994: 60–74.

Crary, Jonathan. *Techniques of the Observer: On Vision and Modernity in the Nineteenth Century*. Cambridge and London: MIT Press, 1992.

Dale, Richard. *The First Crash: Lessons from the South Sea Bubble*. Princeton and Oxford: Princeton University Press, 2004.

De Bolla, Peter. *The Education of the Eye: Painting, Landscape, and Architecture in Eighteenth-Century Britain*. Stanford: Stanford University Press, 2003.

De Forest, T. *Storytelling in the Pulps, Comics, and Radio: How Technology Changed Popular Fiction in America*. Jefferson, NC: McFarland, 2004.

Delisle, Guy. *Pyongyang. A Journey in North Korea*. London: Jonathan Cape, 2006.

Dorr, Gregory P. Review of *Pride and Prejudice* (2005). *DVD Journal*. 17 April 2007. <http://www.dvdjournal.com/quick reviews/p/prideandprejudice05.q.shtml> (22/03/09).

Duin, Steve, and Mike Richardson. *Comics: Between the Panels.* Mikwaukie: Dark Horse, 1998.

Eco, Umberto. "Innovation and Repetition. Between Modern and Postmodern Aesthetics" in *Daedalus* 134 (Fall, 2005): 191–207.

_____. "The Myth of Superman." *Diacritics* 2/1 (Spring, 1972): 14–22.

_____. *The Open Work.* tr. Anna Cancogni. Cambridge: Harvard University Press, 1989.

Edkins, Jenny. "Ground Zero: Reflections on Trauma, In/distinction and Response," in *Journal of Cultural Research*, vol.8:3: 248–270.

Eisner, Will. *Comics and Sequential Art.* Tamarac: Poorhouse Press, 1985.

Elliott, Kamilla. "Literary Film Adaptation and the Form/Content Dilemma." *Narrative across Media.* Ed. Marie-Laure Ryan. Lincoln: Nebraska University Press, 2004.

Ellis, Warren, et al. *Planetary 1: All Over the World and Other Tales.* La Jolla: Wildstorm, 2000.

_____. *Planetary 2: The Fourth Man.* La Jolla: Wildstorm, 2001.

_____. *Planetary 3: Leaving the 20th Century.* La Jolla: Wildstorm, 2004.

_____. *Planetary: Crossing Worlds.* La Jolla: Wildstorm, 2004.

Ellison, Harlan. "Comic of the Absurd." *All in Color for a Dime.* Eds. Dick Lupoff and Maggie Thompson. Iola, WI: Krause, 1970. 240–248.

_____. "Roses in December." *Mangle Tangle Tales.* 1:1 1990. 1–4.

Ferstl, Paul. "Novel-based Comics." *Comics as a Nexus of Cultures.* Ed. Mark Berninger, Jochen Ecke and Gideon Haberkorn. Jefferson, N.C.: McFarland, 2010: 60–69.

Flyvbjerg, Bent. *Making Social Science Matter: Why Social Inquiry Fails and How It Can Succeed Again.* New York: Cambridge University Press, 2001.

Fort, Bernadette and Angela Rosenthal. "The Analysis of Difference," *The Other Hogarth: Aesthetics of Difference,* Ed. Fort and Rosenthal. New Jersey: Princeton University Press, 2001.

Foucault, Michel. *The Archaeology of Knowledge.* London: Tavistock, 1972 (1969).

_____. *The Order of Things.* New York and London: Vintage Books, 1994.

_____. "What Is an Author?" *Aesthetics, Method, and Epistemology.* Ed. James D. Faubion. New York: The New Press, 1998. 205–22.

Frahm, O. "Too Much Is Too Much. The Never Innocent Laughter of the Comics." <http://www.imageandnarrative.be/graphicnovel/olefrahm.htm> (05/04/09).

Friedberg, Anne. *Window Shopping: Cinema and the Postmodern.* Berkeley and Los Angeles: University of California Press, 1993.

Gaiman, Neil, and Andy Kubert. Marvel *1602.* New York: Marvel Comics, 2003.

Gardner, Martin. "Introduction." *Peter Puzzlemaker Returns.* Palo Alto, CA: Dale Seymour Publications, 1994.

_____. "John Martin's Book: An Almost Forgotten Children's Magazine." *Children's Literature,* vol. 18 (1990): 145–159.

Gaudreault, André, *Du littéraire au filmique. Système du récit.* Paris: Méridiens Klincksieck, 1989.

Georgel, Pierre. "'The Most Contemptible Meanness That Lines Can Be Formed into': Hogarth and the 'Other' Arts," *The Dumb show: Image and society in the works of William Hogarth.* Ed. Ogée, Frédéric. Oxford: Voltaire Foundation, 1997.

Goggin, Joyce. "'Nigella's Deep-Frying a Snickers Bar!': The Gilmore Girls and Addiction as a Social Construct." *Screwball Television: Gilmore Girls.* Ed. David Scott Diffrient and David Lavery. SUNY University Press, 257–283.

Goldman, Jonathan E. "Joyce, the Propheteer." *Novel: A Forum on Fiction.* 38.1. (Spring 2004): 84–103.

Goldstein, Nancy. *Jackie Ormes: The First African American Woman Cartoonist.* Ann Arbor: University of Michigan Press, 2008.

Gomringer, Eugen. *The Book of Hours and Constellations.* Trans. Jerome Rothenberg. New York: Something Else Press, 1968.

Goscinni, René, and Albert Uderzo. *Asterix and the Chieftain's Shield.* Trans. Anthea Bell and Derek Hockridge. London: Hodder Dargaud, 1977.

Goulart, Ron. *Great American Comic Books.* Lincolnwood, IL: Publications International, 2001.

Greenburg, Kenneth S., ed. *The Confessions of Nat Turner and Related Documents.* Boston: Bedford/St. Martins Press, 1996.

Groensteen, Thierry. *The System of Comics.* Trans. Bart Beaty and Nick Nguyen. Jackson: University of Mississippi Press, 2007.

_____. "Why Are Comics Still in Search of a Cultural Legitimization?" *Comics and Culture: Analytical and Theoretical Approaches to Comics.* Copenhagen: Museum of Tusculanum Press, 2000: 29–41.

Grover, Jan Zita. "The First Living-Room War: The Civil War in the Illustrated Press," in *Afterimage* (February 1984): 8–11.

Guralnik, David B. "Superstar, Supermom, Super Glue, Superdooper, Superman." *Superman at Fifty!: The Persistence of a Legend.* Ed. Gary D. Engle and Dennis Dooley. New York: Collier Books, 1988.

Hamilton, Lisa. "The Importance of Recognizing Oscar: The Dandy and the Culture of Celebrity." *The Center and Clark Newsletter* 33 (1999): 3–5.

Hatfield, Charles. *Alternative Comics: An Emerging Literature.* Jackson: University Press of Mississippi, 2005.

Hayward, Jennifer. *Consuming Pleasures: Active Audiences and Serial Fictions from Dickens to Soap Opera.* Lexington, KY: University Press of Kentucky, 1997.

Hegerfeldt, Anne. *Lies That Tell the Truth. Magic Realism Seen Through Contemporary Fiction from Britain.* Amsterdam: Rodopi, 2005.

Hein, Michael, et al., eds. *Ästhetik des Comics.* Berlin: Erich Schmidt Verlag, 2002.

Hill, Annette. *Restyling Factual TV: Audiences and News, Documentary, and Reality Genres.* New York: Routledge, 2007.

Hogarth, William. *The Analysis of Beauty.* Ed. Ronald Paulson. New Haven: Yale University Press, 1997.

Hudlin, Reginald, and John Romita, Jr. *Black Panther,* vol. III. New York: Marvel Comics, 2005.

Hutcheon, Linda. *A Theory of Adaptation.* New York: Routledge, 2006.

Iser, Wolfgang. *The Act of Reading: A Theory of Aesthetic Response.* Baltimore: Johns Hopkins University Press, 1978.

_____. *The Implied Reader: Patterns of Communication in Prose Fiction from Bunyan to Beckett.* Baltimore: Johns Hopkins University Press, 1974.

Jaafar, Ali. "Iran's Up in Arms Over WB's '300.'" *Variety.* 13 March 2007. <http://www.variety.com/article/VR1117961076.html?categoryid=13&cs=1&query=300+iran> (22/03/09).

Jackson, Rosemary. *Fantasy: The Literature of Subversion.* London: Methuen, 1981.

Jaffe, Aaron. *Modernism in the Age of Celebrity.* Cambridge: Cambridge University Press, 2005

Jay, Martin. *Songs of Experience: Modern American and European Variations on a Universal Theme.* Berkeley: University of California Press, 2005.

Jeffers, H. Paul. *Freemasons: Inside the World's Oldest Secret Society.* New York: Citadel, 2005.

Kafalenos, Emma. "The Power of Double Coding to Represent New Forms of Representation: *The Truman Show, Dorian Gray,* "Blow-Up," and Whistler's *Caprice in Purple and Gold.*" *Poetics Today* 24:1 (2003): 1–33.

Kafka, Franz. *The Metamorphisis.* Adaptation by Peter Kuper. Trans. Kerstin Hasenpusch. New York: Three Rivers Press, 2003.

Kahane, David. "*300* Shocker." *National Review Online.* 12 March 2007. <http://article.nationalreview.com/?q=ZjM0NDEyZjM1M2JlNjE0ZGMwNDEwMzk5MzlkZjJmYjA=> (22/03/09).

Kannenberg, Gene, Jr. "The Comics of Chris Ware: Text, Image, and Visual Narrative Strategies." *The Language of Comics: Word and Image.* Eds. Robin Varnum and Christina T. Gibbons. Jackson: University Press Mississippi, 2001: 174–198.

Kasson, John F. *Houdini, Tarzan, and the Perfect Man.* New York: Hill and Wang, 2001.

Kavanagh, Barry. "The Alan Moore Interview." *Blather,* 2000. <http://www.

blather.net/articles/amoore/from_hell1. html> (28/03/08).

Keebaugh, Cari. "The Many Sides of Hank: Modifications, Adjustments, and Adaptations of Mark Twain's *A Connecticut Yankee in King Arthur's Court*." *Image-TexT: Interdisciplinary Comics Studies*, Vol. 3, No. 3, 2007. <http://www.english. ufl.edu/imagetext/archives/v3_3/ keebaugh/ > (05/03/ 08).

Kirby, Jack. *The Black Panther* (reprint of issues 1–7, Vol. I). New York: Marvel Comics, 2005.

Klock, Geoff. *How to Read Superhero Comics and Why*. New York: Continuum, 2002.

Klucinskas, Jean. "Le corps immaculé : l'image d'Antinoüs chez Hogarth et Diderot." *Le corps romanesque: images et usages topiques sous l'Anciens Régime*. Presses de l'Université Laval, Québec, 2009.

Knight, Stephen. *Jack the Ripper: The Final Solution*. London: HarperCollins, 1994.

Kohn, Hans. *Nationalism: Its Meaning and History*. New York: Van Nostrand Reinhold Co., 1965.

Kovach, Bill, and T. Rosenstiel. *The Elements of Journalism: What Newspeople Should Know and the Public Should Expect*. New York: Crown, 2001.

Kowaleski-Wallace, Elizabeth. *Consuming Subjects: Women, Shopping, and Business in the Eighteenth Century*. New York: Columbia University Press, 1997.

Kukkonen, Karin. *Neue Perspektiven auf die Superhelden: Polyphonie in Alan Moores Watchmen*. Marburg: Tectum, 2008.

Lacey, Josh. "Mirror Writing." *The Guardian*. February 5, 2005. <http://books.guardian. co.uk/review/story/0,12084,1405330,00.h tml#article> (05/03/08).

Lentricchia, Frank, and Jody McAuliffe. "Groundzeroland." in *South Atlantic Quarterly* (vol. 101:2): 349–359.

Lessing, Gotthold Ephraim. *Laocoon: An Essay on the Limits of Painting and Poetry*. Trans. E.C. Beasley. London: Longman, Brown, Green and Longmans, 1853. Googlebooks, <http://books.google. de/books?id=Sn0NAAAAQAAJ> (11/07/ 08).

Lévi, Éliphas. *Transcendental Magic, its Doc-trine and Ritual*. Trans. Arthur Edward Waite. New York: S. Weiser, 1970.

Lévi-Strauss, Claude. *Myth and Meaning*. London: Routledge & Kegan Paul, 1978.
_____. "Structure and Form: Reflections on a Work by Vladimir Propp." *Propp*. 1984: 167–188.

Levitz, Paul, ed. *9/11 Artists Respond*. New York: DC Comics, 2002.

Lewis, Pericles. "Walter Benjamin in the Information Age? On the Limited Possibilities for a Defetishizing Critique of Culture." *Mapping Benjamin: The Work of Art in the Digital Age*. Ed. Hans Ulrich Gumbrecht and Michael Marrinan. Stanford: Stanford University Press, 2003: 221–29.

Lock, Helen. "'Building Up from Fragments': The Oral Memory Process in Some Recent African-American Written Narratives," in *College Literature*, vol. 22:3: 109–120.

Loeb, Jeph, et al. *Fallen Son: The Death of Captain America*. New York: Marvel Comics, 2007.
_____, and Tim Sale. *Batman: The Long Halloween*. New York: DC Comics, 1999.
_____, and _____. *Spider-Man: Blue*. New York: Marvel Comics, 2001.

Lotman, Yuri M. "The Text within the Text." Trans. Jerry Leo and Amy Mandelker. *PMLA* 109.3 (1994): 377–384.

Lund, Michael. *America's Continuing Story: An Introduction to Serial Fiction: 1850—1900*. Detroit: Wayne State University Press, 1992.

Lupoff, Dick, and Maggie Thompson. "Introduction to 'Comic of the Absurd.'" *All in Color for a Dime*. Iola, WI: Krause Publications, 1997: 240.

Lyotard, Jean-François. *The Postmodern Condition: A Report on Knowledge*. Trans. Geoff Bennington and Brian Massumi. Manchester: Manchester University Press, 1997.

Making of 300 Video Journal: 1— First Look. 17 April 2007. <http://www.300the movie.com> (22/03/09).

Marion, Philippe, *Traces en cases. Travail graphique, figuration narrative, et partic-ipation du lecteur. Essai sur la bande dess-*

inée. Université Catholique de Louvain: Academia, 1993.

Marshall, Monica. *Joe Sacco.* New York: Rosen, 2005.

Marshall, P. David. *Celebrity and Power.* Minneapolis: University of Minnesota Press, 1997.

Mason, Jeff, ed. *9/11 Emergency Relief.* Gainesville: Alternative Comics, 2002.

McBride, Melanie. "The Transmetropolitan Condition: An Interview with Warren Ellis." <http://www.mindjack.com/interviews/ellis.html > (06/06/2008).

McCloud, Scott. *Reinventing Comics.* New York: Harper Perennial, 2000.

_____. *Understanding Comics: The Invisible Art.* Northampton: Harper Perennial, 1994.

McDonald, George. *The Princess and the Goblin* [1872]. <http://www.pagebypage books.com/George_MacDonald/The_Princess_and_the_Goblin/Why_the_Princess_Has_a_Story_About_Her_p1.html> (11/07/08).

McGrath, Charles. "Not Funnies." *New York Times Magazine,* 11 July 2004: 24–33, 46, 55–56.

McGruder, Aaron, Reginald Hudlin, and Kyle Baker. *Birth of a Nation: A Comic Novel.* New York: Three Rivers Press/ Crown Publishing, 2004.

Melville, Herman. *Moby Dick.* Adaptation by Bill Sienkiewicz. New York: Classics Illustrated, 1990.

_____. *Moby Dick.* Adaption by Pocket Classics (no author named). West Haven Co.: Academic Industries, 1984.

Miles, Simon. "The Reptilian Agenda: The Ghost of a Flea." *Reptilian Agenda,* 2000. <http://www.reptilianagenda.com/img/i0 20100a.shtml> (22/03/09).

Millar, Mark, and Dave Johnson. *Superman: Red Son.* New York: DC Comics, 2003.

Miller, Frank. Interview with Steve Daly. "Miller's Tales." *EW.com.* 6 March 2007. <http://www.ew.com/ew/article/0,,20014175,00.html> (22/03/09).

_____, et al. *Batman: The Dark Knight Returns.* New York: DC, 2002 (1986).

_____, and Dave Gibbons. *Give Me Liberty: An American Dream.* Milwaukie: Dark Horse Comics, 1990.

_____, and Dave Mazzucchelli. *Batman: Year One.* New York: DC Comics, 1987.

_____, and Lynn Varley. *300.* Milwaukie: Dark Horse Books, 1999.

_____, and Robert Rodriguez. Audio commentary *Sin City.* Dir. Frank Miller and Robert Rodriguez. 2005. DVD. Buena Vista Home Entertainment. 2006.

Miller, Nancy. "'Portraits of Grief': Telling Details and the Testimony of Trauma," in *Differences: A Journal of Feminist Cultural Studies,* vol.14:3: 112–135.

Mitchell, W. J. T. *Iconology: Image, Text, Ideology.* Chicago: University Chicago Press, 1986.

Moench, Doug and Kelley Jones. *Batman and Dracula: Red Rain.* New York: DC Comics 1991.

Moore, Alan. "Planetary Consciousness" in *Planetary 1: All Over the World and Other Tales.* Warren Ellis et al. La Jolla: Wildstorm, 2000.

_____, and Dave Gibbons. *Watchmen.* New York: DC Comics 1986.

_____, and Eddie Campbell. *From Hell: The Compleat Scripts.* Brooklandville, MD: Borderline Press, 1994.

_____, and _____. *From Hell,* 1–16. London: Knockabout Comics, 2000.

_____, and Kevin O'Neill. *The League of Extraordinary Gentlemen.* Vol. 1. #1–6. La Jolla: America's Best Comics, 1999–2000.

_____, and _____. *The League of Extraordinary Gentlemen.* Vol. 2. #1–6. La Jolla: America's Best Comics, 2002–2003.

_____, and _____. *The League of Extraordinary Gentlemen: The Black Dossier.* La Jolla: America's Best Comics, 2008.

Moore, Roger. "*300* as Fascist Art." *Orlando Sentinel.* 7 March 2007. <http://blogs.orlandosentinel.com/entertainment_movies_blog/2007/03/300_as_fascist_.html> (22/03/09).

Morrison, Grant, and McKean, D. *Arkham Asylum.* New York: DC Comics, 1989.

Moses, Wilson Jeremiah, ed. *Classical Black Nationalism: From the Revolution to Marcus Garvey.* New York: New York University Press, 1996.

Neal, Arthur. *National Trauma and Collective Identity: Extraordinary Events in the*

American Experience. New York: M.E. Sharpe, 1988.

Neale, Steve. "Questions of Genre." *Film and Theory: An Anthology.* Ed. Robert Stam and Toby Miller. Malden, MA: Blackwell, 2000: 157–78.

Nichols, Bill. *Introduction to Documentary.* Bloomington: Indiana University Press, 2001.

Nora, Pierre. *Realms of Memory, Rethinking the French Past (Volume1, Conflicts and Division).* New York: Columbia University Press, 1996.

Norlund, Christopher. "Imagining Terrorists before Sept. 11: Marvel's GI Joe Comic Books, 1982–1994." *ImageText,* Vol. 3, No. 1.

North, Douglass C., and Barry R. Weingast. "Constitutions and Commitment: The Evolution of Institutions Governing Public Choice in Seventeenth-Century England." *The Journal of Economic History,* No. 4, 1989: 803–832.

Noys, Benjamin. Review of *In the Shadow of No Towers.* In *Rethinking History,* vol.9 Issue 2/3: 365–375.

Nyberg, Amy Kiste. "Theorizing Comics Journalism." *International Journal of Comic Art* 8.2 (2006): 98–112.

Ogée, Frédéric. "The Flesh of Theory: The Erotics of Hogarth's Lines." *The Other Hogarth: Aesthetics of Difference.* Ed. Bernadette Fort and Angela Rosenthal. Princeton and Oxford: Princeton University Press, 2001: 120–142.

Patten, Robert L. "Serialized Retrospection in The Pickwick Papers." *Literature in the Marketplace: Nineteenth-Century British Publishing and Reading Practices.* Cambridge: Cambridge University Press, 1995: 123–42.

Paul, Helen Julia. *The South Sea Bubble.* New York and London: Routledge, forthcoming.

Paulson, Ronald. "The Harlot's Progress and the Origins of the Novel." *Hogarth in Context: Ten Essays and a Bibliography.* Ed. Joachim Möller. Marburg: Jonas Verlag, 1996: 36–48.

_____. *Hogarth: Art and Politics, 1750–1764.*

Vol. III. New Jersey: Rutgers University, 1993.

_____. *Hogarth: The Modern Moral Subject, 1697–1732.* Vol. I New Haven: Yale University Press, 1971.

Peeters, Benoit. "'Four Conceptions of the Page' from 'Case, planche, récit: lire la bande dessinée.'" Trans. Jesse Cohn. *ImageTexT: Interdisciplinary Comics Studies.* 3.3 (2007). Dept of English, University of Florida. 29 May 2008. <http://www.english.ufl.edu/imagetext/archives/v3_3/peeters/>.

_____. *Lire la Bande Dessinée.* Paris: Flammarion, 1998.

Pratt, Hugo. *Corto Maltese en Sibérie.* Casterman, 2000.

_____. *La Lagune des mystères.* Casterman, 2002.

Priest, Christopher, and Mark Texeira. *Black Panther,* Vol. II. New York: Marvel Comics, 1998–2001.

Prince, Gerald. *Dictionary of Narratology. Revised Edition.* Lincoln & London: University of Nebraska Press, 2003.

Propp, Vladimir. *Morphology of the Folktale.* Austin: University of Texas Press, 1968.

_____. *Theory and History of Folklore.* Manchester: Manchester University Press, 1984.

Proust, Marcel. *Remembrance of Things Past.* Adaptation by Stéphane Heuet. Trans. Joe Johnson. New York: Nantier, Beall, Minoustchine, 2001.

_____. *Time Regained.* Trans. Stephen Hudson. <ebooks.adelaide.edu.au/proust/marcel/p96t/chapter3.html> (11/07/08).

Pustz, Matthew J. *Comic Book Culture: Fanboys and True Believers.* Jackson: University Press Mississippi, 1999.

Ray, Robert B. "The Field of 'Literature and Film.'" *Film Adaptation.* James Naremore Ed. New Brunswick and Jew Jersey: Rutgers University Press, 2000: 38–53.

Reitberger, Reinhold, and Wolfgang Fuchs. *Comics: Anatomy of a Mass Medium.* Boston: Little Brown, 1971.

Ridley, Jasper. *The Freemasons.* London: Constable & Robinson, 2000.

Riehl, Joseph E. "Charles Lamb's 'Old China,' Hogarth, and Perspective Painting." *South Central Review*, vol. 10, No. 1, 1993: 38–48.

Robinson, Dean E. *Black Nationalism in American Politics and Thought*. New York: Cambridge University Press, 2001.

Rosenthal, Angela. "Unfolding Gender: Women and the 'Secret' Sign Language of Fans in Hogarth's Work." *The Other Hogarth: Aesthetics of Difference*. Ed. Bernadette Fort and Angela Rosenthal. Princeton and Oxford: Princeton University Press, 2001: 120–142.

Ryan, Marie-Laure. "Narrative and Digitality: Learning to Think With the Medium." *A Companion to Narrative Theory*. Eds. James Phelan and Peter J. Rabinowitz. Blackwell Publishing, 2005. 515–528.

Sacco, Joe. *The Fixer: A Story from Sarajevo*. Montreal: Drawn & Quarterly, 2003.

_____. *Notes from a Defeatist*. Seattle: Fantagraphics, 2003.

_____. *Palestine: The Special Edition*. Seattle: Fantagraphics, 2007.

_____. Personal interview with Bethany Lindsay. April, 2005.

_____. *Safe Area Goražde: The War in Eastern Bosnia 1992–95*. Seattle: Fantagraphics, 2001.

_____. *War's End: Profiles from Bosnia 1995–96*. Montreal: Drawn & Quarterly, 2005.

Said, Edward. "Homage to Joe Sacco." *Palestine: The Special Edition*. Seattle, WA: Fantagraphics, 2007: v–vii.

Saraceni, Mario. *The Language of Comics*. London and New York: Routledge, 2003.

Schickel, Richard. *Intimate Strangers*. New York: Fromm International Publishing Company, 1986.

Sharrett, Christopher. "Batman and the Twilight of the Idols: An Interview with Frank Miller." *The Many Lives of the Batman*. Ed. Roberta E. Pearson and William Uricchio. New York: Routledge, 1991: 33–46.

Shesgreen, Sean. "Hogarth's Industry and Idleness: A Reading," *Eighteenth-Century Studies*, Vol. 9, No. 4, 1976: 569–598.

Smith, Erin A. "'The Ragtag and Bobtail of the Fiction Parade': Pulp Magazines and the Literary Marketplace." *Scorned Literature: Essays on the History and Criticism of Popular Mass-Produced Fiction in America*. Westport: Greenwood, 2002: 123–45.

Smith, Kevin. *Green Arrow*. New York: DC Comics, 2003.

Snyder, Zack. Interview with Jonah Weiland. "300 Post-Game: One-on-One with Zack Snyder." *Comic Book Resources*. 14 March 2007. <http://www.comicbookresources.com/news/newsitem.cgi?id=9982> (22/03/09).

Spiegelman, Art. *In the Shadow of No Towers*. New York: Pantheon Press, 2004.

Stam, Robert. "Beyond Fidelity: The Dialogics of Adaptation." *Film Adaptation*. Ed. James Naremore. New Brunswick and New Jersey: Rutgers University Press, 2000: 54–76.

Standish, David. *The Art of Money: The History and Design of Paper Currency from around the World*. San Francisco: Chronicle Books, 2000.

Stevens, Dana. "A Movie Only a Spartan Could Love: The Battle Epic *300*." *Slate*. 8 March 2007. <http://www.slate.com/id/2161450/> (22/03/09).

Stevenson, Robert Louis. *Doktor Jekyll and Mister Hyde*. Adaptation by Lorenzo Mattotti and Jerry Kramsky. Trans. Rossi Schreiber. Hamburg: Carlsen, 2001.

Swanson, Don R. "Toward a Psychology of Metaphor." *On Metaphor*, Ed. S. Sacks. Chicago: University of Chicago Press, 1978: 161–164.

Todorov, Tzvetan. *The Fantastic: A Structural Approach to a Literary Genre*. New York: Cornell University Press, 1975.

Tolkien, J.R.R. *The Annotated Hobbit*. Ed. Douglas A. Anderson. Boston and New York, Houghton Mifflin, 2002.

_____. *The Hobbit*. Adaptation by Charles Dixon and David Wenzel. London: Harper Collins, 2006.

Uglow, Jenny. *Hogarth: A Life and a World*. London: Faber & Faber, 1997.

Van Deburg, William L., ed. *Modern Black Nationalism: From Marcus Garvey to Louis Farrakhan*. New York: New York University Press, 1997.

Verano, Frank. "Invisible Spectacles, Invisible Limits: Grant Morrison, Situationist Theory, and Real Unrealities." *Interna-*

tional Journal of Comic Art, 8.2, (2006): 319–329.

Vickroy, Laura. *Trauma and Survival in Contemporary Fiction*. Charlottesville: University of Virginia Press, 2002.

Wagner-Pacifici, Robin. "Memories in the Making: The Shapes of Things That Went," in *Qualitative Sociology*, vol.19:3: 301–321.

Ware, Chris. *The ACME Novelty Library 2–4*. Seattle: Fantagraphics, 1994.

Weber, Max. *The Methodology of the Social Sciences*. Trans. and eds. Edward A. Shils and Henry A. Finch. New York: Free Press, 1949.

Weber, Samuel. *Unwrapping Balzac: A Reading of* La Peau de Chagrin. Toronto: University of Toronto Press, 1979.

White, Hayden. *Metahistory: The Historical Imagination in Nineteenth Century Europe*. Baltimore: Johns Hopkins University Press, 1973.

Whooley, Owen. "The Political Work of Narratives: A Dialogic Analysis of Two Slave Narratives." *Narrative Inquiry* 16:2 (2006), 295–318.

Wilde, Oscar. *The Picture of Dorian Gray*. (1889.) *The Complete Works of Oscar Wilde*. Great Britain: HarperCollins, 1966.

Williams, Kristian. "The Case for Comics Journalism: Artist-Reporters Leap Tall Conventions in a Single Bound." *Columbia Journalism Review*, March–April, 2005: 51–55.

Williams, Martin. "About George Carlson." *The Smithsonian Book of Comic-book Comics*. Eds. Michael Barrier and Martin Williams. New York: Abrams, 1981: 127–128.

Wolf, Werner. "Pictorial Narrativity." Eds. David Herman, Manfred Jahn and Marie-Laure Ryan,. *Routledge Encyclopedia of Narrative Theory*. New York: Routledge, 2005: 431–435.

Wolk, Douglas. *Reading Comics: How Graphic Novels Work and What They Mean*. Cambridge: Da Capo Press, 2007.

Wough, Coulton. *The Comics*. Jackson: University of Mississippi Press, 1947 (reprint edition).

Wright, Bradford W. *Comic Book Nation: The Transformation of Youth Culture in America*. Baltimore: Johns Hopkins University Press, 2001.

Wright, Nicky. *The Classic Era of American Comics*. London: Prion, 2000.

Yezbick, Daniel. Interviews with Henry Bishop. 4 and (29/05/2008).

_____. Interview with June Bishop. 5 May, 2008.

_____. "Riddles of Engagement: Narrative Play in the Children's Media and Comic Art of George Carlson." *ImageTexT: Interdisciplinary Comics Studies*. 3.3 (2007). Department of English, University of Florida. 29 May 2008. <http://www.english.ufl.edu/imagetext/archives/v3_3/yezbick/>.

Žižek, Slavoj. "The True Hollywood Left." *Lacan.com*. 13 May 2008. <http://www.lacan.com/zizhollywood.htm> (22/03/09).

Index